Buying a property
CYPRUS

CADOGANguides

Contents

09
References 171

About the authors

Sue Bryant is an award-winning journalist who has written and edited 16 guidebooks on Mediterranean destinations for publishers including Insight Guides, Berlitz and New Holland. She has contributed to many UK and international travel magazines and news-papers on topics as diverse as business travel, adventure, winter sports, cruising, family travel and travel health. She has also appeared on many television and radio programmes, including Radio Four's Today, BBC Business Breakfast and BBS News 24, as a commentator on the travel industry. Sue has a long-standing passion for Cyprus and has visited the island many times over the last 20 years, writing about everything from hiking in the Troodos mountains to spas, golf, honeymoons and business tourism, as well as property.

James Franklin is the author and publisher of *The Cyprus Croc*, a free pocket-sized listings magazine popular with tourists and expatriates alike and *Moving to and Living in Cyprus*, a definitive guide to the Republic. He also publishes the official guide to the rural wineries of Cyprus and is currently working on other publications promoting Cyprus.

Conceived and produced for Cadogan Guides by **Navigator Guides Ltd**, The Old Post Office, Swanton Novers, Melton Constable, Norfolk, NR24 2AJ
info@navigatorguides.com
www.navigatorguides.com

Cadogan Guides
Network House
1 Ariel Way
London W12 7SL
info@cadoganguides.co.uk
www.cadoganguides.com

The Globe Pequot Press
246 Goose Lane, PO Box 480, Guilford, Connecticut 06437–0480

Cover design: Sarah Rianhard-Gardner
Cover photographs: © Oliver Ben/Alamy/Paul Hellander
Photo essay photographs: © Paul Hellander
Editor: Susannah Wight
Proofreader: Mary Sheridan
Indexing: Isobel McLean

Printed in Finland by WS Bookwell Oy

A catalogue record for this book is available from the British Library
ISBN 1-86011-123-8

Introduction

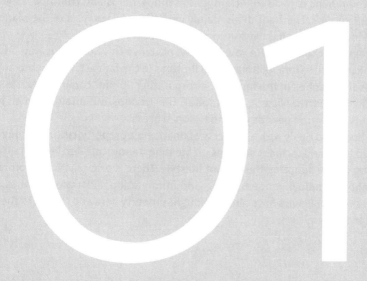

01

There is something indefinable about Cyprus that draws people back, again and again. What the island lacks in sweeping sandy beaches it makes up for in its raw, mountainous beauty. Although pockets of the coastline are highly developed, there are great swathes of rugged countryside to explore, peppered with sleepy villages, vineyards and olive groves.

To residents of chilly northern Europe, the year-round sunshine is a big draw. Most of all, however, it's the warmth of the Cypriot people that brings holidaymakers back to the island as homeowners. You'll hear it over and over again, but it's genuine. In Cyprus, people have time. They're relaxed, easy-going and endlessly welcoming to visitors. Many expats in Cyprus find it relatively easy to integrate into the local community, aided by the fact that most Cypriots speak English. Furthermore, a lot have close ties with Britain and the two cultures merge happily. Russian, German, Dutch and American visitors are also buying here, although not in such great numbers as the British.

Cyprus is currently going through a property boom, with a gold-rush mentality sweeping the island. Everybody from local millionaires to taxi drivers has suddenly become a property developer. Compared with some European countries it is not too difficult to buy in Cyprus but there are important concepts to understand, such as land ownership, zoning, construction and modification of property, all of which are explained in this book.

At the time of writing, Cyprus is still divided into two: the northern part is occupied by Turkey, a situation not recognized by any United Nations country except Turkey; the southern, Greek-speaking part of Cyprus is where the bulk of development is focused. Attempts to reunify the island continue, as yet without success. This book deals mainly with the southern part of the island, as buying in the north is a most uncertain process.

To help you choose where you might want to live this book takes you on a tour of the south from Ayia Napa and Protaras in the far east, via Larnaca and Limassol to Paphos in the far west, incorporating up-and-coming Latchi and Polis in the north; Nicosia, the capital; the Troodos Mountains and their foothills; and some new, as yet undeveloped areas.

The book also deals with all aspects of financing a property, cutting through the red tape, and includes sections on building, renovating, letting property, settling in and adopting the Cypriot lifestyle. There is also practical information about employment, education and immigration, illustrated with case studies of people who have already bought property here and moved to their place in the sun.

First Steps and Reasons for Buying

02

Why Cyprus?

There are many reasons to buy a home in Cyprus: 330 days a year of sunshine; the beautiful, rugged mountains; the low crime rate; the highly developed infrastructure; the lack of a language barrier; the booming property market; and, most of all, the friendly people.

Wherever you buy, the mountains will not be more than a couple of hours' drive away, and it will take you less than half an hour to get to the beach. There are also civilised towns, which provide all the shops, culture, schools, bars and restaurants that you need.

Year-round Sunshine

Cyprus has a hot, dry summer and a long, blissfully warm extended spring and autumn, many people's favourite times. Winter, from November to February, has some rain but is rarely cold, except in the Troodos Mountains, where there are a couple of places to ski on the rather wet snow. In February the whole island is shrouded in pale pink, as the almond trees come into blossom. One can enjoy every season, whether by walking on the beach after work in winter, cycling to picnic in the mountains in spring, or making merry at the local wine festival in the autumn.

Another bonus is that there are no dramatic extremes of climate. Floods, hurricanes, very strong winds, tidal waves and big freezes are unheard of. Cyprus used to suffer from droughts in the summer but new desalination plants and an efficient system of dams ensure a steady supply of water.

Friendly People

The Cypriots are warm and hospitable and enjoy excellent relations with the British and other expats living on the island. Many have relatives in the UK or North America – there are some 270,000 Greek Cypriots resident in the UK and 52,000 in North America. The stories you hear about Cypriot hospitality are not just the stuff of holiday brochures; stroll through a village and someone may well invite you in for a drink. Dine in the local taverna and a constant stream of extra dishes will be brought to the table for you to try. Have a business meeting with a Cypriot and you'll probably be invited to dinner with the family that evening. Friends and family are of top importance in Cyprus and affect every aspect of day-to-day living. If you have a problem, a Cypriot will almost always know someone who can solve it.

Cultural Heritage

Cyprus occupies a strategic position in the Eastern Mediterranean, close to Europe, Africa and the Middle East, all of which have shaped the island's history, from the ancient Greeks and Romans to the crusaders. Ancient traditions are kept very much alive, through village festivals, carefully preserved mosaics, amphitheatres and Crusader castles, and live music and dance. While modern life has made its impression, with high-rise buildings and neon lights, the heart of Cyprus lies very much in its heritage.

Accommodation for All Tastes

Most properties sold in Cyprus are new-builds, which vary from small apartments to multi-million-pound villas on the beach or golf course. There is also a growing trend for building traditional stone houses in the mountains. Alternatively, buy a town house, a modern apartment, or something old in a traditional village to renovate; there are government grants available and the letting potential is good as 'agro-tourism' (the phrase for tourism with an environmental slant) grows. Planning regulations on colour and style of properties are very strict, to preserve the 'village' feel of the island, but there is a great variety of locations and styles within this.

A Healthy Lifestyle

Everything about Cyprus points towards a healthy lifestyle, provided you take precautions in the sun. The famed Mediterranean diet consists of fresh, locally produced organic food, which is cooked in olive oil and washed down with a glass or two of red wine. There are plentiful opportunities for leading an outdoor life of walking, swimming, cycling, sailing, golf and even skiing. The glorious sunshine encourages residents to spend more time outdoors and the laid-back atmosphere helps to melt away stress. And finally, should you need it, there is an excellent health care system.

The Property Boom

Cyprus has been enjoying a property boom since the beginning of the 21st century and prices are still rising, particularly of new-builds, which are being bought off-plan and sold for a hefty profit even before completion. The boom is unlikely to be sustainable at this rate but Cyprus does represent a good investment, with plenty of areas still likely to bear fruit.

Why Buy?

The mere fact that you are reading this book suggests that you like the idea of Cyprus, but is it really necessary to buy? Only you can answer that. Whether you want a second home, an investment or a complete relocation, you won't be alone, as thousands of Brits have already bought property on the island. If you've fallen in love with the place or visit regularly anyway, or if you have the funds for a deposit and you are prepared to manage your investment property from afar, then Cyprus could be the answer. If you're hoping to relocate but are not quite sure whether to take the plunge, why not rent for a few months while you look around for a house? If you're having something built, many developers will help you find somewhere to rent, or may even put you up in one of their own properties.

A Second Home

The idea of having a second home in Cyprus is appealing, but bear in mind that it is unlikely to be practical to have a weekend home there, with a flight time of four and a half hours from the UK, and a two-hour time difference. Flying out on a Friday morning would get you into Larnaca by 4pm, giving you just Saturday and until mid-afternoon on Sunday before having to hop onto the afternoon flight back to London. This is just an example, using the most popular Cyprus Airways timings; there are night flights and, of course, plenty of regional flights, but if you add it all up – an hour to check in on departure, the flight, the time difference and an hour to get from aircraft to accommodation – it takes the best part of a day's travelling time (eight and a half hours) to get there. It's not the same as nipping across to Mallorca or the south of France for a weekend.

On the plus side, if you're planning to enjoy your property in chunks of, say, half-term weeks and school holidays, the season is very long, indeed year-round in some areas (Limassol, Larnaca and Paphos, less so in Ayia Napa and Polis/Latchi). There is no time of the year when Cyprus is to be avoided, although there is likely to be some rain in November to February.

Buying to Let

The holiday letting market is good for the season from around Easter to the end of October and tails off in the winter months. There is also potential for longer-term lets, fuelled in part by the property boom. A lot of buyers choose to rent for six months or a year while their house is being built. Bear in mind that with so many properties being built the potential for holiday lettings will ultimately be diluted. Do not take seriously any developer or seller who talks about 'guaranteed' letting income, as there are no guarantees.

Investment

Cyprus represents an excellent investment opportunity, looking at current trends. Property prices are increasing dramatically and houses are cheaper than in other sunshine destinations like Mallorca, the Costa del Sol and the Côte d'Azur. If you can spot an up-and-coming area and are prepared to take a risk on it, the spoils can be even greater. Speculative buying and selling can accelerate your path up the property ladder, as can the buying and selling of land (if you can get your hands on it, which is not easy). Returns on real estate are currently 5–8 per cent each year.

But – as with all property purchases – property can decrease in value as well as increase. The rate of appreciation can also slow down and may well do so when the curve of the building boom levels out. The lettings market cannot be guaranteed. Cyprus has the potential, as a tourist destination, to expand into new markets, but its proximity to the Middle East and the presence of British army bases put some people off. And while the cost of living is still low, prices are rising now that the island is a member of the EU and the rate of VAT in Cyprus has increased to 15 per cent. Despite this, Cyprus has not yet fulfilled its tourism potential. With three championship golf courses already built and more planned, as well as government investment in marinas, casinos, a new airport terminal for Larnaca and road improvements, the island will continue to expand and diversify the tourism industry on which it is so heavily dependent.

A new trend identified in the UK in 2004 also bodes well for the property investor – for the first time since the advent of the package holiday, individual holiday arrangements have outstripped traditional package deals. This is partly because of the number of low-cost airlines operating in Europe (including Helios Airways in Cyprus) and partly because of the property boom, as more and more people buy holiday homes.

One big question is when or whether the northern, Turkish-occupied part of the island will be reunified with the southern, Greek Cypriot part, and what happens to Cyprus then. Property values in the east around Protaras (close to the beautiful but Turkish-controlled town of Famagusta and its long, sandy beaches) are likely to rocket. A great deal of land will be reclaimed by its rightful owners but eventually opportunities will open up in the north – and foreigners are allowed to own more than one property.

Retiring or Relocating

At the moment, for half the price of a four-bedroom semi in West London you could snap up a luxury villa in Cyprus, with a great deal more entertaining space, marble floors, air conditioning, private swimming pool, five or six bedrooms and a decent garden. For under £150,000 you can buy a smart four-bedroom property with pool and outdoor space.

Many people who have paid off their UK mortgage are selling up and moving to Cyprus to a better house, with a couple of hundred thousand pounds in the bank. The only places where Cypriot property prices are on a par with the UK are the very rare beachfront properties and on the golf courses, where you pay a huge premium for the views and proximity of the golf course. So, in general, Cyprus is a good place to start again with an easier life and money in the bank.

Relocation is not just something for retirees, either. Cyprus has several good English and American schools and a solid education system. Salaries are much lower than in the UK, but so is the cost of living. A couple owning a house and a car could comfortably live on CY£350 a month. Brits can work in Cyprus now with relative ease, as the island is a member of the EU. More and more young people are moving to the island with their children in search of a more peaceful, carefree life.

However, be aware that if you relocate and downsize it may be difficult to get back on the property ladder should you return to the UK. Moving to Cyprus is not like moving to France; it's an island in the far eastern corner of the Mediterranean and you can't drive there or just nip backwards and forwards. Life is quiet compared with somewhere like London or Manchester and getting to other parts of Europe can be expensive.

Who's Buying in Cyprus?

The British are the largest expat market, and include a large community of British Cypriots who were born and raised in the UK but have decided to go back to their roots for the better quality of life. The largest British community is in Limassol, although Paphos and its suburbs are fast catching up.

Germans are also snapping up property, particularly in Paphos and Pissouri, while Russians buy in Limassol or in small pockets all over the island, often for the purposes of development. Cypriots are the biggest buyers of property in Nicosia, the capital. Although Nicosia is a charming and sophisticated city, its lack of a nearby beach puts off most British buyers. There is also growing interest in the island from Middle Eastern buyers, whether they are British expats who no longer want to live in the region, or natives of Middle Eastern countries who are buying as an investment.

Red Tape

Living in Cyprus

If you want to settle, work, run a business or retire in Cyprus, there are procedures that must be followed. The process is much simpler than it used to be for citizens of European Union countries, now that Cyprus has joined the EU. But be warned that a lot of the information on the Internet, and even some material published by the Cyprus Tourism Organisation, might be pre-EU and out of date.

Visas and Permits

Citizens of any EU country and of countries in the European Economic Area which are not in the EU (Iceland, Liechtenstein, Norway and Switzerland) can enter the Republic of Cyprus with an identity card or a valid passport. Dependants – spouses and children – enjoy the same rights as the European citizen whom they accompany but a dependant who is not a national of an EU country must have a visa. Citizens of Australia, Canada, Japan and the USA require no visa.

Tourists may stay up to three months and are not allowed to work. If you decide to stay longer, you need to apply for a temporary residence permit. If you've got a stamp in your passport issued by the Turkish Republic of Northern Cyprus you will probably have trouble getting into the Republic of Cyprus (the south). The only legal points of entry are the airports at Larnaca and Paphos and the ports of Limassol and Larnaca.

Residence

European citizens who wish to live in Cyprus are required to register with the Department of the Population and Migration Archive or with an office of the Aliens and Migration Service of the police. Once registered, you are allowed to look for work. European citizens who work and reside legally in Cyprus and their dependants have the same rights as citizens of Cyprus as regards pay, working conditions, residence, social insurance and trade union membership.

Residence Permits for EU citizens

When you first arrive, you must apply within eight days for an **alien registration certificate (ARC)** at the local immigration branch of the police (issued automatically for monitoring purposes). A fee of CY£20 is paid for the issue of this. When you have a job, you must also apply for a social insurance number.

If you and your family wish to stay in Cyprus for more than three months, or work in Cyprus, you should apply for a **residence permit** through the local district aliens and immigration branch of the police. Application forms for the issue of a residence permit are available at the Civil Registry and Migration Department of the Ministry of Interior and at the district aliens and immigration branches of the police. They are also available at **www.moi.gov.cy**.

The application form must be submitted within three months of entry in the Republic. The residence permit is issued within a maximum period of six months from the date of submission of the application. The first permit you will receive will be valid for five years, and will be renewable indefinitely.

You must supply the original and a photocopy of each of the following:

- **your passport.**
- **two recent passport photos.**
- **details of all visits to Cyprus for the last five years.**
- **all up-to-date bank statements and investment details (such as share certificates).**
- **statement of all income (royalties, annuities).**

- deeds or contract of purchase of any property in Cyprus or of house rent.
- certificate of medical insurance.
- anything else that demonstrates that you are solvent and not likely to become a burden to the Cypriot state.

After a few months, you will receive a '**pink slip**' to attach to the alien's visitor permit.

After two years, you can apply for a **permanent residence permit**. It is best to do this about 18 months before the pink slip expires, to avoid having to renew the pink slip while the new permit is being processed. This procedure is fairly similar, except that you will also be invited to attend an interview at the District Office by the person responsible for the municipality where you reside.

If you intend to work, you need a **confirmation of engagement** from your employer or a **certificate of employment** stamped by the Labour Department of the Ministry of Labour and Social Insurance, in which the duration and type of the work you are doing is stated. You can still work while the formalities of obtaining the residence permit are being carried out.

Citizenship

There are two ways to apply for Cypriot citizenship: by naturalisation and as a result of marriage to a Cypriot citizen.

Anyone over 18 years old and of 'full capacity', who has been legally residing in Cyprus for at least seven years or has accumulated a total of at least seven years' residence in the Republic, of which residence in Cyprus in the year before the date of application was continuous, is entitled to apply for Cypriot citizenship. A birth certificate, copy of passport, good character certificate, two photographs and the publication in a Cypriot newspaper for two consecutive days of the applicant's intention to apply for naturalisation are required. The application must be submitted on form M127.

Persons married to a Cypriot are entitled to apply for Cypriot citizenship after completing three years of marriage in 'harmonious cohabitation' with their Cypriot spouse. The marriage certificate, a good character certificate, the birth certificate of the applicant and particulars of the Cypriot spouse (a copy of their Cypriot passport) are required. It is also necessary to have a certificate issued by the chairman of the Communal Council (Muktar) stating that the applicant and their spouse have been living continuously in his or her sector for at least two years immediately before the date of application. Applicants must be residing in Cyprus legally. The application must be submitted in duplicate on form M125.

For forms and further information contact:

- **Migration Department**, Ministry of the Interior, 1457 Lefkosia (Nicosia), t 22 80 45 10, f 22 67 69 44, **migration@crmd.moi.gov.cy.**
- **Citizen's Charter of the Ministry of the Interior** at **www.moi.gov.cy/cc.**

Working in Cyprus

The following categories of people are allowed to work in Cyprus:

- **citizens of Cyprus and of the other countries of the EU/EEA.**
- **foreign nationals who are of Cypriot origin on their mother's or father's side (proof is needed).**
- **political refugees.**
- **foreign spouses of Cyprus nationals.**

Seasonal Work

A European citizen who wishes to work in Cyprus for a period of less than three months must declare their presence to the Department of the Population and Migration Archive or to an office of the Aliens and Migration Service of the police within eight days of entering the country.

European citizens can enter Cyprus without an employment contract and look for work for a period of up to three months. Those who find work must contact the Department of the Population and Migration Archive or an office of the Aliens and Migration Service of the police, again, in order to be registered in the relevant archives.

Long-term Work

Those want to work for a period longer than three months must register with the Department of the Population and Migration Archive or with an office of the Aliens and Migration Service of the police. When they find a job, the statement of recruitment must be stamped by the Department of Labour of the Ministry of Labour. The statement of recruitment should state the duration of the employment, the job description and other relevant particulars.

Dependants who accompany a citizen of Europe who wishes to work in Cyprus must register with the Department of the Population and Migration Archive or with an office of the Aliens and Migration Service of the police. Relevant documents such as a birth certificate, a marriage certificate and evidence of funds for maintenance will need to be presented for dependants.

Cyprus is home to many offshore companies, which are governed by different rules; executives from these companies need to apply for a temporary residence and employment permit through the Central Bank of Cyprus with a form obtained from their lawyer or accountant. Permits are granted readily. Non-executive staff must apply through their relevant district labour office. Cypriot workers are given priority for non-executive jobs in offshore companies.

For further information contact:

- **Migration Department**, Ministry of the Interior, 1457 Lefkosia (Nicosia), **t** 22 80 44 35 or **t** 22 80 44 33, **f** 22 67 69 44, **migration@crmd.moi.gov.cy**.

Starting a Business

Many British residents have started small businesses on moving to Cyprus, running anything from pubs and restaurants to video hire shops and water-sports rentals. Local English language newspapers and property websites like Living Cyprus (**www.living-cyprus.com**) advertise businesses for sale.

Setting up as self-employed in Cyprus is easier than it used to be before the island joined the EU, when you needed a Cypriot partner and a minimum level of investment. Investors from the European Union are now allowed 100 per cent equity participation in any enterprise in Cyprus without a minimum level of capital investment (apart from businesses involved in land development, which are subject to different rules). Applications for projects that may create environmental problems or be detrimental to the country's economy or national security may be rejected, and businesses relating to stockbrokering, financial advice and services are subject to more strict criteria.

EU citizens can register a foreign direct investment company with the office of the Registrar of Companies. They must submit a statistical declaration, which is available in electronic form (from **www.centralbank.gov.cy**) to the Central Bank of Cyprus, purely for statistical purposes.

For further information contact:

- **Foreign Investments Section (International Division)**, 80 Kennedy Avenue, PO Box 25529, 1395 Lefkosia, Nicosia, **t** 22 71 43 39, **f** 22 37 81 64, **idfi@centralbank.gov.uk**.
- **Ministry of Commerce, Industry and Tourism**, Foreign Investors Services Centre, **t** 22 86 72 39, **f** 22 37 55 41, **mcindustry2@cytanet.com.cy**.
- **Registrar of Companies**, 1427 Lefkosia (Nicosia), **t** 22 40 43 01 or 22 40 44 82, **f** 22 30 48 87, **deppcomp@rcor.gov.cy**, **www.mcit.gov.cy/drcor**.

Educating Children

Education is compulsory until the age of 15, and the state system provides education for children from the age of three. Many Cypriot students remain at school until they are 18 and then go on to study at an institute of higher education. The school year is divided into three terms of three months, with attendance on five days of the week. School hours can be a considerable problem for working mothers, as school finishes at around 1.30pm. After-school clubs exist but many Cypriot mothers rely on their extended family to provide childcare, so such clubs are few and far between. For more information about education in Cyprus, see 'Education', pp.137–8.

Retiring in Cyprus

It is relatively simple to retire in Cyprus; see 'Retirement', pp.124–5.

Culture and Politics

The Cypriots

Cypriot families are extended and close-knit and an extremely important influence on society. Family members are very protective of one another. In business nepotism is rife, with parents often encouraging their children to follow in their footsteps and promoting them within the company once they have done so. *See also* 'The Family and Everyday Life', pp.153–6, and 'The Role of Women in Cyprus', p.154.

The majority of the population of Cyprus (84.1 per cent) is Greek Cypriot and Christian Orthodox. Turkish Cypriots, who make up 11.7 per cent of the population, are Sunnite Muslims. Young people are encouraged to go to church and almost all marriages take place in church, but church attendance is in decline among younger Cypriots. *See* 'Religion', p.156.

Cypriot Ties with the UK

Great Britain administered Cyprus as a colony from 1878 to 1960. With the treaties of Zurich and London of 1959, Cyprus was given independence while Turkey, Greece and the United Kingdom reserved for themselves special rights as guarantor powers, bound to maintain the independence, territorial integrity and security of the republic with the right of intervention to restore the constitution. The UK retained two sovereign base areas for its own defence purposes. Consequently, Britain retains strong ties with the island and has left its legacy, including driving on the left, a similar legal system to that of the UK, and a widespread understanding of English.

There are currently some 270,000 Cypriots living in the UK, out of an estimated half a million living overseas. Around 30,000 live in the USA and 22,000 in Canada, but the British Cypriot expat population is by far the largest. So every Cypriot you meet will know someone in the UK, have lived in the UK, have a business connection with the UK or at least have some understanding of where you come from and what it's like there.

Military Presence in Cyprus

There are British military bases at Akrotiri/Episkopi and Dhekelia, covering 98 square miles, or 2.74 per cent of the country's territory. The bases were retained by Britain under the 1960 treaty that gave Cyprus its independence. The bases enable the UK to maintain a permanent military presence at a strategic point in the eastern Mediterranean. The Army presence includes the Joint Service Signals Unit at Akrotiri and 62 Cyprus Support Squadron Royal Engineers and 16 Flight Army Air Corps at Dhekelia, alongside a variety of supporting arms.

RAF Akrotiri is an important staging post for military aircraft and the communication facilities are an important element of the UK's worldwide links. Either base can be used for a variety of military and humanitarian operations.

A UN peacekeeping force, UNFICYP, comprising 1,209 military personnel, has been on the island since 1964. It arrived after the outbreak of fighting in December 1963 and Turkish threats to invade. Its chief task is to supervise the buffer zone between the Republic of Cyprus in the south and the area in the north occupied by Turkey. The peacekeeping force is also present to maintain the ceasefire and is an important reassurance to Greek Cypriots, given that 35,000 Turkish troops occupy the north of the island.

It is also possible to find up to a regiment's worth of British soldiers serving with these United Nations Forces in Cyprus, although there is no operational link between British soldiers serving in the sovereign base areas and UNFICYP. These soldiers serve on an unaccompanied six-month tour of duty as United Nations soldiers, during which they wear UN berets and receive the UN medal for their efforts.

The Impact of Tourism

Tourism plays an important role in the Cyprus economy and its continuing growth is vital for the success of the buy-to-let market. According to the Cyprus Tourism Organisation (CTO), in 2003 tourism contributed about 8.7 per cent to GDP and 10.5 per cent of the workforce was engaged in the industry. That year, over 2.3 million tourists visited Cyprus, mainly from the UK (58 per cent). Some 5.6 per cent came from Germany and 4.7 per cent from Greece. Growing markets included the Republic of Ireland, Eastern Europe and the Middle East, with most other markets showing a slight downward trend. This was, however, an unusual year, because of the war in Iraq and the threat of SARS to international flying.

The Cyprus Tourism Organisation has developed a 10-year plan with various goals, including to increase the length of stay of visitors, to get them to spend more and to get them to travel more out of season. The success of this plan will have a direct impact on the holiday letting market. Various 'target' types of visitor have been identified, including those interested in culture, nature, walking and hiking, golf, cycling, yachting, weddings, honeymoons and cruises. If the CTO is successful in promoting the island to these markets, more opportunities will be opened up to home-owners looking for letting opportunities.

Where in Cyprus?

The areas in the Republic of Cyprus have clearly defined characteristics: different landscapes, different architecture, and even different types of people attracted to them. Ayia Napa, for example, is heaving with young people, clubs and bars in summer but is extremely quiet in winter. Limassol boasts of its easy access to the Troodos mountains, its wine-growing industry and its attractive old town centre. Paphos attracts the Brits, with its pretty waterfront, hill villages and nearby beaches and mountain scenery. Larnaca, something of a poor relation, is undergoing a renaissance to become a sophisticated, upscale beach resort, while Nicosia, the capital, is cosmopolitan and lively. Then there are the 'new' areas: Coral Bay, outside Paphos, with its vast homes and rolling agricultural landscape, or the sleepy towns of Polis and Latchi in the northwest.

All around the expanding urban areas are villages, each with its own sense of community, and the choice of many buyers looking for village life in proximity to a big town. Finally, for those who want to go right back to nature, the whole Troodos mountain range and its foothills is peppered with tiny villages and hamlets, where more and more people are buying plots, or old village houses to renovate.

Cyprus is officially divided into six districts: Famagusta, Kyrenia, Larnaca, Limassol, Nicosia and Paphos. The Turkish Cypriot area's administrative divisions include Kyrenia, all but a small part of Famagusta, and small parts of Nicosia and Larnaca.

One thing you'll notice straight away on the island is the use of alternative place names. In recent years, using an official system of transliteration from the Greek alphabet, these names have changed:

- Nicosia has become Lefkosia.
- Limassol has become Lemesos.
- Paphos has become Pafos.
- Ayia Napa has become Agia Napa.
- Larnaca has become Larnaka.
- Famagusta has become Ammochostos.

Buying Property in Northern Cyprus

This book deals only with buying in the south of the island. At present, the north is occupied by Turkey, so any purchase would be through a Turkish, rather than Greek Cypriot, agent, in Turkish lire rather than Cyprus pounds, and subject to the legal system of Turkey. Land ownership in the north is under heavy dispute and emotions run high when it comes to property development. If you buy here, you must be aware that the land you purchase may once have belonged to a displaced Greek Cypriot, whatever the vendor tells you. When the island is reunified, they will be back to claim it and you will potentially have a lawsuit on your hands. There is certainly a thriving property market in the north, but nothing like that of the south.

Larnaca

For many years Larnaca has been overshadowed by the other Cypriot towns as far as tourism is concerned. It hasn't enjoyed the development of Limassol, and it doesn't have the scenic beauty of Paphos or the legendary nightlife of Ayia Napa, but it is a lively town with a great history and some good property deals.

Larnaca sprawls along a sandy beach, the length of the wide half-moon of Larnaca Bay. From a distance, the town looks almost Middle Eastern – low-rise, sand-coloured houses, a tangle of TV aerials and water tanks on their roofs, backed by scrub-covered hills and almost desert-like plains, the metallic glint of the Mediterranean in the distance. Just south of the town is the airport, opposite a curious salt lake. The lake dries up in summer and forms a white-crusted dustbowl, but for the rest of the year it's very attractive, with varied bird life, including flamingos. The Hala Sultan Tekke mosque (*see box on p.18*) on the western bank is an important Muslim shrine and despite its incongruous setting is well worth a visit.

Larnaca is built on the foundations of the ancient city of Kition, dating back to the 13th century BC. The city never gained much importance, as it was often damaged by earthquakes, but it became an important trading centre in the Ottoman period (1571–1878). There's very little left today: bits of the acropolis, a small Mycenaean site and the main site, off Leontiou Makhera Street, where you can look at the ongoing excavations. Modern Larnaca's seafront is its greatest charm. The town has a fine, sandy beach, and the whole waterfront was developed a few years ago as a pedestrian zone, lined with restaurants and bars. Further along there are fabulous fish tavernas right on the waterfront. Everybody gathers down on the seafront at weekends, at lunchtimes and in the evenings and there's a great buzz and a sense of camaraderie. It's for this reason that a lot of buyers choose an apartment right in town. Needless to say, those on the seafront come with a premium price tag. The benefit of living right in the centre is that you don't need to drive everywhere. The infrastructure is good, too, with several British or American schools in the town.

The town has a more 'Cypriot' feel than Limassol or Paphos. A lot of service industries are based here and it's a popular shopping centre. Because so many Cypriots live here (and a lot of people from Nicosia have weekend homes as well), the town is busy year-round. It is also well positioned for the salubrious charms of Ayia Napa, half an hour's drive east along the motorway, and the beautiful sandy beaches of Protaras and Cape Greco. Nicosia is only half an hour away and thanks to the motorway linking Larnaca and Limassol, the Troodos Mountains are an easy day trip.

Pilgrimage to Larnaca

On the west bank of the Larnaca salt lake is Hala Sultan Tekke, a very important mosque where Umm Haram, believed to be the maternal aunt of the Prophet Mohammed, is buried. The story has it that she fell from her mule and broke her neck in AD 649 when accompanying Arab raiders to Cyprus. She was buried on the spot, and the mosque was erected over the site in 1816.

This unassuming little mosque is one of the top destinations for Muslim pilgrimages, surpassed in importance only by Mecca, Medina and the Al-Aksa mosque in Jerusalem. As well as the mosque, there's a graceful minaret on the site and a small water garden. It is open daily from 7.30am to 7.30pm, although visitors are not allowed in during prayer times.

Larnaca also has strong links with Christianity. The town's first bishop was Agios Lazaros, brother of Mary and Martha in the New Testament, who settled there after the episode of being raised from the dead by Jesus. Lazaros died in Cyprus and was buried in a church known known as Agios Lazaros. In the 17th century a new church was erected on the site, with a distinctive and very pretty campanile (bell tower), still standing today. His tomb was discovered in 1890 and his remains were stolen.

Larnaca is predicted to be the next big thing on the island, with millions of Cyprus pounds earmarked for investment. It has many advantages to buyers and, if you scratch the surface, great hidden charm. For a start, Larnaca has the island's principal airport, which is to undergo a massive and much-needed renovation, with a brand new passenger terminal. The marina is also to be developed, adding an air of glamour as it attracts bigger yachts (currently the only marinas are in Limassol and Paphos). The government is also aiming to make Larnaca a port of call for cruise ships. An 18-hole golf course with a nine-hole golf academy is to be built to the west of the airport near the small town of Zygi. Perhaps most important to investors, the remodelled seafront is to be extended all the way from the town to the airport.

The Environs of Larnaca

It is perhaps what's happening outside Larnaca that is the most exciting for investors, though. West of the airport is one of the last undeveloped stretches of coastline, ending at the sleepy town of **Zygi**. Most people pass this area by as they head west on the motorway towards Limassol in their rental cars. But take the old road instead of the motorway and you'll pass through rolling fields of carob trees and potatoes, stretching right down to narrow, admittedly gritty beaches, probably the way Limassol and Paphos looked 30 years ago. Smart buyers, mainly Cypriots, have snapped up seafront plots here and put up lavish villas, and developers are beginning to build, either on the waterfront where it's permitted, or on the inland side of the road, overlooking the fields towards the beaches. Zygi is a gorgeous little village, famous for its fish tavernas. It is marred only by a large refinery on the horizon, but most of the new developments will not be able to see this.

There are several villages behind Larnaca where people are recognising a good bargain, too. The landscape around the town is scrubby and flat – almost desert-like in places – but on a slight hillside, **Pervolia** has some very attractive developments with sweeping views across the town to the sea. **Kiti** is extremely quiet, with a few pockets of development, while **Tersafanou** is perched on a hill, with cobbled streets in the village centre giving a feel of authenticity. Prices are considerably lower here than in other parts of the island – for example, a five-bedroomed house is around CY£170,000, a new-build in Kiti around CY£155,000 for four bedrooms, and an apartment in Pervolia around CY£59,000.

Ayia Napa and Protaras

Ayia Napa

Ayia Napa is a good investment for holiday lets, but a less attractive prospect for year-round living, as practically everything shuts down in winter. A three-bedroomed house with pool costs around CY£175,000, while a one-bedroomed apartment in the centre can go for as little as CY£35,000.

The Cypriots have succeeded in bringing year-round tourism to Paphos, Larnaca and Limassol but much less so to the eastern end of the island, despite its sunny climate and superb sandy beaches. The town is extremely popular with tourists in the 18–30 age bracket, mainly from Britain and Scandinavia. It's known as the 'second Ibiza' but doesn't yet have the hippy-chic cachet of Ibiza. Despite its rowdy image, Ayia Napa is actually a fairly clean-living place, as the Cypriot government has zero tolerance of drugs. Families manage to coexist happily with the clubbers in summer.

Ayia Napa was once a modest village, sitting close to the end of Cape Greco, the southeastern point of the island. There's essentially one old part of the town – the monastery in the centre, built by the Venetians in the 16th century, with a peaceful cloistered courtyard. Everything else in the town is new, and is geared towards tourism, from large hotels to smaller establishments and apartments. The town is quite attractive but becomes a sea of neon in summer, with music thudding out through the streets. There's a small harbour, lined with tavernas, and one of the island's best beaches. The surrounding country-side is dry and scrubby, and not far to the north is the infamous 'green line', the division between the south and the Turkish-occupied north. By night, Ayia Napa has a real buzz, with people thronging the streets and bars and tavernas open late, but you'd have to be at home in this kind of atmosphere to thrive here. By around October, the whole place is like a ghost town as sanity returns.

There's masses to do centred around the beach in Ayia Napa. Gently shelving Nissi Beach is where the action is, with jetskis and waterski boats buzzing up and down, and plenty of night time attractions including bungee jumping from a crane. It is not especially quiet at any time of day. Macronissos Beach, three minutes away, is more family-orientated. There's also a big water park and various activities like go-karting. To escape all this, jump in the car and head for beautiful Cape Greco, with crystal clear water, rocks and cliffs, and a ban on noisy watersports. It's a romantic place to watch the sunset.

Protaras

A few minutes' drive across the cape is Protaras, a quieter version of Ayia Napa with equally wonderful beaches, particularly in Fig Tree Bay. The development of recent years now stretches all the way from here to neighbouring Paralimni. When the island is reunified, this area is likely to boom, thanks to its proximity to lovely Famagusta, once Cyprus's premier resort, just north of the Green Line.

Limassol and Pissouri

Limassol

At first glance, Limassol looks something of a dusty, urban sprawl, but it has a great deal of charm and is a favourite among Brits. Located just west of the centre of the south coast, Limassol has excellent road connections to the rest of the island – a motorway to the airport (about 40 minutes); a new motorway to Paphos (40 minutes to the west); and reasonable roads due north into the Troodos Mountains, where locals go at the weekends to walk, picnic and smell the pine-scented air.

The town is bordered by the motorway to the north, the archaeological site of Amathous to the east, and the Akrotiri peninsula, British sovereign base territory, to the west. The British base of Episkopi is a short drive west along the old coast road. Limassol's port is the main centre of shipping for the island, with cargo and cruise ships coming and going from all over the world.

There are several distinct areas of development. The Amathous area is a long string of ribbon development to the east, all the prime beach spots dominated by four- and five-star hotels. The main road forms a strip of bars, clubs and restaurants all the way up to the edge of the commercial centre of the old part of town. Many of these are geared to British tastes, with pub food, draught bitter and sport on TV. It's not at all Cypriot, in the traditional sense, but it draws the crowds year-round.

The town is extending northwards beyond the motorway, and various villages like Germasogia and Mesa Gitonia have now practically become suburbs. Prices are high in these popular areas; a luxury new home in a village, with five bedrooms, pool and a large plot, will command as much as CY£420,000, while a smaller new-build with garden and pool on a development in a village costs from CY£140,000. A large maisonette in Limassol itself, with three bedrooms, will cost around CY£118,000.

Limassol centre has shops, offices, hypermarkets and a lot of new development, as well as some waterfront apartments in established blocks. Prices range from CY£50,000 for a small two-bedroom apartment to CY£140,000 for a superior beach-front flat. The old centre is gorgeous, its narrow streets clustered around the hulking Limassol Castle, which houses an excellent medieval museum. The Grand Mosque, still in use, is close by and the old streets conceal some excellent restaurants, not to mention a variety of shops and market stalls. If you want to brush up on Cypriot history while you're looking for property, pay a visit to the new Time Elevator, in the old carob mill just behind the castle. It's a thrilling multimedia ride with amazing special effects that propel you through 10,000 years of history (with an admittedly daft script).

One of the best things about Limassol is the constant sense of antiquity. The Amathous excavation site to the east is fascinating, with some of the remains dating back to 1000 BC. Artefacts and parts of ancient buildings pop up everywhere – part of an old necropolis, for example, is carefully protected within the grounds of the Amathus Beach Hotel. There are rare stories of people buying plots of land, discovering something as they dig, going ahead and building around it and then having to allow visitors constant access to the site, as all antiquities must be made available to the public.

Limassol's other big attractions are Kolossi Castle, 14km to the west, built by the Knights Hospitallers, and nearby Kourion, a second-century amphitheatre still in superb condition. The theatre seats 3,500 and is often used for outdoor

Richard the Lionheart

Richard the Lionheart landed at Limassol in 1191 en route to his third crusade, accompanied by his French fiancée, Berengaria of Navarra, when their ship was wrecked in a storm. Richard's stay turned out to be longer than planned as he ended up in battle against the island's ruler, Isaac Comnenos, and after defeating him married Berengaria at Limassol Castle, crowning her Queen of England.

Richard had conquered Cyprus but was short of funding for his crusades, so sold the island to the Knights Templars in 1192 to raise money for an army. However, the conditions of the sale made the Templars unable to rule, as they did not have the necessary funds to pay Richard any more after they had put down four-tenths of the price he asked. To raise the rest of the money, they taxed the Cypriot people, who rebelled and were cruelly crushed by the Templars. The Templars eventually gave Cyprus back to Richard, who promptly sold it to Guy de Lusignan, a Norman knight, whose family ruled the island for nearly 300 years, until the Venetians annexed it for themselves in 1489.

dance, music and theatre productions, which on a balmy summer's night is a magical experience.

One thing Limassol doesn't have in abundance is beaches. The town beach is clean but grey and narrow, backed by pine trees. All the hotels have beaches but for the best sunbathing areas you need to head out of town. Governor's Beach, 29km to the east, is a startling sight of dark grey sand at the foot of towering white cliffs. It's pleasant out of season but gets very crowded in the height of summer and at weekends. Lady's Mile Beach, on the Akrotiri Peninsula, is long and sandy but also gets crowded. It's worth giving serious consideration to a pool if you're building or buying in Limassol!

Just a little further north from Limassol, 20 minutes' drive from the centre, behind a low ridge of hills, is another world of tiny, sleepy agricultural villages with quaint churches and one taverna which forms the epicentre of village life. **Fasoula**, **Spitali** and **Paramytha** are especially beautiful. Bear in mind that if you buy or build here, you will need to drive everywhere.

Pissouri

Even more exclusive is the up-and-coming area of Pissouri, a beautiful and typically Cypriot mountain village perched on a precipitous hill halfway between Limassol and Paphos. Pissouri is close to the exclusive Aphrodite Hills golf development and Petra tou Romiou, the alleged birthplace of Aphrodite, where if you swim at full moon, you can (maybe) unlock the key to eternal youth. The light around this beach is incredible, reflecting off the white cliffs and the vast chunk of rock (Aphrodite's Rock) on which you can climb. The sea has an almost turquoise quality. There are not many facilities, just a simple tourist pavilion in the car park, and the beach is often relatively empty out of season.

Pissouri and the surrounding developments of upscale villas, perched on the hillsides, appeal to people looking for a quieter life, who don't mind driving to Paphos or Limassol for the facilities of a larger town. Prices around here are high – CY£170,000–325,000 for a three-bedroomed house. What you pay for is the view – uninterrupted vistas of hills, olive groves and the long, sandy expanse of Pissouri Beach. A vacation at a couple of luxury hotels on the beach has lured holidaymakers back as home-owners, and the area is popular with Germans. The prices are likely to remain healthy as people look for something quieter than Paphos and more affordable than the golf course developments. The steep hills are an added advantage, as your view is never likely to be blocked.

Paphos

Paphos is in the southwest of the island and, like Limassol, has expanded beyond recognition over the last 10 years. The original town of Paphos is up a

Case Study: Villa in Pissouri

Cliff and Sheila Morrison bought a villa off-plan in the pretty Pissouri area between Paphos and Limassol. 'We looked at France and Spain first, but there was going to be a language problem for us in both,' says Sheila. 'I had already lived in Cyprus for three years, so we decided to go and have a look. I already knew it had a perfect climate, and they drive on the left and speak English. We didn't want to live in the Turkish north because of the potential land ownership issues still not resolved, or at the more commercialised Larnaca end. We looked at the lower mountains around Limassol and the area to the northwest of Paphos, near Akamas. We're both very interested in wildlife and my husband is a keen bird-watcher. That area is on the migratory routes for a lot of birds.'

The couple looked at houses that had already been built, and a number of plots, through the Paphos-based agent Nicholas & Tsokkas. 'It was quite by chance, really, that they introduced us to the developer Yiannis Liasides,' says Sheila. 'We had seen a couple of places we liked and were going home to think about it and perhaps make an offer. Yiannis said he had a nice plot on the cliff at Pissouri. I remember standing on the plot for the first time. You could see Pissouri village, Akrotiri Point, the mountains and the sea, all at once. I don't know how long that will last, but we know that nobody can build in front of us.

'Yiannis took us round some of his other projects and his work is excellent. His attention to detail is superb. He seems to take other properties that have been put up as a rush job and turn them into something really nice. We signed the initial papers just three hours before our flight took off.'

The villa will have four bedrooms, two of them en suite; a sitting room; dining room and kitchen; and a large garden with a pool. The main bedroom has a large balcony looking out to sea, with wonderful views. 'We will let Yiannis use it as a show home for a while, and then we'll take over,' says Sheila. 'We are not moving permanently to Cyprus straight away as my husband has not retired yet but we may well up sticks eventually.' The Morrisons' home will be ready in summer 2005 and they have built penalty clauses into the contract in the event of late completion of the work. Their lawyer has power of attorney to make the payments from their Cypriot bank account to the developer. 'Everybody has been incredibly helpful,' Sheila says. 'We certainly didn't feel any pressure to buy, although that was possibly because we got in at the very start of the development. If we'd been buying at Aphrodite Hills, it might have been different.'

What advice would she offer to anybody considering buying in Cyprus? 'Make sure you go to a legitimate real estate agent and check their background,' she says. 'I've heard of some horrible cases of people who have handed over all their money and had the agent run off with it. I'd also say, go and stay in the area at different times of year to make sure you like it. When I lived in Cyprus one of the things that I remember was that we skied in the morning at Troodos and swam in the sea in the afternoon.'

gentle hill from Kato Paphos, the beach and harbour area. In Kato Paphos there's a pretty seafront leading to a busy marina and solid, 600-year-old fort. Inland from here are some spectacular mosaics and the Tombs of the Kings, a necropolis of 100 tombs dating back to the 3rd century bc. These major archaeological attractions, combined with a string of chic, five-star hotels along the beach, give the resort a classy, upmarket feel.

There is no beachfront residential property in Kato Paphos itself; all the land is occupied by or designated for hotels and tourist apartments. Behind these, however, is one of the biggest areas of property development, the vast Universal Gardens (named after Universal Bank, which used to own the land). This area is ideal for a bargain-priced town house or apartment close to the centre of town and within reach of the beaches. When the land was sold it was divided into small chunks and sold off to individual developers, so there are a number of architectural styles (within the constraints of the planning allowances) and fairly dense land use. The area lacks character and at present there are few facilities serving the hundreds of plots, although a vast, empty tract in the middle has been designated for shops, schools and restaurants. It's hard to see how Universal will ever have true Cypriot character, but for some it will represent a good investment and the bars and clubs are within walking distance.

The Environs of Paphos

The development out towards Coral Bay starts at the Tombs of the Kings, where once-empty plots along a 13km stretch are now filling up fast with pastel-coloured villas. Beyond Coral Bay, continuing west, is the exclusive **St George** area, which stretches as far as the Sea Caves, a stunning coastal spot of towering cliffs, translucent blue water and caves and rock formations. Expect to pay London prices for a four-bedroomed villa with pool here and into the millions for a lavish mansion on a seafront plot.

Beyond the Sea Caves is the wild **Akamas Peninsula**, one of Cyprus's last spots of wilderness, heavily protected from development. The walking and beaches here are stunning, and wildlife includes griffon vultures and loggerhead turtles. There are no facilities and if you go into Akamas, you'll need a four-wheel drive and a supply of water. Akamas will never be developed (under current legislation, anyway), so Paphos cannot extend any further west.

To the northwest the coast road leads through banana plantations out to **Coral Bay**, an almost entirely artificial development, now extremely popular with property developers. There are several villages that are popular with British buyers. **Emba** is particularly pretty, with an old-fashioned village square and tavernas and some smaller, tasteful developments. **Pegia** is gorgeous, clinging to the side of a steep hill with breathtaking views across the whole Paphos plain down to the harbour. Pegia is not to everybody's taste, though: of the 10,000 inhabitants, some 8,000 are British. A detached house with pool is around

Case Study: Investment Property in Paphos

David and Angela Gabb of Gloucestershire were looking for a holiday home in the sun to use as an investment, to generate income in their retirement, and to use themselves. 'We had looked at Crete but we were on a limited budget,' explains David. 'We went to a property show in Birmingham and someone said we should look at Cyprus, where there were more opportunities. This turned out to be the case and we decided to fly out and have a look.'

The couple had not visited Cyprus before and ended up having rather a dramatic introduction to the island. 'We had a day looking around by ourselves, and the next day were shown around by Kypros from Nicholas & Tsokkas in Paphos,' David says. 'I liked him immediately and felt that he wasn't going to mess us around. We saw a property that was under construction that day and decided to go for it. It was brand new, a mile from the beach and convenient for the airport, and it only cost CY£76,000. Because my wife is disabled, we would need to make some changes to things like the bathroom, where we wanted rails and a shower instead of a bath, which Kypros agreed to.'

Unfortunately, the next day, Angela fell in the hotel and broke her arm. She was rushed to hospital and had to stay there for the rest of the week, after which she was taken by ambulance to the airport. 'This didn't prevent things from happening,' says David. 'Kypros helped us with opening a bank account, found us a lawyer and at one point, they all turned up at the hospital for the papers to be signed! They were really kind to us. His family visited us, and brought wine and cookies to the hospital room. The hospital, St George's in Paphos, was also superb. They let me sleep there on a bed, and fed me for the entire week. The apartment won't be ready for a few months but we're considering going back before then, as we have to choose furniture and it's been four months since we saw it. We intend to let the property out for holiday rentals when it's finished, and we already feel as though we know people and have friends on the island.'

And, unlike most investors, the couple already have extensive experience of the medical service!

CY£230,000, although you should expect a lovely view and features like stone floors and air-conditioning for this price.

Towards the east there are more villages between Paphos and Kato Paphos and the airport, 15km out of town. It's cheaper to buy here than to the west side of the town; a house in **Anarita** will cost around 50 per cent less than Pegia, for example. Some of the villages are extremely pretty, although the land is flatter on this side. **Mandria** has a lot of character; a lot of the plots are Turkish Cypriot owned and so at present are being used for agriculture, and the village has a charming, slightly crumbling feel. A three-bedroomed house here is around CY£130,000, as opposed to CY£170,000 in Emba.

When the island is eventually reunified, these Turkish Cypriot plots are likely to be developed and prices will rise, so it could be a good investment, depending on your analysis of what the future holds for Cyprus. A development of 85 houses here was sold off-plan within four months.

Golf at Paphos

Another reason for the popularity of Paphos is the golf. There are three 18-hole courses at present. The original one is at **Tsada**, opened in 1994 in the hills to the north of the town. The second course to open was at **Secret Valley**, on the old Paphos–Limassol road. The valley is hidden from the road, with views of the sea glittering in the distance, and the course runs along the valley floor. The villa developments seem slightly spartan at present; resale houses are going for a healthy (and many would say overpriced) CY£500,000, but there is not much 'village' atmosphere as such.

The third course, **Aphrodite Hills**, is a swanky and ambitious development sprawling across two hilltops, the course running across both plateaux with an impressive signature hole down in the valley between the two hills. The course opened in 2002 and accommodation has been launched in phases, with one hill devoted to 'village-style' houses and apartments, as well as a resort hotel, a luxury spa, and facilities including a village 'square' with shops and restaurants, and even a small chapel. The second hilltop is being used for luxury villa development, with a mere 8 per cent building density (which means each villa has a big garden). A four-bedroom villa costs upwards of CY£628,000, including all furnishings and a large garden with pool. The price does not, however, include membership of the golf club.

Nicosia

Capital of Cyprus since the 10th century, Nicosia is a lively, cosmopolitan city, with the dubious distinction of being Europe's last divided capital; the 'Green Line' separating north and south runs through the middle.

Because Nicosia is located inland and gets extremely hot in summer, an expat would have to have good reason, probably business, to buy here. It's not really a retirement spot, and there isn't much in the way of holiday letting, although it has a busy buy-to-let market. The city also has all the infrastructure you'd expect of a capital, with good international schools.

Although restrictions on crossing the Green Line were eased recently, there is still a slightly strange feeling about the Cypriot capital, with minarets gracing the skyline on the northern side and orthodox churches to the south. The old part was once entirely enclosed by dense stone walls, built by the Venetians, and the original gates – the Ammochostos Gate and Pafos Gate in the south and the Kyrenia Gate in the north – have been carefully preserved. Parts of the walls are in remarkably good condition. In the centre there are also several excellent museums, dedicated to folk art, handicrafts, Byzantine icons and archaeology. Even if you only end up visiting occasionally, don't miss the Museum of National Struggle, or the tiny, poignant museum on Ledra Street dedicated to those who are still missing as a result of the 1974 invasion.

One of the most appealing places in Nicosia is Laiki Geitonia, the pedestrianised area just inside the old walls. This charming neighbourhood has been carefully restored and you can wander round the narrow, vine-covered streets for hours, browsing in handicraft shops and looking at the enticing menus of the many tavernas. Food here is excellent and reasonably priced, and there's a great atmosphere from lunchtime until the small hours.

Property is reasonably priced in Nicosia, a 600 square metre plot with a five-bedroomed house in a quiet area will cost as little as CY£210,000. There's less development than on the coast but should you buy here and crave beach life you won't have to go far to Larnaca and its beaches, which are only half an hour down the motorway.

Polis and Latchi

Inland from Paphos, a main road (soon to become a motorway) runs due north to the quiet communities of Polis, an agricultural town, and Latchi, a fishing village, on the north side of the Akamas peninsula. Polis is slightly inland, and Latchi is directly on the coast with a wonderfully laid-back feel. The village has a colourful fishing harbour and a long, sandy beach with breathtaking views towards the surrounding hills. The atmosphere here is one of a quiet but pleasant holiday resort, with some excellent fish tavernas on the beach. You won't find nightclubs, theme parks or thumping music in Latchi.

Polis attracts people looking for a quiet, rural life. The town centre has several cafés and tavernas and a friendly, relaxed feel. Polis is actually built on the site of the ancient city-kingdom of Marion, which was an important centre for trade in Hellenic and Classical times. Some of the older houses, dating back over a hundred years, are fine examples of turn-of-the-last-century architecture.

Both towns are within easy reach of beauty spots like the Akamas Peninsula and the Baths of Aphrodite, which is just along the coast from Latchi and is a major tourist attraction. According to myth, Aphrodite would take her beauty baths in the pool of this natural grotto, which is shaded by a fig tree, and has a continuous run of water from the overhead rocks. It's a popular picnic and excursion spot today. On Akamas there's hiking, bird-watching and swimming from beautiful beaches where the drone of jetskis won't disturb you.

Polis and Latchi are popular with Germans as well as Brits and do well for holiday lets. Both are very quiet in winter, although there is a permanent community in each. At present, they have between 500 and 600 British-owned houses. There's quite a bit of development, both on the beach and inland. Prices are moderate – from as little as CY£62,000 for a small apartment on a development outside Polis to around CY£166,000 for a two-bedroomed bungalow on the beach at Latchi. If it's beach living you're after, this is one of the few areas of the island where you can find a decent villa right on the waterfront. Expect to pay about CY£340,000 for four bedrooms.

Property prices could rocket here once the new motorway opens, linking Polis to Paphos. While the existing road is in good condition, the chances are you'll be stuck behind a construction lorry, and the journey from Paphos can easily take 45 minutes or more.

The Environs of Polis and Latchi

The rugged, mountainous scenery between the two coasts is dotted with gorgeous, tranquil villages set among vineyards and olive groves, like **Souni**, **Choulou** and **Polemi**, places where time has stood still and old men gather at the café every day to play backgammon, and where the taverna is the centre of village life. Facilities are limited in these places – a village store at the most – but many expats are buying here, for the endless views, the solitude and the peace. Paphos is only 30 minutes away from the southern villages, so banks, bars and restaurants are within easy reach.

In these rural areas plots will have much lower building density regulations, so you have to buy more land to be able to put up a decent-sized house. As a result people are snapping up plots with fields, olive orchards and even vineyards. There's a growing trend to put up traditional stone houses, which is expensive but has enormous aesthetic appeal and keeps the house cooler inside, too. Specialist builders can be hired who are skilled in the art of stone-cutting.

Selecting a Property

04

Travelling to Cyprus

By Air

Cyprus is well served by flights from the UK. Cyprus Airways is the national airline; it operates a non-smoking, two-class service to various European and Middle Eastern countries, with regular services to London.

Cyprus has two international airports: Larnaca and Paphos. Larnaca Airport is about to undergo a big expansion, not before time, as it's packed in summer with several charter flights coming and going at any one time. Paphos Airport is fairly primitive, but adequate, with facilities and duty free shops. Larnaca Airport is only 10 minutes from downtown, while Paphos Airport to Kato Paphos takes about 20 minutes. Flying time from London to Cyprus is about four and a half hours. Key operators are:

- **Cyprus Airways, t** (020) 8359 1333, **www.cyprusairways.com**. Daily flights from London Heathrow to Larnaca; weekly from Heathrow to Paphos; twice a week from Stansted to Larnaca and Paphos; weekly from Birmingham to Paphos; three times a week from Manchester to Larnaca via Paphos. The airline has good links to the rest of Europe and onwards from Cyprus to the Middle East. From the USA, it's possible to connect via Amsterdam, Brussels, Paris, Rome or Vienna.

- **Helios Airways, t** 0870 750 2750, **www.helios-airways.com**. Low-cost airline with flights from Birmingham to Larnaca; Dublin to Paphos and Larnaca; Gatwick to Paphos; Heathrow to Larnaca; Luton to Larnaca and Paphos; and Manchester to Larnaca and Paphos.

- **British Airways, t** 0870 850 9850, **www.ba.com**. Daily flights from Heathrow to Larnaca; three times a week from Gatwick to Paphos operating as **GB Airways, t** (01293) 664000, **www.gbairways.com**.

By Sea

Limassol port is connected by ferry to Piraeas (Athens) and Haifa (Israel), as well as to some of the Greek islands in summer. Book through:

- **Salamis Tours, t** 25 86 06 00, **www.salamis-tours.com**. Salamis also operates short cruises in summer to Egypt, Greece, Lebanon and Syria.

Travelling around Cyprus

Cyprus has very little public transport infrastructure. There are no trains and no internal flights. The only options are private car, taxi or bus. You really need to

have a car to live here, or even the most basic journeys like trips to the supermarket become difficult.

By Bus

Bus services are inter-urban, urban and rural. They tend to be slow. The village
bus services may have rustic charm in the beginning but are pretty basic and
infrequent.

Intercity buses operate between Nicosia and Larnaca, Nicosia and Limassol
and Limassol and Larnaca; t 22 66 58 14 for timetables. Other services are:

- **Alepa Bus, t** 26 93 68 22. **Operates from Nicosia to Paphos and Limassol,
and between Paphos and Polis.**

- **Eman Buses, t** 23 72 13 21. **Between Larnaca, Protaras and Ayia Napa.**

There is an urban bus service in each town. For timetable information, telephone as follows:

- Nicosia, **t** 22 66 58 14.
- Ayia Napa, **t** 23 72 13 21.
- Larnaca, **t** 24 65 04 77.
- Limassol, **t** 25 37 05 92.
- Paphos, **t** 26 93 44 10.
- Paralimni, **t** 23 82 13 18.
- Polis, **t** 26 32 11 14.

By Inter-urban Service Taxi

Service taxis are slightly more comfortable than the bus and operate every
half-hour between main towns. Book by phone. The taxi will drop you anywhere
within the municipal boundary and most seat between four and eight people.
Needless to say, allow a lot of time if you have an appointment – you may be the
first pickup, with (at worst) seven further stops. Service taxis do not connect
towns and villages, or serve the airports. Taxis operate Monday to Friday
6am–6pm (7pm in summer) and weekends 7am–5pm. There is no service on
bank holidays.

The various companies are grouped together as **Travel & Express (Cyprus
Inter-urban Taxi Co. Ltd)** and can be contacted by telephone:

- Nicosia, **t** 22 73 08 88.
- Larnaca, **t** 24 66 10 10.
- Limassol, **t** 25 36 41 14.
- Paphos, **t** 26 93 31 81.

By Rural Taxi

Rural taxis can only be hired from their base stations, although they are allowed to collect from the airports or sea ports. They are not metered but do have fixed tariffs. Check the cost when you book.

By Urban Taxi

Urban taxis operate in towns, 24 hours a day. They can be booked by telephone or hailed in the street. They are metered and start charging as soon as you get into the car.

With all taxis, it is not necessary to tip the driver, although 10 per cent is appreciated, or a rounding up of the total.

By Car

Cyprus has an excellent road network and anybody moving here after living in a British city will be delighted with the comparative emptiness of the roads, and the free parking in most towns. They will be less impressed with Cypriot drivers. Although driving on the left makes the transition easy for Brits, there are some unpleasant local habits, including common failure to give way, and tailgating on the motorway or country roads, so keep your wits about you.

Three-lane motorways connect Nicosia, Larnaca, Limassol and Paphos, with the road from Larnaca to Ayia Napa and Protaras motorway in part. A new motorway is proposed to connect Paphos with Polis, although at the time of writing, construction hasn't started. The non-motorway roads are one or two lane and mostly tarred, although a four-wheel drive is advisable to visit Akamas, where most roads are dirt tracks with big potholes.

Signposting is excellent on the motorways and reasonable on the main roads. In villages, signs are often dusty or obscured, although almost all are in English as well as Greek. Tourist attractions are clearly signposted in brown.

Larnaca airport has numerous car hire companies, from big operators like Europcar (**www.europcar.com**), Alamo (**www.alamo.com**), Holiday Autos (**www.holidayautos.com**) and Hertz (**www.hertz.com**) to smaller, local firms. Cars are graded from A to G, G being the largest. If you're looking for property in the height of summer, you'll need a vehicle with air conditioning unless you want to arrive hot and uncomfortable at every viewing. Take a good pair of sunglasses, too – driving west in the afternoon can be dazzling and consequently exhausting. Take out windscreen replacement insurance if you're going off the beaten track, as there will be flying pebbles.

All rental cars have red licence plates and registration numbers starting with a Z. *See* 'Cars', pp.130–33, for information about bringing your car to Cyprus, buying a car in Cyprus and rules of the road.

Climate and Geography

Climate

Cyprus has a Mediterranean climate of mild, sometimes wet winters and long, hot summers. The climate is one of the biggest factors that attracts people to move to the island; it has the longest summer season in Europe, apart from the Canary Islands.

Spring comes around mid-February, with the almond trees in blossom and the whole island carpeted with flowers. Daytime temperatures are around 19°C (65°F), 9°C (40°F) at night. April to mid-May is just about perfect, with hot, sunny days and cooler nights. True summer starts in mid-May – until mid-October there are high temperatures, cloudless skies and cooling breezes from the sea. Evenings are cooler and more bearable in the mountains and on the coast. Expect an average of 32°C (90°F) on the coast and up to 40°C in Nicosia. The humidity is slightly less on the eastern end of the island, which is drier-looking than the west.

September and October are still sunny and the water is easily warm enough for comfortable swimming in the sea. Towards the end of October evenings tend to get cooler, although you can still sit out at night. Autumn comes by the end of November, when the trees in the Troodos Mountains begin to shed their leaves. December and January are the months of Mediterranean winter, bringing the possibility of rain, but still an average of six hours of bright sunshine a day.

Geography

Cyprus is the third-largest island in the Mediterranean after Sardinia and Sicily, at 240km long and 100km wide. A spine of mountains, the Troodos, runs horizontally along the centre of the southern part, while the north (occupied by Turkey) consists of a plain rising up to the Kyrenia mountains.

The Troodos are volcanic in origin and Cyprus today suffers the occasional earth tremor, although the last quake of any significant size was half a century ago. All houses are built on a metal frame to resist tremors of up to seven on the seismic scale. The island's highest point is Mount Olympus in the Troodos, at almost 2,000m. The mountains are especially beautiful in winter, when it's warm on the coast and snowy at the peak of Olympus. There is even a short ski season, although for a keen skier it's nothing to get too excited about as the snow is usually mushy.

Vegetation in the mountains is mainly pine and oak, with vines, olives and citrus groves on the lower slopes. You'll notice a lot of dams around the lower slopes, creating reservoirs to collect the meltwater and winter rains. The water is pumped to the towns and agricultural areas and some of the reservoirs are used for recreation, such as freshwater fishing. Water shortages used to be a problem, particularly when the island started developing golf courses, but desalination plants have changed that.

The island's coastline varies from towering cliffs to long, sandy beaches, to smaller, sheltered coves. Much of it is highly developed. Agriculture on the coastal plains includes cultivation of potatoes, citrus fruits, olives and bananas, while the vineyards tend to be inland, in the hills.

The island supports a great variety of wildlife, although some of it is struggling hard to survive. You'll spot the occasional mouflon (mountain sheep) and on the Akamas Peninsula, look out for the mighty griffon vulture, with a 2.5m wingspan. Eleanora's Falcon also breeds here. In winter, thousands of flamingos turn the salt lakes at Larnaca and Akrotiri into a great swath of pink, and on the northwest coast you might see loggerhead turtles and monk seals. On Lara Beach, part of the Akamas Peninsula, there's a turtle hatchery where volunteers protect the baby turtles from inquisitive tourists. Other interesting species to look out for are chameleons and vipers.

The Akamas Forest was declared a National Park in 1989, but elsewhere deforestation is rife. There are active conservation groups but the Cypriot population in general has not embraced environmental issues yet.

Choosing a Location

You've chosen the island, now you've got to pick your spot! This is the single most important decision in the purchase. Take a deep breath before you buy. Think it through, do your research and don't be pushed into anything just because it's a beautiful day and you can see yourself lying by that pool, as the developer stands next to you making noises about a 'once in a lifetime opportunity'. Think hard about why you're buying, what the property will be used for and what will happen when you sell.

A lot of people, particularly those who do not know Cyprus very well, question whether they should buy in the north or the south. This book deals only with the south as the legal situation – in fact, the whole process – in the north is completely different. There is also a very serious risk, for example, of moving into your dream home only to find that some displaced Greek Cypriot owns the land and, once the island is finally reunified, they will be fighting very hard to claim it back, whether it is occupied by you or by a Turkish Cypriot.

Here are some points for you to think about when considering where to buy:

  • **Decide whether you want to live in a town, in a village or in the countryside. The towns along the coast have all the infrastructure you'll need, but village life will be quieter.**

• Think about whether you want a new house that you can buy off-plan, or one that's already built on a new development. Or do you prefer an older house? Or do you want to acquire your own plot and design your dream home on it?

• Bear in mind the seasonality of resorts like Polis, Latchi, Protaras, Paralimni and Ayia Napa, which practically shut down outside the summer season. Even Paphos is much quieter in winter. Limassol and Larnaca are busy all year round.

• Consider whether you want to be near the beach, or whether you want a pool. Or are you not bothered about either? Many Cypriot buyers don't bother with a pool and prefer to spend their free time at the beach, although developers usually include the option of a pool in plots over a certain size. If you are buying in winter when it's cool, try to picture day after day of 40°C, when a pool will become the focal point of your life. Similarly, don't laugh when you're buying in August and the developer mentions central heating. The mountains in particular are cool in winter and many houses come with a fireplace.

• Speak to other expats who have bought in the area, who will be able to tell you about any pitfalls. A good estate agent or developer will be glad to put you in touch with other buyers.

• Be clear about your motives for buying: is it for rental purposes, relocation or resale? Holiday rentals will want a pool, or proximity to the beach. If you're buying your dream home, check all possible avenues to make sure nobody is going to put up a housing estate in your perfect view or, if they are, that it will not totally obscure your view.

• Think about how much renovation you can face when you're considering that tumbledown stable block, and remember that you are operating in a country where you are probably not familiar with the system. You will need a good lawyer, architect and builder, and someone to manage the project.

• If you are buying a plot, check that the land you are buying is the land you are being shown and make sure that there is permission to build there – you don't want to find out that you've bought land which can only be used for agriculture.

• If you are hoping to build your own property, make sure the plot you've chosen has permission for your preferred style of construction. There are strict rules on the colour and form of houses, so a Scandinavian-style chalet or something in a dazzling hue might not be permitted.

• Find out who else lives in the area. Other expats? Or is the community mainly retired Cypriots? Or is it a Russian, German or English enclave? Think carefully about whom you would like as neighbours. If you do like the idea of a rural life, be prepared to learn Greek if you want to get along.

• Look at what amenities are close by. If you don't mind being in the middle of nowhere, fine, but think twice about building a family-style house in a very remote area with no shops or schools – it may be impossible to sell and you will spend a lot of time commuting.

• If you're developing and hoping to sell to the overseas market, don't do something out of keeping with expatriate tastes, for example, build a huge, expensive villa with pool and a tiny garden, or a stunning house with no view.

• If you are buying a town centre apartment, try to avoid the ground and first floors. Besides the roar of traffic keeping you awake, you may have to contend with late night restaurants and bars, and early shop opening hours. Steer clear of flats where central heating and hot water bills are shared, or you'll be in danger of falling out with your neighbours.

• Selling your property can be considerably more complicated than buying it. Think about how desirable your property will be to others before handing over any cash.

• Visit your location in summer and winter. What's buzzing in summer may be dead in December, and what's a charming rural idyll in February may be overrun with tourists in July.

• If you're planning a home for long weekends only, don't choose something too far from the airports.

• Don't set your heart on a waterfront property, especially in Limassol or Paphos. There simply isn't enough to go round and plots on the seafront are few and far between. A mountain with a view is more realistic, or a property near the beach but possibly with a road, field or hotel between you and the Mediterranean.

• If your heart is set on a huge garden, your property will need to be in a rural area, where the density of land development is much lower. It's extremely rare to find an urban property with much outside space.

• Consider whether you want to live on a new development, where you will probably be part of an expat community. Would you prefer to be integrated into Cypriot life?

• Think carefully about where you live within your chosen area. The tourist strip in Limassol is the Amathus area, a long string of development along the beach. Though there's masses going on, it will be noisy in summer. In Paphos, Kato Paphos is the tourist area and, again, gets very busy in summer. Out towards Coral Bay is quieter, but again has much less going on in winter. Polis or Latchi may seem charming in summer, but are very quiet indeed in winter. Ayia Napa is attempting to introduce more of a year-round atmosphere but is also quiet off-season.

Case Study: Living on the Beach

Stella Clarke, 32, visited Cyprus, where she had friends, three years ago, and ended up staying and buying a flat with her partner. 'First, it was a bit of a holiday,' she says. 'But then I got a job in an offshore company. I rented a flat for three years and started looking for somewhere to buy around March 2004.'

Stella began to look in the Limassol area. 'There might be better job opportunities in Nicosia but I wasn't going to come from London and move somewhere that wasn't by the sea,' she says. 'Besides, there are quite a few offshore companies based in Limassol and they're looking for people with good English, French or German.' She started looking in the local paper and on the Internet and visited several agents. 'I saw the website of ECR and noticed that they had an office in the UK, so I thought they might be easy to talk to. Loukas, the agent there, was very helpful and spoke English. He showed me places in my price range – there was no messing around with things I couldn't afford. So I trusted him, and eventually something came up.'

Stella bought a recently renovated three-bedroom flat right on the seafront in Limassol for CY£140,000. 'I suppose it is a bit more expensive than similar flats in town, but it's still a lot cheaper than in the UK. It's centrally located, there are facilities all around me and at weekends I go to the beach. Life here is good compared to England. It's more relaxed, with less hustle and bustle.' The whole buying process was remarkably straightforward thanks to Stella's having a good estate agent. 'Loukas even came with me to the Land Registry Office,' she says. 'I had heard that there could be snags, buying property in Cyprus but, for us, there were no complications and it was absolutely fine.'

Where the Expats Live

There are British communities all over Cyprus and over 80,000 Brits are estimated to have bought in the southern part of the island alone. This includes a large community of British Cypriots who were born and raised in the UK but have decided to come back to their roots for the better quality of life. The largest British community is in Limassol, with Paphos hot on its heels, particularly the village of Peyia.

Germans are also snapping up property, particularly in Paphos and Pissouri, while Russians buy in Limassol and in small pockets all over the island, which they develop. Cypriots are the biggest buyers of property in Nicosia, the capital. Although Nicosia is a charming and sophisticated town, its lack of a nearby beach puts off most British buyers. With the growing number of businesses setting up on the island, though, Nicosia is worth considering if you are planning to enter the buy-to-let market. There is also growing interest in the island from Middle Eastern buyers, whether they are British expats who no longer want to live in the region, or natives of Middle Eastern countries who are buying as an investment.

Case Study: Emigrating to Cyprus

The Munro family bought a three-bedroom detached home with a swimming pool near Larnaca as a holiday home and ended up living in it full time. 'We bought our house about two years ago although we didn't move to Cyprus until spring of 2004,' says John Munro. 'We had holidayed in the Greek islands and Cyprus and property prices were pretty good at the time we decided to buy. We assumed property values would increase significantly once Cyprus got into the EU and this has proven to be the case. We ended up in Larnaca probably by luck. Initially I wanted to live in Paralimni but I didn't see anything I liked there that was the right price. I saw the work of the A&K Developers in this area and I liked it very much and thought it good value for money. We were definitely not attracted to Paphos and we didn't really like Limassol; I prefer the east. It's less humid and quieter, and the beaches are better. Larnaca is perhaps not the most beautiful place in the world – even slightly industrialised when you first see it – but we have grown to like it very much. The Cypriots have invested a lot of money in Larnaca and intend to invest a lot more.

'Initially, we were just going to buy a holiday home but my wife was offered a job and I saw a reasonable business opportunity so we decided to live there permanently. We had been on holiday to our house a couple of times and it got harder and harder to leave. I got quite friendly with the developer and I had a conversation with him during which I told him that my wife was a nurse. He said he could find her a job tomorrow if she wanted. I didn't really pay much attention but two weeks later, when we were back in Scotland, we had a call from a doctor asking when she could start at his clinic! We came out again in April to see how serious he was and what the clinic was like. Property prices by then in Scotland were going through the roof so we decided to sell up.'

The age range of expats varies from young parents who are raising their children on the island, to those who buy to let or to have a holiday home, to retirees looking for a place in the sun. Cyprus has excellent healthcare and education, so is appealing to younger people. It's by no means a retirement island.

There are various ways to meet other expats, including numerous message boards on the Internet. On the island, there are branches of the **United Kingdom Citizens Association (UKCA; t** 25 34 45 78, **info@ukca.com.cy, www.ukca.com.cy)** in Larnaca, Limassol and Paphos, all of which hold regular social events and are highly useful for settling in and getting to know people. Membership is CY£12 a year, joining fee CY£15 (plus VAT).

Choosing a Property

The Cypriot government is careful to keep new developments relatively homogenous, and different building zones have restrictions regarding colour,

The next thing was for John to find something to do. He is an electrical engineer by trade, but didn't see anything appropriate in Cyprus. 'Because we had a holiday home, I was aware that it was difficult to look after and let out,' he says. 'I thought there might be a business opportunity there as so many British people are buying around here.' Absolute Property Services was founded (**www.absolutelycyprus.com**) and, four months on, John is getting busier, working in part with the developer from whom he bought.

The family took the unusual step of putting their two children, aged nine and 10, into a Cypriot school. 'They've got to learn Greek,' says John, 'and we figured that total immersion was the way to do it. We thought, we're not going to go back to Scotland and I want to make sure they have every opportunity when the time comes to work in Cyprus. It has become apparent to us that most good jobs here require fluent English and Greek.

'We are amazed at how quickly they are picking it up. We thought we would give them a year in the local school and, as long as they were not slipping backwards and were not unhappy, we would keep them there. They've made lots of friends and they skip off to school nowadays. We are only four months into the first year and I can safely say there is no way we'll change our plans. We did have a private tutor for a while, but the local ministry also provides three classes a week for them to learn Greek over and above the school day.'

So how has life changed since moving to Cyprus? 'Life is slower,' says John. 'My wife is working full-time but it's still not the same meaning as full-time at home. It is a different lifestyle, the Mediterranean way, and it has been quite hard to adapt, coming from a reasonably high-pressure job, as well as having the pressure to get my business up and running. But I am starting to enjoy the pace of life and we definitely get a lot more family time.'

style, height and so on. So while you'll find a mixed development of town houses, low-rise apartments and bungalows, you won't find one among them with a purple exterior, or a different coloured roof, or seven storeys. When you look carefully, there are actually many different styles of property, but at first glance this isn't so apparent.

Many people fantasise about a 'typical' Cypriot home. This might, in your dreams, be a lovely stone house surrounded by olive trees, goats and chickens scratching in the yard, and with uninterrupted views across the hillside. This sort of house may exist in rural areas, but in towns and their suburbs 'typical' houses are more likely to be boxy-looking, often with bare wires sticking out of the top layer (so that another floor may be added if the building density regulation for the area changes or the family comes into some money). They may have an unsightly water tank and solar panels on the flat roof, and a giant satellite dish attached to the front. Not quite so romantic! It's hardly surprising that new developments are so popular. You certainly won't find architecture in Cyprus comparable to, say, the Cyclades, or Ibiza, with quaint whitewashed houses with

The Rules of Land Development

It helps to understand the system of land development before you start looking at plans and new-builds; and it's essential if you want to build your own house. All land in Cyprus comes with a building density rating attached. In towns, developers are allowed to build on a greater proportion of the plot. In the countryside, if a building density right is, say, 10 per cent, it means that a developer can only put a 50 sq m house on a 500 sq m plot, in other words, 10 per cent of the size of the plot. So for a decent-sized house, you'll need a very big plot. In town, building density may be several hundred per cent, which means you can put an apartment block on your chosen plot. The height of buildings is restricted, depending on their location, as is the colour.

Each new development must also have a 'green area', which is often a token gesture located next to the last house in a row. The green space won't actually belong to that house, but it will be nicer than staring straight through your neighbour's window. Always identify this green area when you're looking at plans.

Unfortunately, the rules of density are a moveable feast. So if you've bought a nice countryside plot with 10 per cent building density, there is nothing to say that the local government won't move the goalposts next year and the plot next to you will be granted a higher density. Next thing you know, a small housing estate has popped up at the bottom of your vineyard. There is nothing you can do about this, and really very little way of finding out what might change, other than chatting to developers and keeping your ear to the ground.

Another term to understand is 'donums', the unit of land in which plots in Cyprus used to be, and in some cases, still are measured. One donum measures 1,335 sq m (14,000 sq ft) one-third of an acre. Nowadays, it's more common to use hectares (10,000 sq m).

dazzling blue shutters. You will, however, find new-builds of excellent quality, in good areas, and the occasional dream cottage in the mountains.

There are various types of property you're likely to consider buying: an apartment, a town house, a villa, a traditional village house or something you decide to build yourself.

When to Buy

Estate agents are at their most receptive and helpful in the autumn – September to December – and the winter. The summer rush is over and serious buyers come to see properties. Greedy developers are more likely to hike their prices in summer, when the island is packed with tourists who are easily seduced into putting down a deposit after a good holiday. If you're planning an inspection trip, remember that the temperatures are much more tolerable outside the summer months.

Types of Home

Apartments

Apartments are cheaper in the city centre than on the seafront, for obvious reasons. Beware of something at street level, particularly in a busy resort like Limassol, as it could be very noisy. And in summer the cooling breeze higher up could be welcome!

Apartment blocks are always served by a lift and usually have underground parking, or a car park attached. Apartments generally have a compact kitchen, good living and entertaining space, a guest bathroom and a decent-sized balcony or roof terrace. Many new developments have a communal pool for the apartments. In older buildings, beware of agreements where the utilities bills are split between the tenants, which can lead to disagreements. There are some very good apartments on new developments in semi-rural areas, mixed in with town houses and villas.

Traditional Houses

The traditional Cypriot house is built of stone and surrounded by a plot of land. There is a fireplace in the living room and an outside oven for cooking bread or meat. There may well be a cellar and an attic. Windows are small to keep out the burning summer heat, and there is no air-conditioning; the stone walls keep the inside cool. There probably isn't any central heating, either. The kitchen will often be open plan to the living room. Bathrooms are simple, with a shower rather than a bathtub. The surrounding plot will be used for cultivating vines, olive, lemon and pomegranate trees, and growing tomatoes, cucumbers and lettuces. It's rare to see a Cypriot garden in full bloom; growing lemons to squeeze over the souvlaki is more important than raising prize-winning roses. Note that if you are buying in a rural area outside a village, your house may not be connected to the mains and will probably have a septic tank, which you will have to maintain.

In towns, houses and apartments will traditionally have roof terraces and balconies rather than a garden, although some very old houses are built around a central yard. Some of these can represent a real bargain, although they may need an enormous amount of work. You need vision, but a crumbling ruin with one communal family room, one stable, basic plumbing, a big, flat roof, a central yard and a gnarled olive tree can actually be turned into something stunning and there are such wrecks to be snapped up in pretty villages for CY£40,000.

If you want to do up a wreck, you may qualify for a government grant, but a project of this scale should not be managed from another country unless you have a brilliant and trustworthy project manager. Most old village houses are listed buildings and you will not be allowed to change the outside. You will also need a fluent Greek-speaker to help with the bureaucracy.

Modern Houses

Modern homes have retained a few of the traditional elements, but not many. Compared with many British developers, Cypriot architects are generous with room size. In a two-bedroomed house, for example, expect two decent-sized rooms rather than a master bedroom and a box room. A master bedroom in a new development will usually have an en-suite shower room and, often, a balcony. Some properties have double-height ceilings, creating a sense of space.

Most new houses are built with provision for air-conditioning and central heating. Not many have a fireplace, sadly, and the outdoor oven has been replaced by the barbecue, although there are plenty of clay ovens for sale in the big pottery outlets on the outskirts of towns. Pipes and cables are laid under the floor, rather than in the walls. All new houses are built to withstand earthquakes of up to seven on the Richter scale (which represents a pretty terrifying shaking). They are either suspended from a steel frame, or built by embedding steel rods into supporting concrete pillars. Windows are large, often with wooden shutters. Special screens keep out the flies. Kitchens are still open-plan to the living room, even in some houses in the half-million-pound range. There is usually a separate utility room.

Outdoor space is limited in towns and you may have to make do with a terrace, or a large balcony. Many Cypriots seem more concerned about having somewhere to put their car than having a patch of lawn. Larger developments usually come with the option of a pool. The water tank will be on the roof, probably alongside solar heating panels. Most households have satellite TV, and dishes in Cyprus are large and unsightly. Inside, expect marble or stripped wood floors, and fitted wooden cupboards. Most new houses have a bathtub as well as a shower, although water is sometimes rationed in summer. Larger plots of land usually come with a borehole.

Villas are in hot demand in Cyprus and many Brits like to have a pool. It often seems amazing that a pool can be crammed into the seemingly tiny amount of space around a villa, once it's up, but it can and they usually look good. But don't expect an expanse of lawn; big gardens in town really are rare. Most developers offer a choice of covering for the garden – gravel, paving, grass – and a lot of people, particularly those who will not be living in Cyprus year-round, opt for the low-maintenance option.

New Developments: Buying Off-plan

There are about 10 big developers on Cyprus and hundreds of smaller ones. Many of the new properties are charming and can be snapped up for reasonable prices if you buy off-plan. Expect even-sized rooms: a separate utility room; guest bathroom, generous entertaining space and, in town, probably not much garden. Houses are often built quite close together with the obligatory 'green zone' left carelessly to one end, next door to the end house.

Case Study: Neil and Elaine

Neil Murray, an IT specialist, and his wife Elaine , a hairdresser, are planning to move to Cyprus as soon as their stone bungalow is completed. 'We wanted to buy something slightly unusual,' explains Elaine. 'We looked at houses all around Paphos but the developments seemed a bit samey and, while some of the houses were pretty, we particularly wanted a village with character. We didn't want to be surrounded by Brits and we weren't particularly bothered about being near the sea.

'In the end, we found a developer who was building a row of bungalows on a hillside in the mountains outside Paphos, using traditional Cypriot stone. We just drove past the site, thought it looked good and took their number from the board at the entrance. There was a fantastic view and a tiny village nearby. We decided to go for it and have returned to the island several times to look at the construction. We chose a lawyer in Limassol and most of the correspondence with him has been by e-mail.

'The whole development is taking about a year to build, although it seems longer. It can be frustrating at times; you ask for something to be done and when you come back on your next visit, nothing has changed. The developer is very obliging and often turns up in person at the site, but we have had a few heated exchanges. We were very nervous, buying off-plan, about how the bungalows were going to look, but we really like what we have seen so far. We also wondered who our neighbours would be, as the bungalows are on a steep hillside and are quite close together. Most of them are British, with some Germans, and everybody seems very nice.

'The next thing to do is to choose all our fixtures and fittings, which has been quite good fun. Luckily, we chose a developer who was fairly relaxed about what we could have; I have heard stories of people being given very little choice. Because these are traditional stone houses, I think quite a few of the buyers are very picky and want everything to be just right.

'Our bungalow will be ready in spring 2005, when we are planning to leave our jobs and moved to Cyprus full-time. Having spent part of last summer on the island, I'm really glad we have chosen a location in the hills, as it gets incredibly hot. We have a pool, although it takes up most of our garden.

'We may start a family in the near future and I expect then we will question why we chose somewhere so remote, but for now it is our dream home. If we need to move out, I expect we will let this one out and buy something else built from scratch, as it has been relatively easy this time round.'

A good developer will allow you to choose your own tiles, kitchen and flooring from a range, and allow you to upgrade if you want something special and are prepared to pay the difference. Do not buy from a developer who won't give you any choice; it simply means they're getting a kickback from the tile and flooring suppliers, which you should not have to finance.

Case Study: Buying Off-plan

Maureen and Gordon Mckay from Edinburgh bought a two-bedroom apartment in a small development outside Larnaca, in the village of Oroklini, in April 2004. They paid CY£59,000. 'We had always thought about buying somewhere overseas,' says Maureen. 'We knew my husband was going to be made redundant at the end of the year so we went to Cyprus in April with the intention of buying. 'I did a lot of Internet research and I came across the Living-cyprus.com website. The people there were very helpful and they set up appointments for us on our trip to Cyprus.'

What is unusual about this situation is that Maureen and Gordon had never even been to Cyprus! 'I knew that a lot of English people went there and I didn't want to live in a Little Britain,' explains Maureen. 'I knew that they drove on the same side of the road as we do, which helps. I thought it might be like some of the nicer bits of the Canaries. I knew a lot of people would speak English and I knew the climate would be good. '

So how did they end up choosing the Larnaca area? 'We didn't want to live in Paphos as it seemed prices were quite a bit higher there,' Maureen continues. 'We actually stayed in Limassol on our visit but it seemed very touristy. Where we have ended up is only 15 minutes' drive from the airport. We had a look at one other development in Oroklini but it seemed to be mainly larger apartment blocks. When we saw our development, we knew it was what we wanted – six apartments and four houses just five minutes' walk from the village.

'We were really impressed with the developer, A&K Developers. They were very accommodating; in Cyprus you are supposed to put down a deposit of 30 per cent. I said this was not an option as my husband was being made redundant at the end of the year, and they just said, well, what *could* we afford to put down?

'We have been back to Cyprus to see the building work and they arranged accommodation for us in the same village. They have also been great when it

Some of the new developments are around the three, soon to be four, championship golf courses. Aphrodite Hills is the most expensive and prestigious, while Tsada and Secret Valley, also in the Paphos area, are longer-established and equally pretty. A new course has been announced at Tersefanou, a village outside Larnaca, with villas and apartments, a health spa and country club by the time it is completed. Houses on golf courses always carry a large premium and, strangely, do not always include membership of the club. If you're a keen golfer, look at properties near but not necessarily on the golf course to save money.

comes to furnishing the apartment – they said anything we wanted them to get, they would sort out, and we could pay them when we arrived. You hear about people having bad experiences but ours has been nothing but good.'

The Mckays ended up buying a slightly bigger property than they had intended to. 'We wanted a one-bedroom flat but then we thought if we were to spend longer in Cyprus we would want family to come and visit, so we went for the two-bedroom flat in the end,' says Maureen. 'Eventually we plan to live there. I'm not interested in renting it out in the meantime, though.'

The apartment has two bedrooms, one with an en-suite bathroom, a large open-plan area, a communal pool and parking. There are large balconies to the front and rear of the building.

So have there been any problems? 'The only drawback we've found is access to Larnaca from Scotland,' says Maureen. 'Charter flights are very expensive and one route we have found ends up taking us via Prague.'

So what advice would Maureen gave to prospective buyers? 'I would say research as much as you can on the Internet and find a good agent,' she says. 'Andrew at Living Cyprus was excellent and I really felt I could trust him. We told them what we wanted to spend and they never took us to see anything over that price.'

In fact, Maureen and Gordon were so enthusiastic about their purchase that on their return from Cyprus, Maureen's sister, Margaret, immediately bought an apartment on the same development, for CY£43,000. Margaret says: 'I had thought about doing it anyway and when Maureen came back with all the plans and information, I thought I would take the plunge. I had never been to Cyprus and I still haven't but I know lots of people who have and have loved it. I thought it would be a good time to buy, before Cyprus joined the EU. I have a one-bedroom flat next door to Maureen. We have never even been on holiday together! But I think I have made a good purchase – we were very quick getting in and the properties had not even been advertised.'

Sample Costs

Property prices in Cyprus rose by 17 per cent in 2004, according to one of the island's biggest property groups. Asking prices were up by 7.7 per cent over the first six months of the year, while the number of sales rose by 8.6 per cent. Uncertainty about the referendum over reunification in April 2004 caused a blip in the market, as did Cyprus' accession to the EU and the imposition of VAT on property. Prices are as at December 2004.

Larnaca

- One-bedroom apartment, built 1985, town centre: CY£22,000
- Town centre apartment (off-plan), two bedrooms: CY£135,000
- Two-bedroom semi-detached house, Pyla, communal pool (off-plan): CY£85,000
- Five-bedroom detached house with pool: CY£168,000

Limassol

- Two-bedroom apartment, town centre: CY£50,000
- Three-bedroom detached house, Kolossi, pool optional: CY£125,000
- Detached house, four bedrooms, Fasoula: CY£190,000

Paphos Area

- One-bedroom apartment, Kato Paphos, communal pool: CY£55,000
- Two-bedroom semi-detached house, Peyia, communal pool: CY£92,900
- Three-bedroom detached villa with pool, Tala: CY£139,000
- Three-bedroom house, Coral Bay, private pool: CY£235,000

Polis

- Stone village house, one bedroom, Polemi: CY£60,000

Ayia Napa

- Two-bedroom apartment, Ayia Napa, communal pool: CY£73,000
- Three-bedroom apartment, Paralimni: CY£73,000
- Two-bedroom detached house, Cape Greco (off-plan): CY£139,500
- Three-bedroom detached house, Protaras, pool: CY£150,000

Nicosia

- One-bedroom apartment, new: CY£51,500
- Two-bedroom apartment, brand new: CY£89,000
- Three-bedroom semi-detached house, no pool: CY£130,000
- Five-bedroom detached house with pool: CY£382,000

Research and Information Sources

The Internet

There is a huge amount of information about buying property in Cyprus on the Internet but proceed with caution as a lot of it is horribly out of date. Most of the websites with 'helpful' information pages have not been updated since

Cyprus joined the EU in 2004, and the rules have changed completely since then, for example, concerning the number of properties a non-Cypriot residing on the island can own. Only take advice from the most trusted sources if you're doing all your research online.

The best way to get a feel for the market before you leave for Cyprus is to look at a mixture of sites: those of the big developers like Aristo and Cybarco (*see* 'Property Developers', pp.56–9), some of smaller developers, and some of estate agents, who sell properties built by the developers as well as older houses. These are some websites that can provide useful guidelines, as well as plans and pictures of new developments:

- **Headlands, www.headlands.co.uk**. A good site for searching for a new property, with plans and photographs online.

- **Living Cyprus, www.living-cyprus.com**. Informative site and with a helpful office in the UK.

- **Serious About Cyprus, www.seriousaboutcyprus.com, t** (01234) 401557. Handles new properties, resales and rentals, and represents a number of developers on the island, so is useful if you want to buy off-plan. The company also has a good investment guide on its website for buy-to-let schemes.

Print Media

The main daily and Sunday newspapers all have travel and property sections and can be a useful place to start, especially as they have articles on overseas property buying in general, aspects of living abroad, and sometimes articles specifically about Cyprus or a region of the country. There are also specialised glossy property magazines that are crammed full of adverts, usually arranged by country.

- *Homes Overseas*, **t** (020) 7939 9888, **www.homesoverseas.co.uk**. A lively, colourful monthly with a worldwide scope but some space for Cyprus. They also organise property exhibitions (*see* below).

- *World of Property*, **t** (01323) 726040, **www.outboundpublishing.com**. A bimonthly publication with worldwide scope, which also organises property exhibitions. Cyprus features in the magazine and in the exhibitions.

- *International Homes*, **t** (01245) 358877, **www.international-homes.com**. A glossy magazine with an international perspective.

- *Private Villas*, **t** (020) 8329 0120, **www.privatevillas.co.uk**. A glossy magazine mainly used by those looking to rent a holiday villa or apartment but also has a 'For Sale' section. Most of the adverts are by estate agents.

- *Dalton's Weekly*, **www.daltonsholidays.com**. Carries ads for Cyprus properties. The website is operated jointly with *Private Villas* (*see* above).

An Encounter Outside an Artist's Studio

Some years ago, James Franklin, the author of the legal and financial chapters of this guide, used to visit Cyprus once or twice a year and grew to love the island. He decided that it might be a nice place to live. One day, exploring the countryside on the way from Limassol to Platres, he came across the most idyllic little village. There happened to be, opposite the village taverna, an artist's studio and, being of a somewhat garrulous nature, he introduced himself to the owner. As it happens the man was a fellow Brit and while they were chatting James mentioned that he too might buy a little cottage in one of the villages. 'Ah,' said the owner of the studio, 'there's a charming cottage owned by an ex-RAF squadron leader for sale just up that little lane there. He's away on holiday but left me the keys so I could keep a weather eye on it. Would you like to look at it?' So James did; and he bought it!

The moral of the story is an obvious one – most of us buy a property because we want to live in a particular location. So, if the hill villages of Cyprus sound attractive to you, rent a car and go exploring. If you find a village you like, have a coffee or whatever (a brandy sour springs to mind!) in the village taverna and get chatting; you are more than likely to find someone who speaks English; and, believe me, the locals know everything that is going on! Conversely, if you are selling your home here in Cyprus, put a notice on your gate saying so...and be sure to tell the owner of your local taverna!

Local Press

The two English speaking newspapers, the *Cyprus Weekly* (**www.cyprusweekly.com.cy**) and the daily *Cyprus Mail* (**www.cyprus-mail.com**), have extensive sections devoted to property advertisements.

Word of Mouth

The best way to buy or sell a property is by word of mouth. That might sound difficult if you live in the UK, but it really is not, although you do need some luck! *See* box, above.

Property Exhibitions

There are various property exhibitions in the UK where buyers and sellers can come together, and where you can chat to Cypriot developers:

- **Homes Overseas, www.homesoverseas.com.** Takes place in Brighton and London.
- The **International Property Show, www.internationalpropertyshow.com.** Takes place in London, Manchester and Dublin in association with the *Daily Mail*.

- **Invest in Property.** Takes place in London and is organised by the same company as Homes Overseas, dealing with property worldwide. The show also has a seminar programme which tackles matters like financial advice.

- **A Place in the Sun.** A show at London's Excel Centre and the Interhol in Bournemouth.

- **Cyprus Wine Festival and Business Exhibition, www.cyprus-winefestival.co.uk.** At Alexandra Palace in London.

Inspection Trips

Fact-finding Inspection Trips

There are various ways of going to look for property in Cyprus. You can go on a hosted buying trip, where you will be shown around by an agent or a developer, or you can arrange the trip yourself, making arrangements with a number of estate agents in different locations. Alternatively, you can make your own travel arrangements but get an agent to set up appointments for you. A good UK agent like Halcyon Properties (**www.halcyon-properties.co.uk**), Headlands (**www.headlands.com.cy**) or Living Cyprus (**www.living-cyprus.com**) will be able to set up a buying trip for you. This is usually more effective than doing it yourself. Remember that sellers in Cyprus almost always go for multiple agents (the commission the seller pays is the same as for a sole agent), so if you arrive and start making appointments, you may find yourself seeing the same property several times, which is a waste.

If your trip is purely exploratory, make sure you have a list of questions to ask, and things like a video camera, or digital stills camera. After about four houses, they all look the same! Also remember either to get plans of each property, or to sketch your own. Make notes as you go round. Avoid travelling over national holidays if you are short of time.

Inspection Trips with a View to Making a Purchase

If you've decided where to live and are on a serious mission to buy, make sure everything is in place for the visit. Property moves so fast that you've got to be ready to commit on the spot, make an offer and pay a reservation deposit (between CY£1,000 and CY£2,000) to reserve the property. Don't expect to visit the island, make an offer on a place and return home to wait for the reply. Within the space of a week you can expect to have made an offer, had it accepted, hired a Cypriot solicitor, gone through the beginnings of the legal process and secured your property.

In Cyprus, unlike in England, the deposit-paying process is legally binding. Gazumping doesn't happen. You'll then have to wait a few days while the contract is drawn up, sign it, and hand over some 20–30 per cent of the value of the property. The developer will work out a schedule of payments for the balance. If it's a re-sale, you pay 10 per cent on exchange of contracts and the remainder on completion.

Transfer of ownership from vendor to purchaser is accomplished by a simple procedure through the Cyprus Land Registry Office, either by the buyer in person or by an appointed third party with power of attorney. The title deeds will be registered in the name of the buyer and will be recorded in the government archives once the 30 per cent deposit has been paid. After this point, the land cannot be sold to anybody else, or leased, transferred or mortgaged. The government archives are confidential. At any time after the purchase, the buyer may sell or dispose of the property at will, provided that a valid contract exists. You can even sell your property before it is built if you want to – many people do.

Having signed a 'contract of sale' for your property, as a formal procedure, you also have to apply to the authorities of the Republic of Cyprus (as a non-Cypriot) for permission to acquire immovable property. This procedure may take up to three months, but in the meantime there is no restriction on taking possession of the property.

On transfer of the property and registration in the purchaser's name, the District Land Registry will charge transfer fees, based on the market value of the property at the time of purchase as follows:

- up to CY£50,000 – 3 per cent.
- CY£50,001–100,000 – 5 per cent.
- more than CY£100,001 – 8 per cent.

Between paying your reservation deposit and putting down the first 30 per cent, you need to instruct your solicitor to carry out a local search. This includes looking at things like who owns the roads, checking that all the building permits are in place, and checking the land density regulations. A search is usually satisfactory but, if it's not, the understanding is that you will get your reservation fee back. Surveys are uncommon in Cyprus although if you're buying a very old property you may want to appoint a chartered surveyor or a structural engineer to have a look at it. This is usually expensive but can be a worthwhile investment. *See* 'Checklist: Do-it yourself Inspection of Property', pp.188–94, for a checklist of points to go through with your surveyor.

The best way to find a solicitor is through word of mouth; it is not worth trying to circumvent the legal process and do the conveyancing yourself. Be very wary of solicitors recommended by estate agents and developers. Everybody knows everybody on Cyprus and you could well be dealing with your agent's cousin or best friend, who may not act in your best interests in the event of a dispute.

Before you embark on a buying spree, remember to sort out your mortgage, if you need one, or some means of transferring your money from the UK.

For more detail on all these issues and the process of buying a property, see the following chapter, **Making the Purchase**.

Hosted Buying Trips

A number of developers will offer to fly you out to Cyprus, all expenses paid, show you round and generally give you a good time. These viewing trips usually last for three or four days. You'll be escorted all the way and shown places of interest as well as several properties.

But be warned! There will almost always be pressure to buy. Do not, absolutely not, commit to something unless you're sure. You will not have free time to visit other developers and you will only be shown properties built by your host. You will be told things like '90 per cent of this development has been sold off-plan already' and taken to see the couple of 'remaining' properties. Other agents will offer you some cashback, say CY£500, ostensibly to offset your travel costs, if you buy from them. This is hardly a big deal. Cypriot developers tend to be quite amenable to bargaining. If you were seriously interested in a property and were paying a decent price, you would probably be able to negotiate CY£500 worth of 'extras' anyway.

If you are uncomfortable with a hosted buying trip, arrange your own trip but make appointments to see agents and developers in advance. Or choose your agent carefully; Halcyon Properties (**www.halcyon-properties.co.uk**) in the UK, for example, won't pay your air fare but will sort out everything else and only arranges trips for individuals, not groups.

Estate Agents

See also **Making the Purchase**, p.69.

Cyprus has thousands of estate agents, some officially recognised and some trading illegally. It is in your interests to deal with a registered agent as you will have no recourse if somebody who is trading illegally runs off with your money. Do not confuse an estate agent with a developer. Estate agents represent a number of developers and private sellers as a third party; developers only sell property they are building themselves. There are one or two dedicated agencies that, while web-based, have offices in Cyprus. These agencies are not estate agents per se – they simply put buyer and seller together.

Estate agents in Cyprus are supposed to be members of the **Cyprus Real Estate Agents Association** (**CREAA**; 17 Hadjiloizi Michaelides Str., PO Box 50563, Limassol, CY-3041, **t** 25 36 74 67, **f** 25 36 51 88, **solo@cytanet.com.cy**). This is a semi-governmental body which regulates the industry, but these agents are not required to have any formal qualifications. Those who deal with unlicensed estate agents are not subject to protection offered by the regulatory body. One of these protections is that licensed estate agents are obliged to carry insurance to protect the purchaser against either the agent or the developer going insolvent. CREAA requires its members to carry indemnity insurance of CY£50,000 per customer; some agents voluntarily carry insurance of CY£100,000 per customer, so you will have some comeback if you feel you have been given bad

Case Study: Building a Traditional Stone House

Retired TV producer Michael Begg wanted to 'flee the country' and, in his search, ended up in Cyprus. 'I looked at Spain, too, but Cyprus seemed good,' he says. 'They speak English. They seem quite cheery. And they make a real attempt to make us feel welcome, with just 5 per cent tax on pensions.'

Begg was shown around the Paphos area by a representative of the estate agent Antonius Loizou & Associates. 'It was the last day and I was getting a bit despondent,' he recalls. 'The coast was a sea of beige; old people in beige polyester. Then the agent said there was a plot in the hills. I originally come from the north of Scotland and the total peace and tranquillity of this plot appealed to me. I like the idea of swallows nesting under my eaves. It's cooler in the hills, too.' The 2,600 sq m plot, and a house that was not yet built, were being sold by a small developer, Christoforou & Sofocleous. It is a beautiful spot in the mountains, with uninterrupted views of fields, orchards and vineyards, and only one neighbour, who lives in another stone house, built by the same developer in the same style. The building rights were for only 10 per cent density, as the plot is in the middle of the countryside.

Begg acquired the plot in March 2004 and drew up a contract with the developer, withholding a considerable amount to be paid on completion as insurance against the project running late. This was a bit of a shot in the dark, as the developer is small and did not have many other projects to show as examples. 'I saw one house they'd done and it was OK but nothing special,' says Begg. 'With alarming candour, Demetrius said he was learning from his mistakes. I was definitely taking a risk.' The house, which is almost complete at the time of writing, has three bedrooms, two bathrooms, a spacious kitchen

advice and need to sue. A second benefit of dealing with a licensed estate agent is that his receipt is deductible from your liability to Capital Gains Tax.

Unfortunately, despite the existence of CREAA, many agents are believed to be trading illegally, including one or two large ones. Some of the 'unlicensed' estate agents are just as good as the licensed ones but others make extortionate claims as to, for instance, the numbers of thousands of 'hits' they get every day on their website. In itself that is not serious; what is much more worrying is the attempt by a few fly-by-night cowboys to sign you up at an exclusive and extortionate rate of commission. According to one estimate, of the 320 estate agencies in Paphos alone, only 20 are registered, and though developers legally operate around 100, the remaining 200 are illegal. By law, in Cyprus all registered estate agents must do searches on their properties and must inform clients about any legal encumbrances or problems related to the property.

Two estate agents to look out for are:

• **Antonis Loizou and Associates, t 22 42 48 53, enquiries@aloizou.com.cy, www.aloizou.com.cy**. One of the biggest groups of estate agents on and living area, a sizeable pool and a large garden, which incorporates part of a vineyard. 'The house has been put together in local stone and it does look good,' says Begg, 'hand-built by master mason Mr Fanis – he had no first name – he was so ancient he could barely lift the honey-coloured rocks, but when he selected one for the wall it would drop into place like a piece of jigsaw.

'I spent CY£190,000 on the house and the plot and CY£10,000 on 'extras', which is a popular term in Cypriot property development. I wanted polished granite floors throughout, which are cooler and look nice, but were expensive. 'I fleetingly considered selling it immediately as it's now been valued between CY£250,000 and CY£270,000 but my wife keeps muttering "my dream home" and now we're both looking forward to moving in to what has turned out to be a beautiful house. Unfortunately, it's sitting on a plot that resembles downtown Baghdad so I need to spend some serious money on landscaping. I plan to keep some of the vines but won't be making any wine. It sounds like a lot of work for an indifferent result. We shall cheat and offer friends a good supermarket plonk, having first steamed the labels off the bottle! But we do intend to put in a full range of fruit trees and keep a small vegetable garden.'

The project has had remarkably few problems, apart from difficulties agreeing on the position of the swimming pool, now resolved. Despite some problems in the course of building Begg is delighted with his purchase and plans to make Cyprus his permanent home very soon. 'Demetrius [the developer] has produced a fine house and should be given credit for his honesty and trustworthiness,' he says. 'Even if giving a quarter of a million pounds to a company without premises, stationery, fixed address and telephone, other than a mobile, is evidence of premature senility...'

Cyprus. The company has offices in all the major cities as well as one in Paralimni and even one in Platres, in the Troodos mountains. The company can help with financial advice and has a strong after-sales service. It claims in its literature not to be 'pushy' and has had many glowing reports in the press.

- **Nicholas & Tsokkas Real Estate Agency**, Apostolou Pavlou 57, 8103 Paphos, Kato Paphos, **t** 26 93 09 35, **f** 26 22 04 38, **www.cyprusproperty finder.com**. A well-established real estate agency based in Paphos, with a mixture of Cypriot and British employees and an enormous database of property. You can walk into the office and use one of the computers there to browse the database. The website is easy to navigate and covers the whole of the island. The agency offers resales, new property, property off-plan, land and custom-designed villas. Property management, mortgage advice and plenty of after-sales support are part of the service. There's even a 'living in Cyprus' helpline, should you have a sudden panic about whether your mobile phone will work or how to get your dog to the island.

UK Estate Agents Selling Properties in Cyprus

For many years estate agents in the UK have been offering properties overseas and nearly all of the specialist UK agents appoint a local agent to actually show you the property and answer your questions. Should you find a property through a UK estate agent, ensure that his or her corresponding Cypriot agent is a licensed estate agent. Agents with representatives in the UK include:

- **ECR properties**, 4 Recreation Road, London SE26 4ST, UK, **t** (020) 8347 0055, **f** (020) 8347 5577, **www.ecrpro.com**; in Cyprus: 243, 28th Oktovriou Str., Christiana Sea View Court 3035 Limassol, Cyprus, **t** 25 81 76 60, **f** 25 81 76 61. Has offices in London and Cyprus and represents property all over the island, working with both developers and private sellers.

- **Halcyon Properties**, **t** (01323) 891639, **f** (01323) 892954, **www.halcyon-properties.co.uk**. Works with developers and licensed estate agents all over the island and aims to offer a personal service, including after-sales care and individual inspection trips.

- **Living Cyprus**, **t** 07050 262596 or 659909, **www.living-cyprus.com**. The company works with some 100 developers on the island and will arrange inspection trips with discounted accommodation and a consultant dedicated to you when you reach Cyprus. It will also refund the cost of the flight if you buy from them.

- **Property Finders International**, **t** 0845 330 1449, **www.newskys.co.uk**. Has a big selection of accommodation for sale all over the island and a useful, newsy website on which you can sign up for a free newsletter. The company represents real estate agents and developers on the island.

- **Serious About Cyprus**, **t** (01234) 401557, **www.seriousaboutcyprus.com**. Handles sales and rentals and represents a number of developers on the island, so is useful if you want to buy off-plan. The company also has a good investment guide on its website for buy-to-let schemes.

Dealing With Estate Agents When You Sell

In a publication about buying a property you may think it irrelevant to be discussing the fees and arrangements to be made with estate agents when selling a property. But many people move house for this or that reason and it may well be that purchasing a property in Cyprus is dependent on your selling your existing Cyprus property.

Be careful with estate agents' contracts. Insist they are in English and read the agreement! Never sign an exclusive agreement. Your property might not sell because the estate agent hasn't bothered to advertise it; you cannot go elsewhere – if you do and another agent sells the property, you are still legally bound to pay the first estate agent as well. Don't allow yourself to be hassled. Unscrupulous estate agents are only interested in getting your signature on their piece of paper. Take it away and consider it at your leisure. If anything concerns you, phone your lawyer and talk it over with him. Finally be aware that there is no specific legislation in Cyprus granting a 'cooling off' period for agreements with estate agents.

Avoid open-ended agreements and give an estate agent a fair amount of time to sell your property. If you have not sold within the time stipulated, you are free to think again. The estate agent's fees for selling property are usually 5 per cent; this percentage has crept up over the years. The prescribed percentage that is legally acceptable is 3 per cent; if estate agents want more they must get the vendor to agree to their terms in writing. Feel free to haggle about the agent's commission – the rule of thumb used to be 4 per cent in town, 5 per cent in the villages. If vendors are in breach of contract with an estate agent, they can only sue the vendor for 3 per cent of the asking price.

Questions to Ask Yourself when Considering a Purchase

- **What is your budget and can your finances support it?** Generally speaking, people spend 1.5 to 2.5 times their annual income on a second home.

- **Do you need to borrow money?** Work out whether you have enough cash, whether you are going to raise equity in the UK, or whether you need a Cypriot mortgage.

- **Do you want to work on your new house?** If you are buying a rural property or something very old there is every chance it will need work done on it, which can be expensive and complicated, particularly if you are not there to oversee it.

- **If you're buying an apartment, how are the expenses of the building divided up between the residents?**

- **Check, check and check again who owns the land**, and whether it has been developed within the restrictions of the law.

- **Is your new property connected to the mains?** If it's not, getting a connection can be very expensive and can take a long time.

- **Is your property in a development zone?** If so, who owns the surrounding land and what do they propose to do with it? The last thing you want is your beautiful sea view ruined.

- **Are you dealing with a reliable developer?** In Cyprus, anybody can set themselves up as a property developer. Be sure to get testimonials from other buyers and look at other properties this developer has built.

- **Are you dealing with a licensed estate agent?** If you are not, you will have no comeback if the agent runs off with your money. Similarly, if your arrangements are all through an agent's representative in the UK, make sure the Cypriot agent is licensed.

Tips for Successful Viewing

• **When viewing properties, ask to look around on your own as well as listening to the agent's spiel.** Not only will you avoid the 'hard sell', but you'll have some privacy to talk about your real concerns with your partner. Be suspicious of people you meet in a bar who have a 'friend with a good deal'. There is a good chance that they could be working on commission although, having said that, many people in Cyprus do indeed have a genuine friend who is a developer and a lot of property exchanges hands through personal recommendation.

• **Spend some time researching the local community and finding out what amenities the area has** with a view to any future letting plans you may have. Pop round to see the neighbours, who should be able to give you a more 'independent' impression of what the area is really like.

• **Check the heating.** Cyprus can get pretty chilly in winter and you want to know how the water is heated. If there are solar panels ask how old they are and ask to see some heating and water bills. If there is a fireplace, check that it works.

• **Find out where your water supply comes from.** Is it mains-fed, spring-fed or does the property have a borehole? Connecting up to the mains can be very expensive. Likewise, find out how the sewage system connects to the property. Is it a cesspit or soakaway and how often does it need emptying?

• **Check the property deeds.** Does anyone have access to the property or any trees planted on it? Can you park your car nearby, and is the parking area shared with anybody else?

• **Check all fixtures and fittings carefully.** Once you've signed for the property you'll have no legal recourse. This includes the swimming pool, which will inevitably need maintaining.

Property Developers

Cyprus has about 10 big developers and hundreds of smaller ones. It would be impossible to list them all here, but a selection of them are described below. Keep your eyes open as you drive around the island, as developers almost always put a board up on their sites with their contact details.

If you are buying from a developer, check what after-sales support is included, particularly if you are buying to let (*see* **Letting Your Property**, pp.157–70). For example, what is the guarantee on the property? Will the developer help you with the application for ownership of the property? Will they sort out things like mains connection and help you to organise bank loans? Do they have a reasonable payment schedule? Will they manage your lettings for you? Not all of the offers are the same, although many developers are extremely professional and will go the extra mile for their buyers. Word of mouth is the best way to make sure you're dealing with a good company.

Most buying stories in Cyprus are positive, but a certain flexibility in attitude is required when dealing with property developers. Mediterranean time is slower than UK time and, while you may expect things to be done to a rigid schedule, your developer will not necessarily achieve this. Naturally, the contract must have penalty clauses built in for not completing by the agreed date – don't be surprised if you turn up on the island to inspect your work in progress and find that not much has happened since you were last there, or that certain goals have not been met.

A favourite ploy of developers is to show you a plan and tell you that almost all the units have been sold, putting you under a certain amount of pressure. This may not be the case and you must only buy if it feels right. If you are one of the first to snap up a property off-plan, it may be some time till the development is finished. The developer will use the money of the first few buyers to build the properties and can run into problems if the rest of the units are slow to sell. Be sure to have those penalty clauses in place. Long delays can be deeply frustrating if you are making plans to move to Cyprus permanently and have given up a job.

Some of the largest developers are listed below, as well as a couple of the medium-sized developers:

- **Aristo**, 8 Apriliou, 1st Str., CY-8101 Paphos, **t** 26 84 28 42, **f** 26 93 82 90, **www.aristodevelopers.com**. One of the largest developers, whose signs you will see all over the island including at the Secret Valley golf course and the Tsada Golf Club. The company has developments in Limassol, Paphos and Pissouri, as well as at Polis on the north coast.

- **Cybarco**, Cybarco House, Dollis Mews, Dollis Park, London N3 THH, **t** (020) 8371 9700, **f** (020) 8371 3999, **info@uk.cybarco.com**, **www.cybarco.com**. A huge developer, with projects island-wide. The company has several plots on Aphrodite Hills and also specialises in construction and civil engineering.

- **Kleanthis Savva**, 133 Archbishop Makarios Ave, 8221 Chlorakas, Paphos, **t** 26 81 54 44, **f** 26 27 13 38, **www.ksavva-developers.com**. One of the medium-sized developers, based in Paphos, with a lot of very attractive villas, town houses and apartments, particularly in the villages to the north and west of the town. The company has an excellent after-sales service and its own design centre (see website), where you can see examples of fixtures and fittings and room layouts – the Cypriot equivalent of a show home.

- **Leptos Estates**, 111 Ap. Pavlou Ave, PO Box 60146, CY-8129 Paphos, **t** 26 88 01 00 or (sales) (00357)-8000 LEPTOS, **f** 26 93 47 19, **Sales@LeptosEstates.com**, **www.leptosestates.com**; in UK: 162 High Road, East Finchley, London

N2 9AS, **t** (020) 8883 2333, **f** (020) 8883 6464, **uk@leptos.demon.co.uk**, **www.leptos.com**. A big company, with over 65 developments in the Paphos area. The company offers a full property management service, financing and retirement advice, and has an excellent, up-to-date website. The company will organise inspection trips at a discounted rate and will put you up in one of its hotels. If you're keen on buying in the Paphos area, this one is worth considering and is particularly strong at Coral Bay.

• **Pafilia**, Glencar House, West Pole Avenue, Cockfosters, London EN4 0AR, **t** (020) 8440 9890, **f** (020) 8440 9399; in Scotland: Suite 58, Abbey Mill Business Centre, Anchor Mill, Paisley, Scotland PA1 1TJ, **t** (0141) 849 1100 or 0845 130 6040, **www.pafilia.com**. One of the biggest developers in Paphos, offering terraced houses, apartments and villas. The company has quite a few developments in the Coral Bay area and in the villages surrounding Paphos. Services include everything from helping you to furnish your property to maintaining your swimming pool, repairs, landscape gardening and managing your property while you are not on the island.

• **Quality Developers**, Quality Group of Companies, 14 United Nations Str., 6042 Larnaca, **t** 24 66 23 33, **f** 24 66 29 22, **sales@qualitydevelopments. com**, **www.qualitydevelopments.com**. If you want to buy in Larnaca, try Quality Developers, which has snapped up a lot of land along the seafront heading west from Larnaca, and developed in some of the villages behind the town. The smart money is on this region to be the next boom area of Cyprus and there are still bargains to be had. The company offers hosted inspection visits and will return your airfare if you end up buying a property. The focus is very much on high-quality accommodation, with a strong after-sales service. There's also a DVD about their developments and Cyprus in general. Represented in the UK by Halcyon Properties (*see* p.54).

Of course, not everybody wants to buy on a development. There are some companies that specialise in traditional stone houses, which are custom-built. **Christoforou & Sofocleous Developers**, **t** 99 46 24 78 or 99 46 45 31, **info@csdevelopers@europe.com**, is a small developer which has built several stone houses in the mountains around Paphos, using a local expert to cut and lay the stone, all of which comes from Cyprus.

Most of the UK-based Cyprus specialist estate agents and marketing companies – Halcyon Properties, International Property Finders, Living Cyprus and Serious About Cyprus, for example – also represent developers.

• **Headlands International**, Station Road, Nene Park, Irthlingborough, Northants NN9 5QF, **t** (01933) 654000; **f** (01933) 654099, **info@headlands. co.uk**, **www.headlands.co.uk**. In Cyprus: 6–7 Frixos Center, 33 Makarios Avenue, 6017 Larnaca, **t** 0845 900 5353, **info@headlands.com.cy**, **www.headlands.com.cy**.One of the big property specialists in the UK, with homes for sale in a number of countries, including Cyprus. It represents a number of developers on Cyprus, so only offers new property. The company is based in the Midlands and has a permanent exhibition suite where you can drop in and browse through property details. Headlands won 'Best Cyprus Estate Agent' at the 2004 Bentley International Property Awards.

Buy to Let

Now that Cyprus is a member of the EU, buy-to-let schemes have become very attractive. The market is buoyant and, for the time being at least, buying to let is worth considering. There may come a point where the market is saturated, but Cyprus has not yet arrived at this. 2002 was the strongest year for housing on record, and 2003 and 2004 showed an equally strong performance, despite the uncertainty of the 2004 referendum and the accession to the EU.

Inclusion in the European Union has lifted restrictions on how many properties a national of an EU country with residence can own in Cyprus (previously, it was only one; now it is unlimited). Also, prices are still rising so fast that there is money to be made by buying off-plan and tapping into one of the many schemes offered by developers whereby they will guarantee your letting income for a number of years. As a result, more and more companies are setting up in Cyprus, opening up the market for corporate lets, particularly around Nicosia, Larnaca and Limassol.

The easy way to buy to let is through a good developer, who will include full management of your property as part of the package. This should include everything from letting and maintenance to administration, advertising, cleaning, rental and client management and, of course, monetary organisation.

The best way to approach a buy-to-let project is to find a developer you like and trust and go for one of the schemes that provides a guaranteed rental income for the first three years. The rental market is so good that developers are prepared to take on this kind of risk. Many of them also have a lettings department and will manage your property once the three years is up. These schemes are relatively foolproof, as all the risk is with the developer. Do, however, make sure you buy in a good area with potential for the future, as you will still be paying a mortgage in three years' time.

A Typical Buy-to-let Scheme

A typical buy-to-let scheme would work like this, a project currently on offer from Serious about Cyprus. You invest in a scheme off-plan, in this case, the 'Iliyianna' project, a development of just 10 three-bedroom luxury homes, 600m from Coral Bay outside Paphos. The properties are all freehold and come with pool and air-conditioning as standard. Possibly the most attractive feature of this development is that each property comes with an annual rental income guaranteed by the developer, for a three-year period commencing on the delivery date of the villa, and paid to you monthly .

During this three-year period, the developer will manage the property and pay all the bills (pool and garden maintenance, cleaning, electricity and water bills), and you are guaranteed the annual sum irrespective of the occupancy rate achieved. A CY£255,500 property would bring in a guaranteed annual rent of CY£13,000. The only expense to the owner is insurance and furnishings. The developer even tries to accommodate owners who want to come on holiday, subject to availability.

For further information about buying to let, including choosing the best location and type of property for letting, and expected rental incomes, *see* **Letting Your Property**, pp.157–70.

Temporary Accommodation

If you are planning to make Cyprus your permanent home, it is highly recommended that you give it a try in rented accommodation before selling up and leaving the UK for good. Some people will rent for a year just to see if they like living on the island, while others will take the plunge, buy off-plan and live in temporary accommodation so they can supervise the building of their home.

There is no shortage of rental property in Cyprus, although it is not the cheapest way to live and at peak times it is difficult to get something without booking in advance. However, a long-term rental is cheaper than spending six months in a hotel and is a much better way to get to know an area and the people who live there. Many developers in Cyprus will offer you temporary accommodation if you have bought off-plan, and include the rental cost in the cost of your property. This makes financial planning easier and gives you a chance to get to know your developer and their style.

If you are renting in the height of summer, consider staying somewhere with a swimming pool or near the beach if you want to get a feel for what living in Cyprus will eventually be like. A long, hot summer will be miserable if you do not have somewhere to cool down.

Landlords can be cunning in Cyprus and you must go and see a property before committing to renting it – a surprising number of people will simply rent off the Internet. Photographs can be taken strategically; often new developments will be shown as artists' impressions with green fields all around them, when in fact these fields are all earmarked for development, or already built on. Do not fall for language like 'a few steps from the beach'; very little residential property in Cyprus is actually on the beach and there could well be a road between you and the sand.

Do your research when it comes to location, too. The pleasant, relatively sleepy village in early spring may be heaving with tourists by July. Make sure you rent somewhere with some facilities nearby, unless you really do want to live the rural life. Wherever you live, you will probably end up driving to the supermarket

6 Stone arch near investment settlement, Paphos region
7 Ruins of Venetian palace, Ammochostos, Famagusta

8 Stone-built mansion, Platres, central Troodos
9 Caledonia Trail, Troodos Mountains
10 Door chain and padlock, rural southern village

11

13

14

11 Typical investment apartments with pool, Paphos

12

15

but a village shop can still make a difference. If you are moving to a mountain village, choose one with a taverna, which will be the focus of village life and help you to get to know the local people.

Do not expect to be able to rely on public transport unless you are extremely patient and very flexible. You really do need a car to live in Cyprus, even if you are only there temporarily, and using a car is also the only way to reach the most beautiful parts of the island, including some of the more remote beaches. Car rental is quite reasonable and there are plenty of companies that will do a long-term deal. Petrol is cheaper than in the UK.

As when you rent in the UK, most landlords will expect you to pay a security deposit and your apartment or villa should come with a full inventory. Check through this carefully, make sure everything works and if there is anything wrong bring it immediately to the attention of the landlord, or you run the risk of not getting your deposit back. If you're renting a villa with a pool, check that the pool is in good working order and also who will maintain it.

There are numerous rental sites on the Internet. A good place to start is with **www.cyprus-property-rentals.com**; if you like the look of a property, you deal direct with the landlord. Another good, no-nonsense site is **www.cyprus.gb.com**. Also look at the sites of the developers and the large estate agents, many of whom offer rentals.

There are a few practical points to note. Utility charges are not usually included in the rent and will be paid direct to the utility company, not via the landlord. If you are renting an apartment in a block, you may find that maintenance charges for things like swimming pools and public areas are shared between all the tenants. You will also have to pay things like refuse collection charges. In Cyprus water is charged according to consumption.

Building from Scratch

Building from scratch requires a lot of resources and energy, but plenty of people do it and in Cyprus it's quite commonplace, much more so than in the UK. You must always take professional advice when building your own property in Cyprus but, broadly speaking, this is the procedure. There are various ways to buy land – through the local press, on the Internet, through real estate agents, through developers and via word of mouth. All advertised land should state the **building density factor**, which is controlled by the local authority: 90 per cent, the maximum permissible coverage of a plot possible, excluding storage areas, refers to one-storey buildings; 100 per cent and over refers to two- or three-storey buildings on smaller pieces of land. Land outside a building zone will have a much lower percentage on which you are allowed to build.

To apply for **building permission** you must submit your application via an approved architect or civil engineer, who will lodge it with the local town plan-

Case Study: Building Your Own House

Lucy and Zenon Zenonos and their two small children moved to Limassol in 2002. Previously, they had been living in a rural village in the hills near Paphos. Lucy, who is English, had met Zenon more than 10 years previously, when she was working as a holiday rep in the area.

'We wanted to move to Limassol partly because Zenon's job took him away from Paphos and Limassol had a good choice of schools,' says Lucy. 'Once we had made the decision, we came here every weekend looking for a property. We thought about living in the old town but we decided it was too noisy, so started to explore villages within a 20-mile radius. But we couldn't find anything that was stone-built and within our budget of up to CY£80,000. Everything seemed to be too small or too large and luxurious with a pool which we didn't need. We really wanted something with character, without the need for renovation, as we had spent many years renovating our village house in Paphos and didn't want more of the same.

'We were shown some new houses in the villages but they all just seemed to be two up, two down – just boring concrete squares, and they were all on tiny plots. We wanted a plot big enough for a garden for the children to play in and a separate area for fruit trees and vegetables.

'Travelling from Paphos with two young children was getting very difficult so we thought we would find our own plot and design our own house. We had a couple of villages on a shortlist and in the end we found our land through a chain of coincidences, from a friend of a land surveyor who was working in the area. It belonged to a developer who wanted to start selling his fields and building. Our plot was outside the building zone and was 2,600 sq m, which meant that we were allowed to put a 180 sq m house on it.

'We sketched a rough plan of what we wanted and a local architect then expanded on it and put it on a computer in 3-D. Then the building work was put out to tender. The house was supposed to be ready in September when the children started school but it wasn't finished until the end of October, so we had to

ning office. Then you need a regular **building permit**, for which you apply with your proposed design at the town district authority or the technical services department of the local municipality. Again, the architect or civil engineer usually does this. Building permits will not be granted unless the plot is on a public road or you have or will receive right of way to it. If you purchase an isolated plot, under Cypriot law the owner of an adjoining plot must give you a three-metre-wide right of access to your plot from a public road across his or her land. You are usually only allowed to put up one house on these isolated plots. When the building design and construction have been approved, the plans will be stamped. The property will be inspected during construction. Once it's finished, you need to apply for a **certificate of completion**.

rent a small flat in the town for a while. Our belongings were stored in the newly built garage, which was the first part of the house to be finished. When we moved in we were connected to electricity straight away and had mains water supplied through a long black hose that carried water for several hundred metres across some fields. Our telephone line took around a year to get after applying for it and a proper mains water pipe took two years, until the village boundary was extended by the district council.'

The house is a large, typically Cypriot stone bungalow on the highest point of the land, which includes spectacular views and an orchard. 'I wanted it to be on one level because I have mild arthritis,' continues Lucy. 'I wanted a big kitchen, although in retrospect I would have had a utility room on the same floor and not down in the garage. We wanted a laundry chute to be put in to lead from the kitchen to the utility room but this failed, as the builder made a hole in the floor in a corner of the kitchen which had a cupboard over it, so it's impossible to put the washing in. Now, we carry the washing all downstairs in a basket.

'I'm not happy with the cellar, which was meant to be for wine but is actually a garage that gets terribly hot in the summer due to its southwest aspect. Our idea of a cellar was of an underground room reached by a flight of downward stairs without any outside doors or windows. I also wanted a loft and I had assumed that the design included the whole house, but at the moment it's just an open space up there and it's not safe for the children.

'Generally, though, we're very pleased with the house and its situation. The land cost CY£30,000 in 2001 and the house cost CY£79,000. However, we spent an additional CY£20,000 for some extra stonework and then about another CY£20,000 on the fittings, so in the end we went quite a bit over our budget. We are saddled with a very large mortgage, which is quite a financial burden, but on the other hand, the property is now worth about CY£250,000.'

The pretty village of Spitali is already being developed by the same developer who sold Lucy and Zenon their land. Just down the road, he has built some bungalows, all of which have been sold, mainly to older, English people.

Local authorities have different rules about what they do and do not have to supply you with. The local water authority should, but is not obliged to, supply you with a quote for mains connection. The electricity authority is obliged to supply you and will give you a quote on request, as will the telephone company.

Advantages

Some advantages of building from scratch:

- You get a home designed to your specific requirements.
- You have more control over the materials used. You get to choose every-thing: roof tiles, windows, flooring, doors, lighting, tiles, bathroom and

kitchen fittings, carpentry, plumbing, insulation. You won't be sold any 'extras' by a developer and you can go for quality brands for essentials like plumbing and solar heating.

• Everybody on the project is working for you. If you buy from a developer, the contractors will work for that developer, not for you. On a self-build project, you are the client and your architect or construction engineer instructs the builder and makes sure the work is up to scratch. If they feel something has been missed, they are within their rights to make the builder undo it and start again. You can also hire specialists to handle the wiring and plumbing, rather than a mate of the developer's, or a builder who happens to work on the project and has some spare time.

• You can get competitive quotes from a number of builders. You can brief several builders – at least three is a good idea – and get a much better feel for the value of the job. When you buy from a developer, you pay what the market will bear. Be sure to inspect other work by your architect and builder and get personal recommendations from their other clients.

• You have more control over when work is done. You won't be tied to a developer and their own agenda about when the project should be completed. Do not, however, insist that your builder works in double-quick time just so you can move in (and they have better cash flow). Concrete needs time to 'cure' and your architect should advise you on a realistic time scale.

Disadvantages

Some disadvantages of building from scratch:

• A self-build project will probably cost more because of the fees of the architect, construction engineer and surveyor. You will not be able to bulk-buy finishes and fittings as a developer would. The process is slower than buying off-plan because of all the preparatory work involved, not least designing the house.

• You will need to be more involved personally than you would if you were buying from a developer; even if you have a good project manager, you ultimately have to oversee the work, not to mention getting in all the quotes and choosing everything. And you may, of course, have no experience in building project management, or house design.

Making the Purchase

James Franklin

05

Acknowledgements

A significant proportion of this chapter has been written with the help and assistance of the Limassol-based law firm, Chrysses Demetriades. I am particularly grateful to Mrs Lenia Economou and Mrs Anthea Nutt-Keane of their Conveyancing Department. Chrysses Demetriades assert the accuracy of the facts contained within this chapter so far as Cyprus law is concerned as at November 2004. Any other errors that may have crept in are mine alone.

I must also give particular thanks to the Bank of Cyprus for explaining their policies on mortgages, to Nick Skelton of Nick Skelton Homes who explained aspects of property development, and to John Murphy of HPL Superior Real Estate who gave me insight into some of the trickeries practised by the less honest estate agents; let us hope that those like him who have introduced an informal British standard code of practice – and indeed those honest Cypriot agents who have long since done so – prevail.

Buying a property in the Republic of Cyprus is certainly not as safe as buying a property in the UK – but, given the right caveats and taking the appropriate action, it can be. The primary purpose of this book is to explain some of the fundamental differences between purchasing a property in the Republic of Cyprus and purchasing a property in the UK. That is most emphatically *not* to say that this book is in any way a DIY guide. Do not even dream about undertaking a purchase of immovable property in Cyprus – whether a house, villa or land – without competent, independent professional advice at every step along the way. The purpose of this fundamental advice is not to make professional lawyers, accountants and financial advisers rich – it is to prevent you from falling into any of the potential traps that could cost you tens of thousands of pounds, to say nothing of the time and hassle to which you may be exposed.

This book is about buying a property in Cyprus, but while the Republic is in fact the whole of Cyprus, the term 'Cyprus' as used in this and the next chapter refers specifically to the southern part of the island not under occupation. We offer no advice about buying property in the occupied northern part of Cyprus other than to say be very, very careful indeed. You may well be purchasing a property built on land that is legally owned by a refugee and the 'owner' of any such property can never be considered to be the bona fide owner – in other words, at some stage in the future you could lose the whole of your investment. The problems of the northern part of Cyprus are beyond the remit and scope of this book.

Disclaimer

This publication has been prepared primarily for British citizens thinking of purchasing a property in the Republic of Cyprus – that part of the island not under occupation. The topics discussed in this and the next chapter have been put together to the best of our ability but you should be aware that in a regime where laws are changing rapidly to enable the Republic to accord to the requirements of the rules laid down by the European Union – certain aspects may be out of date by the time you read this book. Accordingly, before proceeding with any arrangements, you are strongly advised to confirm directly with the competent authorities of the Republic of Cyprus whether any changes to the information on these pages have taken place.

In any eventuality, neither the author, nor his legal, financial or other advisers, nor the publisher, can accept liability for any errors and it is up to readers to satisfy themselves about the accuracy of facts and comments presented.

Finding a Property in Cyprus

Since Cyprus acceded to the European Union on 1 May 2004, the property market, which had enjoyed something of a flurry, has flattened out somewhat. At the time of going to press in 2005 it is neither a buyers' market nor a sellers' market. However, that has not stopped the developers and new property is being constructed pretty much everywhere. Equally, the number of estate agents and websites seeking to put buyer and seller together has grown rapidly over the last year or so. In the more popular destinations where British expat residents tend to congregate – Paphos, Limassol and, to a lesser extent, Larnaca and Paralimni – there is no shortage of properties to look at. In the secluded villages of the Troodos uplands, there are fewer possibilities.

What Preparations Should You Make?

Understand the System

Although the procedures of buying and selling immovable property are not so dissimilar from those in the UK, you may be forgiven for believing that the procedures with which you, as a property owner in the UK, are familiar are the same in Cyprus. They are not. Then, too, there is the attitude of the average Cypriot vendor. While most have an easygoing attitude towards life – rather as the way of life here is considerably less frenetic than it is in the UK – be aware that a small minority of vendors are little short of being outright sharks. There are horror stories of improperly constructed or improperly finished houses and villas; worse are the stories of vendors selling the same property to more than one buyer or of vendors selling people a property that they don't own in the first place. If you read these pages and follow the advice they contain, you will be more aware of how the system works and how to avoid the pitfalls that await the unwary.

Consult a Lawyer

When you are ready to commit yourself to purchasing a property, the very first thing you should do is to seek out a reputable lawyer. It is probably best to do this even before looking at properties, but it is essential that you do so before committing yourself to any specific property. Quite apart from the fact that it would be extremely foolish to commit yourself to a property before the lawyer has reviewed the sale agreement with you and undertaken the preliminary checks of title, there are other fundamental matters to consider. Depending on your financial circumstances you may also need to seek out a reputable accountant or independent financial adviser. You will wish to discuss a number of topics in the light of the different taxation regime in Cyprus and in consideration of your particular circumstances. These topics may include the following:

- **In whose name should the property be registered? For information about the options available to you, *see* 'Who Should Own the Property?', on p.80.**

- **Whether you should take out a mortgage – either because it is the only way you can make the purchase, or because it is tax effective for you to do so. If so, where should your mortgage provider be situated – in Cyprus, in the UK, offshore? And in what currency is it most effective for you to pay the mortgage instalments?**

- **How will you provide the Cyprus pounds necessary to pay for the property?**

- **If you intend to be resident in Cyprus, what you are going to do about your domicile and residence status so as to minimise your global tax liability? What other financial instruments, such as trusts, might you employ to minimise your estate's potential liability to death duties?**

At your initial meeting your lawyer will be able to recommend the whole range of other professionals you may need – banks, surveyors, valuers, mortgage providers, accountants and financial consultants. This book contains the names and addresses of the associations to which these professionals will be affiliated – so before you start house-hunting contact these associations and arm yourself with their various lists of members. It also contains the title of another publication by this author which contains the names and contact details of individuals and companies involved in these professions who have, to a greater or lesser extent, been vetted or otherwise recommended by other expats who have already done what you intend to do. Using word of mouth recommendations from someone who does not have a vested interest is always preferable.

Decide on Ownership

For tax reasons, it is important to decide on ownership after taking competent advice based on your financial situation and that of your spouse in the light of your intentions about the ultimate disposition of the property. The decision of ownership can save you significant taxes during your life and can avoid unnecessary liability to estate duty on your death. *See* pp.80–82.

Secure Your Financial Position

Work out how much you want to spend on acquiring property and precisely how you will pay for it. If you require a mortgage, or if it is tax efficient for you to take out a mortgage, then decide whether to apply for a UK mortgage, a Cypriot mortgage or an offshore mortgage. Before you start house-hunting you should secure a provisional mortgage offer.

Estate Agents

There are now several British-run estate agencies based in Cyprus and Cypriot estate agents abound. Standards are improving from the days when properties were advertised without price tags and sometimes, when investigated, turned out to have been withdrawn.

Artists' impressions remain the dominant force of the typical display in an estate agent's window but at least the properties they portray tend to be priced nowadays, so you can wander down the road to the next estate agent's window if there is nothing that strikes your eye. The very recent British influence into this industry is positive indeed. For a full discussion of account of the way estate agents operate in Cyprus and contact details, *see* 'Estate Agents', pp.51–6.

Property Inspection

It is surprising how few people purchasing property in Cyprus bother to have a property surveyed before they buy it; it's not a particularly expensive thing to have done and it just might save you from some hefty charges in the future. One memorable incident of which we were made aware when we invited people to tell us their experiences, good and bad, in acquiring property is that of a couple who purchased the last in a line of semi-detached two-storey properties. The retaining wall beneath what is their side balcony has not been properly constructed and the whole side part of the property is moving away. That will be very expensive to fix – something a proper survey would have picked up.

New property comes with a lifetime 'guarantee' for major structural defects, but the onus is on you to prove negligence; the normal guarantee for minor defects is one year. Any subsequent purchaser acquires the residue of the guarantee.

Valuation and Survey

Until very recently, surveys in Cyprus have usually been carried out by a civil engineer and occasionally by an architect. For contact details of the Cyprus Civil

> ### A Cautionary Tale
> One of the author's personal experiences was attempting to get a valuation for a friend of a plot of land in one of the more desirable districts of Limassol. I found two agents, both of whom told me on the phone that if my friend was prepared to put the piece of land on their books for sale they would be delighted to inspect the land, enquire of the District Land Registry Office as to what the building coefficient for that area is, and give us a fair estimate of the value of the plot. In both cases we met at the agreed time – something unusual in itself, as time in Cyprus does not quite have the same meaning as it does back home! – and in both cases when asked for their opinion as to the plot's value we were asked, 'Well, how much do you want for it?'!!!

Engineers and Architects Association (CCEAA) *see* 'Professional Bodies in Cyprus', p.178. Their website contains a list of members for each district but unless you read Greek you will need someone to translate the website for you.

There is now also a new association of valuers – so new that they only approved the title of the Association in October 2004. The Association of Valuers and Surveyors (*see* 'Professional Bodies in Cyprus', p.178, for contact details) undertakes valuations of land and property for commercial, industrial and residential purposes. They will value your property or the property you are considering purchasing. They also undertake valuations of land and property subject to compulsory acquisitions and valuations for tax purposes. Some of the members also undertake property management, which may be of interest if you wish to let out your property in Cyprus.

Valuations cost something in the order of CY£100 for a typical house or villa and CY£75 upwards for a plot of land. The actual cost varies on the value of the property – more expensive properties are obviously larger so more work is required to ascertain the value – and the distance from the office to the property   to
be valued.

Rule-of-thumb Valuations

As a very rough guide, the **value of property** may be calculated on the square metre covered area of the property – the number of square metres of the ground floor, plus the number of square metres of the other floor(s) as follows:

- Limassol town: CY£1,000 per sq m.
- Desirable suburbs (such as Ayias Tychonas): CY£1,200 per sq m.
- Limassol seafront: CY£2,000 per sq m.
- Paphos town: CY£1,000 per sq m.
- Paphos seafront: CY£2,000 per sq m.
- Desirable villages: CY£1,000 per sq m.
- Other villages: CY£700 per sq m.

All of these figures must be regarded as a guideline only. They may vary in either direction by 25 per cent or more depending on a number of factors: the general state of repair of the property (not including derelict property), the actual immediate location, the views the property commands, and so on.

Those who intend to build their own property will find it is worth knowing the approximate **value of land** and on how much of it you can build. Again these figures are based on early 2005 prices and are approximate. The building coefficient referred to below is the percentage of the plot area on which you are allowed to build. This can vary enormously. In the larger towns and cities the overall coefficient on high-rise properties may be several hundred per cent. In agricultural zones it may be as little as 10 per cent, and that 10 per cent may be restricted to a single building. The allowable building coefficient in nature protection zones is even lower. Development in urban areas is governed by the local development plan for that area while development in rural areas is governed by regulations contained in the government's statement of policy.

Until relatively recently, land in Cyprus was measured in donums, a donum being 1,338 sq m, about one-third of an acre, and this unit of measurement is still used in statute. A normal building plot was half a donum. Today land is measured in metric units, there being two principle measurements: a decarioum being 1,000 sq m and a hectare being 10,000 sq m.

Price of half a donum:

- **Limassol outskirts: CY£35,000–50,000.**
- **village within 20 minutes' drive of Limassol: CY£15,000–30,000.**

Building coefficient:

- **Limassol Town: usually 50–90%.**
- **country villages: minimum 20%.**
- **countryside: minimum 10%..**

Approximate cost to build a typical single-storey property (excluding the price of the land; a two-bedroom bungalow is around 100 sq m, a three-bedroom property 130 sq m):

- **conventional property – minimum CY£500 per sq m (not turnkey), which is about CY£600 per sq m fully fitted; if steel frame construction, somewhat new to Cyprus, may be significantly cheaper.**

Mortgage Lender's Valuation

Unlike in the UK, even if the purchaser requests a copy of the mortgage lender's valuation, the mortgage lender will not normally make a copy available. Most banks consider that their own valuation is their own affair. If a mortgage provider is prepared to let you have a copy of their own valuer's report, then that report will almost certainly be in Greek. In any event, the bank or other mortgage provider is not going to undertake a full survey of the property, so their own valuation is not going to reassure you of much and is certainly no substitute for having a proper survey carried out.

UK Qualified Surveyors Working in Cyprus

Though we are not aware of any independent British qualified surveyors, it is doubtless a niche market which will be discovered in due course so, if you prefer to deal with a fellow Brit in surveying your property, skim through the classified adverts in the two English language newspapers (the *Cyprus Weekly* and the *Cyprus Mail*) or get hold of a copy of the magazines of the British associations in Cyprus such as the Royal British Legion and the UKCA.

Contracts 'Subject to Survey'

While practically unheard of in Cyprus, there is no legal reason that a sale agreement may not be drawn up 'subject to survey'. However, since having a survey done is not a long-drawn-out exercise, any vendor is going to be some-what perplexed by your request and is more likely to tell you to have your survey done, then sign a normal contract if you wish to proceed.

Checklist

You will want to ask your surveyor to report on the following, where appropriate:

- the state of the foundations.
- the state of the damp proof course.
- any sign of rising damp and, if so, the seriousness, cause and likely cost of remedial work required.
- the condition under the floors.
- any sign of cracking in walls and pillars.
- the quality and condition of cement in concrete constructed buildings.
- the quality and condition of woodwork, including a check for dry and wet rot.
- drains and manholes.
- the septic tank.
- the condition of electrical wiring including earth leakage test.
- the heating and air-conditioning equipment.
- the swimming pool and related equipment.
- the roof insulation type and quality.
- the roof tiling.

Raising Finance to Buy a Property in Cyprus

Given the relatively low cost of property in Cyprus in comparison with most of Europe and certainly the UK, many Europeans and, in particular, British are considering purchasing property in Cyprus. Though they have been buying properties here for many years, and despite the fact that Cyprus is undergoing a particularly inflationary period – rather as Spain did when it joined the EU – there seems no apparent slowdown in demand for property from the British sector. Many are happy just to purchase a holiday home, but others buy property in Cyprus with the long-term view of retiring there.

Cypriot developers have not been slow to catch on to this booming market – in fact one can be forgiven for thinking that the outskirts of Limassol and Paphos are one big building site. While one would think that, with the apparent overabundance of property for sale, property prices would at least be stable, in fact house prices in Cyprus seem to march forever onwards and upwards. Yet property prices have risen steadily and mostly consistently in the UK for many years. So the disparity remains – for the cost of a small flat in London one can buy a decent house or even a villa in Paphos or Limassol.

Cypriot developers have been here for a long time but British developers, realising that Cyprus was about to join the EU, have been quick to jump on the bandwagon. In early 2005, just a few months after Cyprus became a member state, there were a lot of new British developers and estate agents on the island. From 2004 there have been regular pull-out property sections in the English language newspapers in Cyprus, and many of these pages feature British-run companies. At the same time, a wider range of options for financing new properties is developing on the island of Aphrodite.

Just two or three years ago it was nigh on impossible for Britons to finance property through any of the major Cypriot banks, simply because they were foreigners. In those relatively recent days a Brit could not even get a bridging loan from a high street bank in the Republic. In the year or so before Cyprus' accession to the EU, banking policy became more fluid and, while unusual, it was theoretically possible for an expat to obtain a Cyprus mortgage from a Cyprus bank. At that time, even in early 2004, there was about as much chance of flying to the moon as walking into your local bank manager's office back home and walking out with a mortgage even partially based on a Cyprus property. Today, slowly, that is changing, even though it may be a few months after this book is published that some of the changes are actually perceptible.

It is assumed that everyone reading this book is aware of the concept of a mortgage. It is, of course, a loan secured on an asset, in this case property. Although a mortgage is often essential – for instance when most of us first climb on the property ladder – a mortgage can also be a handy investment tool when you don't actually have to borrow the cash. It's all a matter of foretelling the future – an educated gamble, so to speak – and that is what every investment is. In the simple case of investing a sum by depositing it with a bank, if the rate of return exceeds the rate of inflation, then you make a net gain. Moving on to stocks and shares, three factors are important: the rate of return (the dividend) as a percentage of the price you paid; the risk factor of the particular investment (how well the company is performing in relation to its competitors and how likely it is to get into financial difficulties); and the market trend for the particular sector in which you are investing. By way of example, any hint of Gulf War Three would depress the value of stocks and shares in businesses involved in tourism while it would boost the value of stocks and shares in businesses involved in armaments. Commodities such as precious metals could also be expected to rise. So, with stocks and shares, you are juggling both an income by way of dividend and a gain (or loss) on the value of the stock you are holding.

Mortgages are not dissimilar. On the income side you have rental income (if your property is rented part or all of the time) plus, in the case of a holiday home, the money you have saved by not renting similar accommodation from someone else. Of course you have to weigh up the costs of upkeep but in doing so you should remember that there is the unquantifiable advantage that it is your home. On the capital side, the gamble is that the percentage increase in value of the property will be greater than the mortgage rate.

Until very recently it was unusual to take out a mortgage secured against property in Cyprus through anyone other than a specialist broker. Today it is generally not possible to take out a mortgage in the UK secured on a Cyprus property. However it is now possible, status permitting, to obtain a mortgage on a property in Cyprus from any of the Cypriot high street banks (see 'Banks in Cyprus' p.179, for contact details of the banks). We have also been assured by Barclays Bank that it expects to be able to offer a similar service very shortly (by the spring of 2005).

It has always been possible to finance borrowing for any purpose by mortgaging or remortgaging your existing UK property, and this is the route many people will continue to choose. Let us look at some of the options available.

Mortgaging or Remortgaging your UK Property

Without doubt this is the easiest way to raise finance for your new property in Cyprus; and unless you are a financial guru looking for offshore funding, it is almost certainly the most convenient and probably the cheapest too. There are a host of mortgage providers in the UK and a bewildering number of packages available, so it is possibly best to take advice from a mortgage broker. There are a number of British financial advisers with offices in Cyprus and the UK who will be able to offer you mortgage packages from either country.

Advantages

- **The loan repayment will be in whatever currency you wish.** It is always a wise move to keep your expenses in the same currency as your income. So if you are British and intend to continue working in the UK, and are perhaps buying a property in Cyprus either as a holiday home or with a view to retiring there in the future, you will most probably want a sterling mortgage. In this way you will not get any nasty shocks if exchange rates fluctuate. The same applies if, for instance, you are paid in dollars. It is perfectly possible to set up a dollar mortgage in the UK.

- **The set-up costs will be low.** If you are remortgaging your existing property, then your existing lender will be able to extend your loan for a nominal arrangement fee. There will be no legal costs and probably no revaluation fee. If you remortgage with a new lender or mortgage for the first time there is fierce competition in the UK to provide finance. Many mortgage providers will undertake to pick up most or all of the legal and valuation charges involved.

- **Flexibility.** There is a greater range of mortgage offers in the UK. In Cyprus, in general only repayment mortgages are available, at least from the major banks. In the UK you have the choice of repayment-only mortgages, pension mortgages, endowment mortgages...to name but a few. Note, however, that some specialist mortgage advisers in Cyprus are able to offer greater flexibility.

Disadvantages

- **Possible devaluation of the Cyprus pound.** You are taking the risk – and it is a big risk – that if the Cyprus pound devalues, a mortgage in Cyprus pounds would have been cheaper to pay off. For some years now in some financial quarters, the consensus of opinion has been that the Cyprus pound is over-valued. The Cyprus government made a commitment to join the European Monetary System (the euro) in 2007. In fact it would appear that Cyprus will be unable to meet that deadline, since certain economic targets are unlikely to be attained within that time scale. This will oblige the Cyprus government to defer entry. Today the Cyprus pound is 'strapped' to the euro. That is to say that the value of the Cyprus pound is linked to the value of the euro, which the Central Bank must maintain within a fairly narrow trading range. When Cyprus is ready to adopt the European Monetary System the Republic of Cyprus is required by European law to un-strap the currency from the euro and let it float freely for a period of two years before the euro is adopted. Unless the Cyprus government voluntarily devalues the Cyprus pound before the two-year period commences, there is a possibility that the currency will devalue steeply. This, of course, is only a considered opinion. It may or may not be correct.

• **Interest rate fluctuations.** One needs to compare the interest rates prevailing in both countries in the light of the mortgage set-up fees, life insurance, valuation costs and other charges.

Cyprus Mortgages

A Cyprus mortgage is a loan taken out from a Cyprus company – which may be the Cyprus offshoot, or subsidiary, of an international company – secured against an immovable property located in the Republic of Cyprus. In early 2005 it was not possible to walk into your local bank in England, Scotland, Wales or Northern Ireland and obtain a mortgage based solely on your intended Cyprus property, though, as mentioned above, we have been led to believe that Barclays Bank will be able to offer this service (contact details are on p.179).

A mortgage is a security for a loan. In this case it is secured against property – whether land, a house or an apartment – and, as with any loan, the capital security may become forfeit if the payments due on the loan are not met in accordance with the loan agreement.

There are a few differences between a Cyprus mortgage and a mortgage obtained in the UK, but these differences are not great and in due course the sophistication of the UK (and European) mortgage industry in general is bound to seep into the Cypriot system, as it will do in every EU member state. In comparison with the UK, the generic Cyprus mortgage industry is very small, relatively young and may be expected to be relatively unsophisticated. What is not unsophisticated is the influence of international corporations, independent financial advisers and the like who can and have set up onshore and offshore companies in Cyprus and who are able to offer very much the same sort of options that you would expect in the UK. In all fairness, the local banks – Alpha Bank, Bank of Cyprus, Laiki, Co-op and so on – are learning fast. Only a year and a half ago Cypriot mortgages were not available to the average expat.

The mortgages offered by the high street banks in Cyprus are normally repayment mortgages; however, there is flexibility on the repayment terms, such as deferred capital repayment, and even some options akin to endowment mortgages. A Cyprus mortgage has the advantage that if you earn income in Cyprus pounds, then you will not be in for any nasty shocks if the exchange rates push up the value of the Cyprus pound. However, a Cyprus lender will be able to offer you a mortgage in whatever major international currency you want. One may take an educated guess that now that Cyprus has acceded to the European Union, the high street banks are not going to sit on their laurels but will be investigating and gradually introduce a greater range of mortgages specifically with the European borrower in mind.

Generally speaking the maximum term of a Cyprus mortgage offer to an expat is 15 years, although that may be subject to an upper age limit for an older borrower. There will probably, and in the case of mortgages with low start-up interest in the early years definitely, be penalties for early redemption – if your circumstances change, perhaps you inherited some money from your Great-Aunt Mabel, you will be penalised if you decide to pay off the capital outstanding on the mortgage early.

How Much Can I Borrow?

Each individual case is assessed on its merits but, in general and subject to your personal financial status and the bank's own survey of your intended property, you will be able to borrow up to 70 per cent of the value of the property. In exceptional circumstances you may be able to borrow up to 75 per cent. The minimum loan available is generally CY£10,000.

The only Cypriot bank that would give us any kind of guideline as to the amount you would be able to secure by way of a mortgage was the Bank of Cyprus. The Bank of Cyprus, whose policies are likely to be similar to the other high street banks in the Republic, are primarily concerned that you will be able to make the mortgage repayments comfortably. For the average person their calculations are based on ability to repay the mortgage as follows:

- **The bank values your intended property at a fair market rate. Up to 70 per cent will normally be available by way of a mortgage subject to their satisfaction as to your income.**

- **In normal circumstances, the bank will assume that you can meet your day to day living costs by expending 65 per cent of your salary or monthly income. This leaves 35 per cent (maximum) available to repay a mortgage. So, if your monthly income is CY£1,000 a month, the bank will assume that you will be able to afford a monthly mortgage repayment of CY£350.**

Depending on the actual plan you opt for, a mortgage of CY£40,000 taken out over a term of 15 years with the Bank of Cyprus would, today (November 2004), involve you in repayments of CY£325 a month for the first two years and CY£360 a month for the next 13 years. Thus an income of CY£1,000 a month would normally secure a mortgage of CY£40,000.

A mortgage of CY£50,000 would involve repayments, as above, of CY£406 a month for the first two years and CY£450 a month for the remaining 13 years. A mortgage of CY£50,000 would be secured with a monthly income of CY£1,285.

The above is not a formula; it is a guideline only. Any mortgage offered will be considered on its own merits. If, for instance, you are in the enviable position of earning CY£10,000 a month, you may well be able to secure a mortgage involving you in mortgage repayments of CY£5,000 a month, which is 50 per cent of your earnings, rather more than the 35 per cent in the model illustrated above. As said, each case is carefully assessed on its own merits.

The mortgage agreement between you and the Cypriot mortgage provider is known in Cyprus as a 'housing loan agreement' and will be recorded as a first charge on the property at the District Land Registry Office.

Timing of a Cypriot Mortgage and First Steps

The preliminary 'approval in principle', that is to say subject to the bank's independent valuation of your intended property and to their verification of personal financial and other information which you will have provided, should not take more than a week. Very often you will receive a verbal indication there and then. You may then expect to receive a formal mortgage offer within 15 days. This offer will usually be valid for 45 days.

The first step in obtaining a mortgage offer is to inform the would-be lender of the identity of the property and give that person a copy of the title deed, unless it is a new development, in which case a specific title deed will not exist. In this instance you will provide a copy of the general title deed of the development – the document the developer requires to obtain a building permit.

Mortgages on New Developments

If you purchase a new apartment, villa, or house from a developer – and this sort of purchase is perhaps the most common purchase that expats make – then you will inevitably be making stage payments (*see* 'Stage Payments', pp.88–90). We mentioned above that your Cypriot mortgage provider will normally provide up to 70 per cent of the finance required. The balance of (usually) 30 per cent will be provided by you directly or via your lawyer in cash (in other words a cheque deposited with your lawyers and held on their client account for your benefit) and this 30 per cent will be the first sum of money applied to the payments schedule to which you agreed in the sale agreement between you and the developer. Only when this sum has been exhausted will your mortgage provider make the balance available to you or your lawyer. The actual payments that the bank makes to the builder (or seller) are via the District Land Registry Office.

Mortgages and Grants for Properties Needing Renovation

Generally speaking there is no problem in obtaining a mortgage for a property that needs renovation, except that one might not obtain the 'usual' maximum 70 per cent finance on the cost of the property in its existing state plus your estimate of the costs of renovation. The mortgage provider may be rather more careful in the assessment of what it will cost to put the property back into a good condition – but will judge each case on its merits.

One thing to note: if you are purchasing a listed building, generous **grants** are available from the government towards the cost of renovation. In urban areas grants of up to 40 per cent of the approved cost of restoration may be obtained, 50 per cent in rural areas. The approved cost of restoration is defined as being the lower of the cost as per the tender submitted by the building contractor and the state-determined cost per square metre. This latter figure was established in 2004 as being:

- **CY£550 per sq m for buildings with an area of under 120 sq m.**
- **C500 per sq m for buildings with an area of between 121 sq m and 1,000 sq m.**
- **CY£300 per sq m for buildings with an area of over 1000 sq m.**

The maximum grant is CY£40,000, with additional tax advantages. The details of these grants and their terms and conditions are beyond the scope of this book. The preservation section of the Department of Town Planning can provide further information; see 'Professional Bodies in Cyprus', p.178, for contact details. The Department publishes a four-page summary in English, which anyone thinking of purchasing a listed building should obtain.

The Cost of Taking out a Mortgage

The ancillary costs of taking out a mortgage can be up to 10 per cent of the amount borrowed, most of which are apportioned during the life of the mortgage. These costs are over and above the normal costs of purchasing a property, which will themselves be between 5 per cent and 12 per cent of the value.

In most cases a mortgage provider will require that the person taking out the mortgage is covered for **term insurance** for the length of the mortgage and for at least the value of the mortgage. If the property is to be registered in joint names the mortgage provider may require that both parties carry life insurance in the full amount of the mortgage. This can be a considerable cost factor depending on age and your state of health. We asked two reputable insurance companies, one in Cyprus, the other in the UK, for quotes. They were asked to quote for term insurance on a mortgage of CY£50,000 (level-term equal to the mortgage amount) for a male in good health aged 30, for a period of 30 years.

The Cyprus quote was obtained, very quickly and without any prevarication at all, from Universal Life in Nicosia. Their quotation was an annual premium of CY£168.50 broken down as CY£138.50, being CY£2.77 per CY£1,000 insured, plus CY£30 policy fee. The UK quote was obtained with considerable hassle from Scottish Widows who quoted £85 per annum for a non-smoker who is a resident of the UK, depending on occupation! We were told that living in Cyprus would add to the cost but Scottish Widows could not (or would not) tell us how much extra it would cost.

So, it would seem that taking out life assurance may be a little cheaper in the UK than in Cyprus, although it seems that there is more hassle in doing so; there is no reason why you should not use UK life cover to back a Cyprus mortgage. All the mortgage provider should be interested in is that the company with whom you have, or intend to have, a policy is reputable – but do check with the mortgage provider before taking out the policy.

Mortgaging your Cyprus Property – Summary

Advantages

• If you wish to let out your property you will be able to get tax relief from the Cyprus taxation authority on the mortgage interest.

• The repayments will normally be in Cyprus pounds. If you opt for a foreign currency mortgage and are paying for it in Cyprus pounds it is going to cost CY£20–30 a month just to buy the required currency. It tends to be more effective to take out a mortgage in the currency in which your income is derived.

• If the Cyprus pound devalues, and your income source is not Cyprus pounds, the mortgage will become cheaper.

Disadvantages

• You will pay Cyprus interest rates. At the time of writing (November 2004) Cyprus mortgage interest rates are slightly more expensive than UK rates. British rates are about 7.5 per cent variable whereas Cyprus rates are about 8 per cent variable.

• Mortgage options are more limited than in the UK.

• The loan will be more expensive to set up.

• You may need extra life insurance.

Who Should Own the Property?

Before Cyprus acceded to the European Union in May 2004, all non-Cypriots, regardless of their residence status, required permission from the Council of Ministers to acquire immovable property and to become the registered owner(s) of that property with the exception of people who have inherited property. Since 1 May 2004 citizens of the European Union residing in Cyprus and in possession of a residence permit (known as a 'pink slip') may acquire immovable property without the approval of the Council of Ministers.

European Union nationals living overseas who do not have a residence permit for the Republic of Cyprus still require the approval of the Council of Ministers when acquiring a house or an apartment. This approval is not required for land or for commercial premises such as shops, hotels or offices. Among the policies enforced by the Council of Ministers is a degree of protection for the tourism industry of the island. A home is intended to be just that; permission for an individual or for a couple to own a residential property is not usually a problem. The couple need not be married; within the last two years it has been possible for a common law husband and wife to register property jointly. Within the last year multiple ownership, where more than one family is involved, has also become permitted.

Before 1 May 2004 a foreigner was only entitled to purchase one property built or to be built on a plot not exceeding two donums (*see* 'Rule-of-thumb Valuations', p.70, for a definition), with the proviso that if the individual(s) concerned can prove the necessity, the two donum limit may be increased to three donums. That law has not yet been revoked, although rumour (from considered sources) has it that it will be in 2007. In any case, if you are exempt from requiring the permission of the Council of Ministers to purchase property (*see* above) you can buy as much land or as many properties as you wish.

For reasons which are not altogether clear to us, until recently the Council of Ministers would not usually grant children under the age of 18 permission to own property, unless they had inherited it.

There are ways around what might appear to be a potential problem by either establishing a trust to deal with ownership of the property or establishing a company in Cyprus to do so. It is outside the scope of this book to go into too much detail about establishing trusts and companies as you will need to discuss your precise situation and requirements with a professional adviser.

Bearing the above comments in mind, there are practical and tax-saving reasons for putting the property in names other than your own, the principal reason being inheritance tax. *See* **Financial Implications**, pp.101–104, for an explanation of what domicile means – if you can change your domicile you will be liable to inheritance tax in Cyprus, not the UK, and inheritance tax in the Republic was abolished some years ago. Remember, though, that unless you force the Inland Revenue in the UK to make a decision, your domicile will only be assessed by the UK Inland Revenue after your death.

The Options

Sole Ownership

For the average couple, whether married or not, it generally does not make sense for tax reasons to have the property in the name of just one individual. It may do so if one of you could conceivably face bankruptcy through the failure of a high-risk business or if one of you is in ill health or there is a large age discrepancy between you and your partner.

Joint Ownership

Joint ownership is perhaps the most common way in which expats purchase property in Cyprus. Your portion is your portion and your partner's is theirs. When one of you dies then that person's portion will be dealt with in accordance with Cyprus law. It will, if you have not changed domicile and/or not devolved yourself of your share by establishing a trust (*see* 'Trusts', p.119), be liable to UK inheritance tax. Since whoever inherits the deceased's portion could insist on the sale of the whole property to liquidate their new asset, you will both want to consider making the surviving partner a lifetime tenant in the property in the terms of your respective wills. Making a will to cover your assets situated in Cyprus is discussed in the next chapter; *see* 'Making a Will', p.117.

Adding your Children to the Title or Making your Children the Legal Owners

If your children are entitled to register title at the Land Registry Office, then you need only remember that that percentage of the property so registered is theirs and they can do what they like with it. Unless you have established a lifetime interest for yourself and for your partner there could be problems if, for instance, one of your children divorces and that child's portion of your Cyprus property becomes part of the divorce settlement.

Limited Company

Apart from being one of the two obvious ways around the problem of having no 'pink slip' and therefore requiring the approval of the Council of Ministers to acquire immovable property, the intentional formation of a company will appeal to a few. First, it completely obviates any question of capital gains tax; a company, in law, is considered as a body corporate – much the same as a living human being – and unless it goes into liquidation it does not 'die'. Secondly, it carries tax advantages, or it may do so. It also carries costs: companies cost money to set up and every year the law proscribes that they have their accounts formally audited by a regulated firm chartered or certified to do so. Your personal situation is important and you need some professional advice to ascertain whether this might be a beneficial way to acquire property.

Trusts

This is the second obvious way around the land registration problem we have discussed, and it may well be a neater and cheaper solution than forming a company. You will certainly need professional advice to establish whether this option is in your personal best interests, as well as in the best interests of those near and dear to you. The formation of a trust will enable you to preserve a lifelong interest both for you and, should you pre-decease your partner, for your partner, and it may be the neatest way to insure against possible problems. As you will see in the next chapter, a trust can be set up to do exactly what you want in any circumstance that you have foreseen and provided for (*see* p.119).

The Process of Buying a Property in Cyprus

General Legal Procedure

The distinct processes involved in purchasing immovable property in the Republic of Cyprus is pretty much the same as in the UK: find a property; check it out; offer to purchase it; sign a contract; pay; sign a deed of ownership. However, there are often a few possible pitfalls along the way and, if you think of the whole procedure in the terms that you would in the UK, you may well be in for some unpleasant surprises. Do *not*, as we have stressed before, even think about doing this yourself unless, that is, you happen to be qualified in Cyprus law! Find a lawyer who can negotiate the minefield on your behalf!

Choosing a Lawyer

A Cyprus Lawyer

Many people purchasing a property in Cyprus, particularly on a development, use the lawyer or law firm that is recommended to them by the vendor. That, as will be seen later, is a mistake. It is important that the lawyer is honest, competent and *independent*. If you use the lawyer recommended to you by whomever you are purchasing the property from, the lawyer's independence is clearly compromised. Quite likely the lawyer is going in to bat for the vendor and will not, by definition, be working solely in your best interests.

There are many competent and professional law firms in Cyprus, but sadly there are some rotten apples. As with every professional you may need to employ – lawyer, accountant, financial adviser – check credentials, ask if they personally know the vendor (to which you would prefer to hear a resounding 'No') and ask for references of other British expats for whom the individual or company has done similar work. Then satisfy yourself about the quality of those references. No professional should be offended by such a request – only those with something to hide might bluster.

Above all, never, never, never use the same lawyer as the seller is using.

A UK Solicitor

I am not personally aware of any UK lawyers who are experienced in dealing with the laws of Cyprus and regulations concerning immovable property although, in surfing the web, we did come across one UK-based firm of international lawyers who purport to do business in Cyprus. Since they could not be bothered to reply to an e-mail requesting further information, they are not mentioned in the reference section at the end of this book.

The Contract Price

The price you will pay for a property is a matter of negotiation between you and the seller. The extent to which you can negotiate a reduction in the asking price will usually depend on the financial climate at the time. In 2004 the market was overstocked with new developments so there may be some room for negotiation. The resale property market was reasonably static, there being no particular excess of demand over supply, or vice versa.

The Amount that Should be Declared in the Sale Agreement

The price in the sale agreement is important because on this figure is computed the amount of capital gains tax the vendor will pay and the amount of land registration transfer fees you will pay (provided that the District Land Registry Office's assessment of the value of your property is the same as the purchase price).

The only legal method of under-declaring the contract price is not really an under-declaration at all. It concerns purchasing a property that is either newly fitted out or, in the case of resale property, part of the purchase price is for fitted appliances which the vendor has agreed to include in the purchase price. Say, for example, that you wish to purchase a three-bedroom apartment and that the purchase price is CY£100,000. For whatever reason the vendor has included in the price the units in the kitchen – electric fan oven, microwave, gas hob, washing machine, dishwasher, fridge, freezer – and has agreed with you to leave the beds in the spare room and perhaps even some, or all, of the furniture. She has also agreed to leave the air-conditioning units. Depending on their age and the make and model of the items, all of this could easily add up to CY£5,000. Assuming that CY£5,000 is a fair figure, it is perfectly acceptable to draw up the sale agreement showing that you are purchasing the property for CY£95,000 and fittings within for a further CY£5,000. The liability to capital gains tax for the vendor (and for you when you eventually sell the property) and the liability to land registration transfer fees for you to pay will be assessed not on the full purchase price of CY£100,000 but on the reduced figure of CY£95,000.

The illegal method is to actually under-declare, paying the amount of the under-declaration 'under the table'. The reason for being tempted to do so is obvious: a lower contract value means less capital gains tax for the vendor and possibly less in land registration transfer fees for you. It is illegal, just as intentionally under-declaring your income is illegal; both are an attempt to defraud the taxation authorities. It is not overly clever either, because when you come to sell, unless you can persuade the subsequent buyer also to under-declare, you will be subject to a greater capital gains tax liability. In any event the value of your property for transfer fee purposes will be assessed by the District Land

Registry Office and if they consider that an obvious under-declaration has been made, transfer fees will be payable based on their assessment of the true value. Finally, in the event of court action the monetary claim of the purchaser will be based on the declared amount, not the actual amount paid. In short we do not advise anyone deliberately to under-declare the purchase price.

How and Where the Sale Price Should be Paid

The sale price may be paid in whatever way the parties agree. The most usual way is to lodge the required money with your lawyer who will deposit it in their client account and, at the time agreed, draw the required funds and pay them either to the vendor's lawyer or directly to the vendor. But there is nothing to prevent your paying the vendor directly in whatever currency you wish and to wherever in the world you both agree. It is a quite common procedure that when a Cypriot property owned by a British person is sold to another British person that the transaction takes place in sterling between the British bank accounts of the two parties. Do remember, though, that if the vendor is subject to capital gains tax, that tax liability must be paid in Cyprus.

General and Specific Enquiries

It is part of your lawyer's remit, or it should be, to search at the District Land Registry Office and specifically check that the vendor actually owns the property in question, whether there is a contract of sale lodged in anyone else's name and whether or not there is a mortgage or other charge lodged against the property.

In the case of land you may be wish to be reassured that the electricity board is not about to install high voltage electricity pylons along your border or that the district council is not about to convert your access road into a dual carriageway. This is not a function usually undertaken by your lawyer; it is something you should appoint a surveyor to check at the planning department.

Your Civil State

Your lawyer will require you to provide your name, address, nationality and passport number. This information will be forwarded to the District Land Registry Office and, if you are the seller, to the Tax Office.

General Legal Procedure and Legal Terms

Whether you are purchasing land, new property or an existing property, the same legal procedure is followed:

- Agreement is reached between parties and a sale agreement is drawn up.

- Four copies of the sale agreement are made and all four copies are presented at the District Land Registry Office. One of these copies is stamped 'Original' and will usually be retained by the purchaser's lawyer on the purchaser's behalf. The other three copies are stamped with a CY£1 stamp and certified as true copies of the original.

- The stamp duty (*see* p.94) is paid by the purchaser or their attorney, authorised by the power of attorney document (*see* below) and one of the copies of the sale agreement is registered with the District Land Registry Office for purposes of specific performance (*see* next section).

- One of the copies of the sale agreement is given to the mortgage provider (if any). The last copy of the sale agreement is given to the vendor.

- The terms of the sale agreement are met and the purchaser takes possession of the property.

- When the title deeds have been drawn up, the parties, or their respective lawyer(s), meet at the District Land Registry Office to pay the land registration transfer fees (*see* p.94), which are payable by the purchaser, and to effect transfer of the property from the vendor to the purchaser.

Specific Performance

We referred above to 'specific performance', and this is a particularly important part of the law of conveyancing, which you need to understand.

The primary purpose of specific performance is to protect the purchaser. While specific performance requires both parties to perform, specifically, their obligations under the terms of the sale agreement, the vendor will always be protected against the wrongful act of the purchaser. What wrongful act can purchasers make? They might be late on a payment. If so, they will probably have to bear interest on the late payment. Depending on the wording of the sale agreement, they might even forfeit part or all of the payments made to date. In any case, the vendor is not going to transfer the property until any transgressions made by the purchaser have been put right to the vendor's satisfaction – until the purchaser has fully complied with all the terms of the sale agreement.

The other way round, it is not so simple. What transgressions might vendors make? The most common reason for invoking the specific performance law is that, for whatever reason, a property developer unreasonably delays transferring title. He might be lazy, he might have health problems, he might not like you! That is not your problem; what is your problem is that you want your deed of title to the property you have paid for.

The law of specific performance provides that, so long as the sale agreement is deposited with the District Land Registry Office, and providing that both parties are in a position to effect transfer, then within six months of notification by the purchaser to the vendor the vendor *must* effect transfer; if he or she does not, you can apply for a court order requiring immediate transfer.

There are two other side-effects of specific performance, both of which act in protection of the buyer:

• **When the certified true copy of the sale agreement is deposited with the District Land Registry Office, the sale agreement acts as an onus, or burden, on the property. The District Land Registry Office is aware that on such and such a date Mr A signed an agreement with Ms B in such a sum of money to purchase the property. Ms B cannot now tear up that agreement and instead sell the property to Mr C. This effectively stops gazumping and acts as a protection to the purchaser.**

• **If the sale agreement is not registered with the District Land Registry Office and subsequently, often several years later as you will see, both parties attend to pay the registration transfer fees, the amount payable will be assessed on the value of the property at the date of the visit. However, if the sale agreement has been registered with the District Land Registry Office, the liability to registration transfer fees will be assessed on the value of the property on the date that the sale agreement was signed. Since the value of property tends to rise, the purchaser will usually prefer to pay on the assessed value of the property at the earlier date.**

Power of Attorney

As you will see below, the processes involved in purchasing a property and obtaining title, particularly from a developer, are many. Most people, whether they live in Cyprus or not, cannot be bothered with all the paperwork – and that is assuming they know the procedures in the first place. If you are still living in the UK, waiting perhaps for your dream villa to be finished, you certainly will not want the extra expense of flying backwards and forwards to get this piece of paper signed or to instruct your bank to do that or to attend to the other hundred and one things that might need doing. So most, nearly all, individuals – buyers and sellers alike – appoint an agent to do the work for them. This appointment is achieved by virtue of signing a power of attorney, and the terms of this document may be as general or specific as you wish. The agent you appoint will usually be your solicitor, whose price for acting as your legal representative should be included in the price he or she first gave you for undertaking to purchase your property. Whoever you have appointed as your attorney may be empowered by you to deal with any or every aspect involved in purchasing (or selling, as the case may be) your property.

Legal Procedure: New Property

The terms and conditions that must be met by the developer will be contained within the sale agreement, as will the timing and amount of the various payments (**stage payments**, *see* below) you will be obliged to make. The sale agreement will be presented to you by the developer and once you have signed the document you will be legally bound to it; there is no cooling-off period prescribed within Cyprus' legislation. So, it's important that the sale agreement is fair and reasonable: do not sign the sale agreement until you and your lawyer are happy with all of its clauses and you have accessed the money you need, including having a firm mortgage offer if desired, to make the payments involved.

There is no given formula for making stage payments; larger developers will tend to be strict in the contractual terms that they lay down whereas smaller developers will be more fluid and a competent lawyer will be more able to vary that particular developer's 'standard' terms of contract in your favour.

Some developers will link stage payments to specific dates; others will link stage payments to work actually undertaken. Since the first option does not give the developer any incentive to actually do any work on your property (until the last minute, that is), any competent lawyer will try to link stage payments to measurable progress being made. Unless there is some exceptional reason for date-linked stage payments, you would be most ill advised to proceed on that basis.

The initial deposit, usually payable on signature of the sale agreement, can vary enormously too. Some developers will only ask for a relatively small deposit; others will attempt to link your first payment with the value of the land on which your particular property will be built. As a generality, a developer will try to get as much as possible from you by way of the initial deposit (20–30 per cent), whereas a competent lawyer will try to reduce the down-payment.

Stage Payments

Having paid the initial downpayment, there will now follow a series of payments, and we reproduce below two actual draft agreements so you can get a better idea of the procedure. The first is relatively simple, the second much more detailed.

Example A

Balance of CY£49,000 as follows:

- **CY£12,000 on completion of the concrete frame.**
- **CY£12,000 on completion of the brickwork.**
- **CY£12,000 on completion of the electrical installations, plastering, flooring and carpentry work.**

- CY£12,000 on delivery.
- CY£1,000 on transfer of title.

Example B

The purchase price of the property is hereby agreed at CY£148,000 (Cyprus Pounds One Hundred and Forty-Eight Thousand). The mode of payment shall be as follows:

- **CY£54,000 on the signing of this agreement, receipt of which is hereby acknowledged by the vendor.**
- **CY£11,000 on completion of preliminary works, excavations and foundations.**
- **CY£24,000 on completion of concrete works and skeleton.**
- **CY£26,000 on completion of brickworks, preliminary electrical, plumbing and mechanical works and placement of all boxes, pipes and provisions; completion of external and internal rendering.**
- **CY£9,000 on placement of floors and tiling.**
- **CY£9,000 on completion of carpentry works, the kitchen and all cupboards.**
- **CY£9,000 on completion of all painting and external works, including the swimming pool and delivery of the property.**
- **CY£3,000 paid 12 months after the delivery of the property.**
- **CY£3,000 on transfer and registration of the property into the purchaser's name.**

Example B is based on the format of one of the larger developers: first, the deposit is well on the high side – a fair deposit, or initial payment, is about 20 per cent of the contract value, although developers will aim to secure 30 per cent or more. Second, both the withholding period and amount of the withholding is on the low side – a competent lawyer will aim to withhold CY£3,000–5,000, preferably for two years – the second year allows more time for the ground to settle. (The reason for the withholding is to give the developer an incentive to fix any problems that subsequently appear in the workmanship). Developers, on the other hand, will not usually offer more than a 2 per cent withholding. Finally, a competent lawyer will aim to withhold as much as possible – at least CY£5,000 – until transfer is effected and clear title is granted. As can be seen in the above case, the lawyer doesn't always succeed!

How Do You Know When a Stage Payment is Due?

The sale agreement will include a clause that the developer must provide you, or your attorney, who is usually your lawyer, with notification that the works for a particular stage are complete and that payment for that stage is now due. That official notification, a '**notice of completion**', will be signed either by the architect or by the supervising civil engineer. After service of the notice of completion, the sale agreement will allow you a short period of grace to make the payment.

Procedure If There is a Mortgage Involved

The mortgage offer will have been based on the original sale agreement, of which your mortgage provider will retain a signed and stamped copy. The bank or other mortgage provider will follow the payment schedule after you have provided evidence that the initial (usually minimum 30 per cent) funding provided directly by yourself has been paid to the developer in compliance with the terms of the sale agreement.

For example, suppose you wish to purchase a property for CY£100,000 and a local bank has agreed to lend you a mortgage of CY£70,000. Suppose that the initial payment is 20 per cent, due on initial signature of the sale agreement, and that the first instalment is 20 per cent, due on completion of foundations and construction of the concrete frame. You will provide evidence that you have made the initial payment (CY£20,000) and, when the first instalment is due, the first CY£10,000 of the CY£20,000 outstanding, thus exhausting the CY£30,000 you injected into the project. Only at that stage does the mortgage kick in, and the bank will pay the CY£10,000 balance of the first instalment as well as all the subsequent instalments.

One word of warning here: if you have taken out a mortgage, then the notice of completion will be referred to your mortgage provider for payment. Cyprus banks have the annoying habit of automatically questioning the competence of the architect and/or the supervising civil engineer and may well send their own valuer or contracted civil engineer to inspect the works – for which they will charge you! If there are many stage payments these 'hidden' charges may well add up to several hundreds of pounds, so check with your intended mortgage provider what their usual procedure is before accepting the offer.

When Do I Start Paying Off the Mortgage?

The Bank of Cyprus offers a number of options:

- **Pay interest only for the first year.**
- **Defer the first year's payments altogether. Repayments must commence one year after completion of the property or (maximum) two years after the first instalment has been paid out by the bank.**

Title Deeds

Title deeds on property developments will only become available after some years – 3 to 5 years is a reasonable period – as a lengthy procedure is involved to separate the land that the property developer initially acquired in order to issue individual title deeds. The earlier you purchased into a development, the longer you will wait; whereas if you are one of the last to purchase then correspondingly your wait for title deeds will be shorter. You may wonder why such a seemingly simple matter should take so long. The legal procedure can only commence when all of the units that comprise a development are completed. That is because when the builder or developer was first granted a building permit he was granted the permit for the whole project, not individual building permits for each individual unit. The reason for that is obvious: the project is more than just the creation of the individual homes; it involves the provision of roads, the installation of services such as water, sewage and electricity and the laying out of 'green' areas.

One does occasionally hear of development properties where the title deeds have been held up for many, many years. This usually happens when the purchaser of a particular unit of the overall development does something to his property which is not in the original plans. For instance, in the second year of a planned five-year development, an individual purchaser decides to build a conservatory on his patio without planning permission. Such a construction is not only unlicensed, but it may have caused the whole development to have exceeded the building coefficient allowed for by the particular district (see 'Rule-of-thumb Valuations', p.70).

Legal Procedure: Existing Property

While the legal procedures are very much along the same lines as already described, purchasing an existing property is a much more simple procedure. First, you will usually be buying from an individual, rather than from a company or developer. Second, a separate title deed will (usually) already exist. That said, there are a few extra jobs that the lawyer will have to undertake on your behalf and the way the sale agreement will be constructed is also different.

The first step that your lawyer will take is to inspect the title deed of the property you intend to acquire at the District Land Registry Office, and check that the deed is correct in its description of the property – for instance that a house is described as a house and not as a field; yes, it has been known to happen! The reason for such inaccuracy is often not sinister but may just be an oversight such as that the original building permit was not registered. Your lawyer will look at the title deed for any other possible problems, such as an outstanding mortgage. (If there is an outstanding mortgage then the first payment that you will make is to the vendor's mortgage company and your lawyer will require, by way of receipt, a certificate of clearance from the mortgage company.)

Your lawyer will then receive a draft sale agreement from the vendor's lawyers and amend it in your best interests. Rather as in the UK, you can normally expect to pay 10 per cent by way of a deposit and the balance of 90 per cent on taking delivery of the property. There may, or may not, be a withholding until the transfer deed is effected. A competent lawyer will most certainly amend the draft sale agreement to withhold CY£3,000–4,000 until the vendor produces evidence that all taxes and other charges are paid. Depending on the value of the property and the status of the vendor, your lawyer may insist on linking a payment to the provision by the vendor of capital gains tax clearance. The other charges referred to above are local rates, immovable property tax, municipal rates, sewerage (if any), refuse collection and common expenses (for a flat or apartment). Apart from capital gains tax and immovable property tax (*see* 'Capital Gains Tax', p.105, and 'Immovable Property Taxes', p.116), these ancillary charges are unlikely to exceed CY£300 a year – but if they haven't been paid for a number of years, they can mount up.

Transfer of the Property

Although quicker than purchasing from a developer, the process of obtaining your own title deed may still take between one and two years. Depending on your circumstances it may be a matter of weeks.

Getting the Money to Cyprus

The first thing to do is to open a bank account in Cyprus; whether you are going to be living here permanently or, if you are buying a holiday home, at least from time to time, it makes sense to open an account with one of the high street banks which has a branch reasonably near you. Look for one that has a cashpoint machine to enable you to access funds whenever you need to. The contact details of the main high street banks are included in the resources section at the end of this book (*see* p.179). My own experience is probably fairly typical: when I decided to move to Cyprus I found the address of the local Limassol head office of three of the main high street banks and visited each in turn. At one I was kept waiting for 20 minutes and walked out. At the next the manager gave me the impression that he really didn't care whether I banked with him or not. At the third I was immediately offered a refreshment and, as the foreign exchange manager didn't speak fluent English, he called in his assistant who did. I have dealt with this bank ever since. Having opened a bank account, you need to send over the money you need to purchase your property. The options are by electronic transfer, as a banker's draft or in cash.

Electronic Transfer

This is by far the quickest and almost certainly the cheapest method of transferring money. It is also secure. You simply instruct your UK bank to despatch the required funds to the SWIFT code of your new Cypriot bank (your Cyprus bank will tell you what this is) for credit to your new account. Your UK bank will charge you £10–20 and the money will usually be in your account in three working days, although the author has known it to be quicker. If you choose to pay the vendor direct (or via your lawyer), remember that you need to pay the bank charges at both ends.

The Bank of Cyprus recently introduced a policy of charging 'commission' on sterling account-to-sterling account transfers, which some of the other high street banks do not charge. Bank of Cyprus rates for incoming same currency transfers is 0.1 per cent subject to a minimum of CY£5 and a maximum of CY£15. The other high street banks will probably follow suit but it is a question you might raise when initially deciding with which bank you wish to do your business. You should also negotiate the best rate of exchange for transferring sterling pounds to Cyprus pounds. You could compare the rate the banks you are choosing from will give on the same day for a given sum of money (such as the value of your new property) to find out if there is any financial benefit in dealing with one bank rather than another. As a guide the Bank of Cyprus' current (November 2004) exchange commission is 0.4 per cent for sums in excess of £20,000. It may also be possible to ask your UK bank to purchase and transmit Cyprus pounds. Check their rates and charges against those of the Cyprus bank.

Banker's Draft

A banker's draft is a certified cheque drawn on your bank (rather than on you) which you send or, preferably, take to your new bank in Cyprus. Even if the banker's draft has been issued by a major UK clearing bank, it is not considered to be cash but is sent for collection, which takes between two and three weeks. It is also more expensive in terms of commissions.

Cash

Don't even think about taking a suitcase full of hard currency. Apart from the fact that you will have to declare it, the receiving bank, even if they deign to accept it, will be obliged to notify MOKA, the Cyprus department responsible for the prevention of 'money laundering' and you will automatically be suspected of drugs-running or arms-dealing. This applies to any amount in excess of CY£10,000 – less if the bank is suspicious. Finally, the exchange rate on cash is always less competitive than cheques or, best of all, electronic transfer.

Exchange Control

All exchange controls for citizens of the EU were removed on 1 May 2004.

The Cost of Buying a Property in Cyprus

Apart from the agreed purchase price, there are several additional costs when you buy a property, as described below.

Lawyers' Fees

Lawyers' fees vary and depend on the amount of time expended by them. The fees are not fixed by statute. A complicated transaction involving multiple ownership in a new development is going to cause the lawyer to spend more time than a simple purchase in a single name on a resale property where title deeds are readily available.

The price a reputable law firm will ask of the purchaser will be in the order of CY£600 (plus an extra CY£250 if approval of the Council of Ministers is required) to CY£2,000. These ballpark figures include the cost of your lawyer acting as your attorney, under the authority of a power of attorney that they will draw up for you to sign, and thereafter handling all aspects of the purchase.

VAT on Property Purchases

VAT is chargeable on new property if the developer of the property applied for a building permit after 1 May 2004. Your lawyer will attempt to ensure that the developer pays the VAT. There is no VAT on resale property.

Land Registration Transfer Fees

This is a significant charge and will cost between 3 and 8 per cent depending on the value of the property. On acquisition of property you will be charged in tranches as follows:

Value up to CY£50,000	3%	Fee payable at CY£50,000	CY£1,500
CY£50,001–100,000	5%	Fee payable at CY£100,000	CY£4,000
Over CY£101,000	8%	Fee payable at CY£150,000	CY£8,000

These bandings are per person. If, for instance, you jointly purchase a property on a 50:50 basis for, say, CY£100,000, you will both be liable to pay CY£1,500 – an overall saving of CY£1,000.

Stamp Duty

Stamp duty is payable by the purchaser on signature of contract at the rate of CY£1.50 per CY£1,000 up to CY£100,000 and CY£2 per thousand thereafter:

Value of property (CY£)	Stamp duty payable (CY£)
50,000	75
100,000	150
150,000	250
200,000	350

Mortgage Costs

Mortgage costs are discussed in 'Raising Finance to Buy a Property in Cyprus', *see* p.79. Typically they will amount to some 5 per cent of the amount borrowed.

Surveyor's Fees

A typical valuation will cost about CY£100 plus VAT.

Miscellaneous Charges

See 'Home Utilities and Services', pp.133–6, for information about the cost of connecting to the utilities.

Property Insurance

Most property owners will take out a comprehensive household policy covering both the building and its contents. Premiums are pretty much the same across the island, if anything a little higher in rural districts – the converse of most other countries. This is principally because the risk of storm damage and damage caused by power outages is higher in the countryside and theft and crime in general in Cyprus is very low. The typical annual rates quoted by **Atlantic Insurance** (one of many insurance companies but particularly geared up to serve the British community) are CY£1.50–1.75 per CY£1,000 insured for property only and CY£2–2.25 per CY£1,000 insured for contents. They offer a combination package and no surcharges are demanded if you leave your property unattended for long periods or, even, if you rent it out. Property insurance is also available from **Intasure**, t 0845 111 0680, **www.intasure.com**.

Key Points

New Property Under Construction

When having your own property built for you or when buying a new property from a developer ensure that:

- **you are perfectly well aware of precisely what you are buying. What will the property look like when it is finished? Are the rooms large enough for your furniture? What facilities will be yours exclusively and which will you share with your neighbours? Are there enough power points in each room (particularly the kitchen)? Are there TV and telephone points where you want them to be? What fixtures and appliances are included in the purchase price?**

- **you have fully considered who should own the property to take full advantage of tax benefits and minimise liabilities to inheritance tax.**

- **your lawyer and you have properly reviewed the contract to ensure that it includes all necessary clauses to protect your best interests.**

- **you have taken the necessary steps to release the capital you require in the currency you require it, and/or that you have secured a mortgage in the** currency you require it, and you are aware when stage payments will be due.

• on delivery, you carefully note all minor defects and draw up a snagging list of problems to be fixed by the developer.

Resale Property

When purchasing an existing property, make sure that:

• you understand exactly what you are buying. What fixtures and fittings are not included in the purchase? What, if any, furniture is included in the purchase? What is the value of these extras? Are they recorded in the contract?

• you have carefully considered whether to have the property surveyed.

• you have fully considered who should own the property to take full advantage of tax benefits and minimise liabilities to inheritance tax.

• your lawyer and you have properly reviewed the contract to ensure that it includes all necessary clauses to protect your best interests.

• you have taken the necessary steps to release the capital you require in the currency you require it and/or you have secured a mortgage in the currency you require it and you are aware when stage payments will be due.

• on delivery of the property, everything included in the sale agreement is in the property.

Older Property

When purchasing a property which was built 50 or so years ago you should further consider:

• that if your first inclination is not to bother with a survey, whether you should think again – a hundred pounds or so can buy you peace of mind – and perhaps save you a lot more!

• whether the property requires any restoration work. If so, have you received estimates of the cost of this work? Is the property a listed building? If so, do you have the necessary information to submit a grant application?

• if you plan to modify the building, whether there are any problems with planning permission – you must discuss this with the planning department to find out.

Apartments and Properties Sharing Facilities

Points to consider in apartments and properties that share facilities are:

• what the communal charges, 'common expenses', are that you will be obliged to pay. How often are they payable? Find out whether there are any major developments in the pipeline which may increase these charges.

• what your neighbours would be like. Try to sound them out – does everyone coexist peacefully? Is the management committee competent? Does everything run smoothly? Have there been any crime problems in the neighbourhood?

• check that you will be eligible to attend community meetings once you are an owner.

• whether there is adequate parking.

Other Matters Arising

Don't forget to think about whether:

• your property and its contents are insured. Maintain a full and complete record of the contents and photograph items of particular value.

• to set up bank accounts in the currencies you wish with a bank reasonably near to you.

• to pay service charges – phone, electricity and so on – by standing order.

• you need to alter your will to cover your assets in Cyprus; make sure that it is drawn up in such a way as to be admissible for probate in Cyprus.

• you need to appoint an accountant; if your affairs are simple the tax office will help you; if your affairs are complicated you will need a local accountant.

Other Publications about Cyprus
by James Franklin

The Cyprus Croc
Annual free listings magazine

Moving to & Living in Cyprus
A definitive guide to the Republic of Cyprus

A Directory of Services
Annual Directory of Goods & Services

The Bacchus Association of Cyprus Wineries Guide

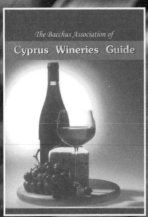

Further information on the above publications may be obtained at www.crocguides
or by post to P.O. Box 54359, 3723 Limassol, Cyprus

Tel: +357 99524445, Fax: +357 25585321, E-Mail: editor@crocguides.com

Financial
Implications

James Franklin

06

Acknowledgements

The sections 'Major Changes in Taxation in 2003–2004', and 'The Social Cohesion Fund Law No. N124(1) of 2002' are adapted from a small part of my *Moving to and Living in Cyprus*, in turn abridged from the article 'Tax News' by KPMG Tax Services, August 2002. KPMG kindly gave me permission to edit their article and include it in my publications. The sections 'Making a Will' and 'Inheritance' are taken from another small part of my *Moving to and Living in Cyprus*, which in turn were abridged from an article written by Stuart McBride, then senior partner of the Limassol law firm Chrysses Demetriades. Mr McBride kindly gave me permission to edit his article and include it in his publications. The accuracy of other sections in this chapter has been checked by the Cypriot accountancy and audit company Photos Arestis & Co, Limassol, and by an independent financial adviser who has a long-standing working experience with British expats worldwide, Chris Clegg of Sumner Holdings Ltd, Limassol.

Taxation

As mentioned before, the term 'Cyprus' refers specifically to the southern part of the Republic of Cyprus – the part of the island not under occupation.

There has been huge British influence over Cyprus in the past and – as with the legal system – the taxation system of the Republic of Cyprus is not wholly dissimilar to that in the UK. That said, there are a great deal of differences! Anyone who has trained in the UK as an accountant will tell you that the British taxation system is extremely complicated, and that new laws and regulations governing the taxation system are constantly ongoing. So it is in Cyprus, particularly in the year before accession to the European Union and in the early months after accession. Like nearly all government departments, the Ministry of Finance has certain obligations to accord with the laws and guidelines with which member states must comply. Like many government departments, a lot of the regulations have still to be worked out in depth before they can be submitted to the House of Representatives, Cyprus' equivalent of the British House of Commons, for incorporation into law.

Many aspects of the taxation regime in Cyprus are outside the scope of this book. They have little relevance to someone buying a house as a holiday home or even for a pensioner retiring there. Nevertheless it is helpful to have a basic grounding in the taxation system of Cyprus, especially in comparison with that of the UK, as it can certainly be advantageous to pay taxes in Cyprus rather than in the UK. We have included a limited amount of information about corporate taxation because Cyprus is a particularly important gateway to the Middle East, and Europeans in general may be considering establishing offices and introducing personnel to staff them, Cyprus being an ideal base to exploit the near Middle East markets such as Egypt, Jordan and Israel.

Individual circumstances will play an important part in making the decision of where to pay tax and if your affairs are even slightly complicated it is very sound advice to seek the guidance of a financial consultant who has ongoing working experience of British and Cypriot taxation regimes. International tax experts who specialise in Cyprus but whose offices are in the UK are a bit thin on the ground, but most of the larger accountancy companies – for instance, Deloitte & Touche, Ernst and Young, PricewaterhouseCoopers – have tax planning departments, and have offices in Cyprus and in the UK. Several local Cypriot tax consultants as well as the partners of the larger local accountancy companies received their training with the large international accountancy companies, and finding a proficient tax consultant in Cyprus is not difficult – and is almost certainly a lot cheaper than employing the services of one of the multinationals! Proficiency, though, is the key and you should ask to see the credentials and qualifications of the partners of any firm you seek to employ. It is also worth asking for the names of two or three expat British residents whom the selected company look after, and to check that these individuals are satisfied with the firm's performance. Just as in your search for a lawyer, it is important to be frank at the outset – to lay out your financial affairs as they affect you in both countries and to be satisfied that you and your financial adviser are in agreement.

Residence for Tax Purposes

As with most countries in Europe, residence is the key factor governing whether or not you are liable to pay taxes in the Republic of Cyprus. Residence for the purpose of taxation in Cyprus – or in any other country for that matter – is a matter of fact: clear tests determine whether you are or are not liable to be assessed to pay taxes in a particular country.

Remember, too, that it is possible to be resident for tax purposes in more than one country at the same time.

The Tests that Determine Residence

United Kingdom

There are two legal categories to be considered, domicile and residence, and these terms are often used interchangeably. However domicile and residence are not synonymous; they have distinctly different legal meanings.

Domicile

Your domicile is pretty much set and for most people it is fairly obvious where your domicile is. Essentially, your domicile is where you come from, it is your base, it is the place you consider to be your natural home and it is the place to which you intend to return when you are away. That does not mean that you were necessarily born there. By way of example, a child born to a British couple who deliberately travelled to the USA for the wife to give birth will have both British and American nationality. But because the parents are British the child will acquire British domicile at birth. So, domicile is more important than residence, for, while residence generally means the place where one lives at any given time, the term 'domicile' generally imparts both physical residence and an intention to remain or return. One may easily be a resident of a particular place without being domiciled there.

Everybody, even a vagrant, has a single domicile at all times; it is not possible to have more than one domicile at any given time and that place of domicile will continue until a new domicile is established. A new domicile is acquired by a person of proper legal capacity establishing a home in a new area with the intent to remain there permanently. Intent is the key issue: a new domicile is not established by merely moving to a new location: it is vital to show the intent to live in the new location permanently.

Generally a wife takes the domicile of her husband, but should she separate or divorce she may choose to acquire a new domicile. A legitimate child acquires the domicile of the father at birth (the domicile of origin) and will keep the father's domicile during minority. An illegitimate child acquires the domicile of the mother. Minors can only change their domicile of origin by being adopted.

So, it is possible to change one's domicile – but it is not easy. One of many tests of British domicile is whether you have purchased a grave plot in a foreign country. If so, and you are resident in that foreign country, you are on your way to changing your domicile to that country, which may have tax advantages. Interestingly, there is no formal court procedure where you could, for instance, swear an affidavit that it was your intention to remain permanently in a new country. So far as Cyprus is concerned, before the country joined the EU retired UK citizens used to be entitled to a 'duty free' car. In obtaining a duty free car, one of the pieces of paperwork involved was a statement that the applicant intended to remain in the Republic. This, together with proof that he or she had subsequently done so (apart from short holidays or trips overseas), was taken as evidence for a change of domicile.

Residence

In English law there are two types of residence, residence and ordinary residence. For tax purposes, **residence** in the UK is established by a person who spends at least six months (183 days) in the country in any given tax year, or who visits for a minimum of three months a year in four consecutive years. **Ordinary residence** is the place where a person normally lives or to where he or she makes regular visits, defined as visits of three months or more a year over four consecutive years.

Someone who is ordinarily resident in the UK does not lose that status just by moving overseas. To be treated as non-resident in the UK you have to convince the Inland Revenue that it is your intention to live abroad for at least three years. The Revenue may allow non-resident status provisionally, to be confirmed by subsequent fact.

Cyprus

Whether or not you are deemed to be liable to tax in Cyprus depends on the following criteria.

For Individuals

If you spend more than 183 days in Cyprus during any financial year (which is the same as the calendar year) then you are considered to be resident and are liable to tax. These 183 days need not be consecutive; the 183-day rule is based on the aggregate of days spent between 1 January and 31 December in any particular year.

For Corporate Bodies

A company is said to be resident for tax purposes when its management and control is exercised in the Republic of Cyprus. The residency test for companies include:

- **where the majority of the directors live**
- **where board meetings are held**
- **where the general policies of the business are formulated.**

Liability to Taxes in More Than One Country

As we mention above, it is quite possible to be liable to pay taxes in more than one country. Suppose, for instance – and many expat British residents do exactly this – that you enjoy the autumn, winter and spring in Cyprus but stay with family in England for the summer and for Christmas. Say that in total you spend 100 days in the UK and 265 days in Cyprus. This automatically qualifies you as liable to Cyprus tax and, under the 90-day rule, you might be adjudged to be resident or ordinarily resident for UK tax purposes too. Since it is clearly unreasonable to pay tax to two different countries for one set of income, Cyprus and England have signed a Double Taxation Treaty, of which more later (*see* p.116).

How to Decide Where To Pay Tax

As we mentioned earlier, if your tax affairs are even slightly complicated you are strongly advised to seek the advice of a professional accountant, specialist lawyer or financial adviser. Between you, you need to consider whether you should change the amount of time you stay in a particular country in order to fall into or out of that country's tax residence, and/or whether you should change your domicile. If a change is desirable, it is important to consider when that change should be made. You will need to keep records of your movements to prove where you were and for how long in the tax year of the countries that may have a claim on your income. These decisions may be critical to the tune of thousands, or even tens of thousands, of pounds.

Taxes Payable in the UK

If you are buying a holiday home in Cyprus, and live for most of the year in the UK, then (presuming that you are not working in Cyprus) you are not liable to income tax in Cyprus other than on rental income; and your British tax situation is unchanged except that you will be liable to pay UK income tax on any rental income earned on your Cypriot property. Since non-residents of Cyprus are liable to pay Cypriot tax on the letting of any property situated in Cyprus, the Inland Revenue will give you credit for any tax for property lettings already paid in Cyprus. Interestingly, there is a law that makes it illegal for a non-Cypriot to let property other than long-term to a Cypriot, and to the best of our knowledge that law has not been rescinded since Cyprus joined the EU! Don't be concerned by this. If the law has not been changed, it will have to be; in any case lots of Brits let out their holiday homes and the 'policy' of foreigners letting property is to ensure that due taxes are paid and that the tourism industry is not affected.

If you live most of the time in Cyprus, but remain either domiciled or ordinarily resident in the UK, in general you will remain liable to pay British tax on:

- **income arising from the rent of land or property situated in the UK; this applies to everyone regardless of nationality, domicile or residence status.**

- **earned income from employment carried out in the UK (UK income tax schedule E).**

- **income derived from a trade or profession in the UK (schedules D1 and D2).**

- **income derived from interest and annuities payable in the UK (usually deducted at source), provided that you are ordinarily resident in the UK (schedule D3).**

- **income derived from businesses and investments not situated in the UK, provided that you are both domiciled and either resident or ordinarily resident in the UK.**

- **income derived from government pensions.**

- **capital gains arising worldwide, provided that you are both domiciled and ordinarily resident in the UK.**

- **inheritance tax derived from your worldwide assets, provided that you are domiciled in the UK.**

Taxes Payable in Cyprus by Residents

Fundamental and dramatic changes in the taxation system in Cyprus were introduced in 2003 and 2004 to comply with the accession of Cyprus to the EU, which took place on 1 May 2004 – *see* 'Major Changes in Taxation in 2003–2004', pp.106ff. The in-depth review completely overhauled the Republic's taxation laws and Cyprus is unlikely to see such major changes in taxation legislation in the foreseeable future. We have therefore examined this legislation in depth.

Overview

Further information may be obtained from the **Ministry of Finance**, Department of Inland Revenue, Nicosia, **www.mof.gov.cy**.

Income Tax

Foreign residents in Cyprus are liable to pay tax – at comparatively advantageous rates in comparison with the UK – on:

- **income earned in Cyprus.**

- **unearned income such as bank interest and interest earned in Cyprus, subject since 1 January 2003 to a 10 per cent 'Defence Fund contribution', which is deducted at source; if income and pension income exceed CY£7,000 in total, the Defence Fund contribution is reduced to 3 per cent.**

- **foreign income remitted to Cyprus.**

See also 'Income Taxes for Individuals', p.113.

Capital Gains Tax

Capital gains tax is levied only on disposal of immovable property at 20 per cent of the gain on property in excess of a lifetime exemption of CY£50,000 if the property is held (and owner-occupied) for five years or CY£10,000 if it is held for less than five years. In calculating the gain, allowance is made for inflation and structural improvements. The CY£50,000 exemption may not be carried forward in part – if an individual purchases a property and after five years has elapsed sells it and makes a CY£30,000 profit (after due allowance is made for inflation and structural improvements), that person may not carry forward the unused CY£20,000 of the CY£50,000 exemption. Nor, strictly, is the CY£50,000 exemption a lifetime exemption. Any person who resides in a second home for 10 years is entitled to a second CY£50,000 exemption, and so on, every 10 years. One caveat: do not move house too often. If the taxation authorities consider that you are 'dealing' in property, not only will you lose the exemption, you will subject yourself to being considered liable to income tax on the profits.

Estate Duty

Estate duty was abolished in 2000. No one, regardless of domicile or residence, is subject to any form of inheritance tax in Cyprus. This may be an important factor for the wealthy if they are considering Cyprus as a permanent home. If that applies to you then take legal and financial advice about changing your domicile to enable your estate to be removed from the clutches of the UK Inland Revenue.

Rates

Each governate (local authority) fixes its own rates, which are levied at a maximum of 25 per cent of the rental value of the property. Rental value is assessed at 5 per cent of the assessed capital value of the property. In practice the liability to rates is likely to be CY£50–150 a year. This tax is for refuse collection, sewerage, street lighting etc. Do not confuse this 'local' rates tax with the annually charged immovable property tax (*see* p.116).

Major Changes in Taxation in 2003–2004

The new Income Tax Law, No. N118 (I) of 2002, came into effect on 1 January 2003. This law consolidates and reforms existing tax legislation and aims to:

- **harmonise the tax laws with EU directives.**
- **simplify and modernise the taxation system.**
- **improve the comparative advantage of Cyprus in the field of international taxation.**

The House of Representatives also amended other laws to bring them in line with the new legislation. The key changes in the taxation system are:

- **to make residence rather than source the criterion of taxation.**
- **to unify the taxation system and rate of corporate tax for international and local business enterprises.**
- **to abolish personal allowances and certain deductions and their replacement by grants.**

Main Definitions Introduced

'Permanent establishment' has the same meaning as defined in the OECD Model Tax Convention on Income and on Capital with the exemption of 'a building site or construction or installation project', which constitutes a permanent establishment only if it lasts more than three months.

'Resident in the Republic', when applied to an individual, means an individual who stays in the Republic for a period or periods exceeding in aggregate 183 days in the year of assessment; when applied to a company it means a company whose management and control is exercised in the Republic. 'Non-resident' or 'Resident outside the Republic' will be construed accordingly.

Income Liable to Tax

Resident individuals or companies are liable to tax on the income accrued or arising from sources within and outside Cyprus. **Non-resident individuals or companies** are liable to tax on the income accrued or arising from sources in Cyprus only for:

- **income from any trade, business, profession or vocation carried on or exercised as far as is attributable to a permanent establishment in Cyprus.**

• profits or other benefits from any office or employment.

• pension received from a past employment exercised in Cyprus, with the exception of any pension paid out of funds created by the government or a local authority.

• rents from property situated in Cyprus.

There is new provision for resident and non-resident persons whereby good-will proceeds, reduced by any amount expended for the purchase of such goodwill, is now subject to income tax. Goodwill proceeds are the sum paid for the fact that the business has a known trade. For instance, were you to buy a restaurant you would pay an amount of 'key money' because the business already trades. Were you to establish a new restaurant you would not pay for goodwill but you would certainly charge goodwill were you to sell the business subsequently.

Exemptions from Tax (Main New Provisions)

Companies and individuals: profits from the activities of a permanent establishment situated outside Cyprus are exempt unless:

• **the permanent establishment directly or indirectly engages in more than 50 per cent of its activities in producing investment income.**

• **the foreign tax burden is *substantially lower* (undefined in the Law) than that in Cyprus.**

Dividends are exempt from tax; however, new provisions have been introduced under the Special Contribution for the Defence of the Republic Law, 2002 ('Special Contribution').

Gains from Trading in Stocks and Shares

Companies only: 50 per cent of income from interest derived by a company is exempt from corporate tax, but the whole interest received or credited is subject to the new provisions of the Special Contribution. Interest derived from ordinary trading activities (undefined in the Law) is only subject to the income tax law provisions, without any exceptions.

Individuals only:

• **The whole income from interest derived by an individual is exempt from tax but the whole interest received or credited is subject to the new provisions of the Special Contribution Law. Interest derived from ordinary trading activities will only be subject to the income tax law provisions, without any exceptions.**

• **Salaries received from a permanent establishment outside Cyprus for an aggregate period of more than 90 days in the year of assessment are exempt.**

• **20 per cent of the emoluments from any employment in Cyprus by an individual who was not a resident of Cyprus before taking up employment** in Cyprus, or CY£5,000, whichever is the lowest, are exempt. This exemption applies for a period of three years commencing from the 1 January of the year following the year of commencement of such employment.

Exemptions Provided in Previous Legislation that Have Been Deleted

Certain exemptions that were provided in previous legislation have now been deleted:

- lump sum or gratuity paid to any individual on retirement.
- up to CY£600 interest received from listed debentures and bank deposits.
- up to CY£1,000 dividends from shares quoted on the Cyprus Stock Exchange.
- travel expenses of foreign employees.
- 60 per cent of professional income earned overseas and remitted to Cyprus.
- 90 per cent of income or dividends from overseas businesses remitted to Cyprus.
- 100 per cent of income from rendering services overseas which is remitted to Cyprus.
- 30 per cent of the amount spent in acquiring shares listed on the Cyprus Stock Exchange.
- 30 per cent of the income of an individual derived from agriculture or animal husbandry.
- interest derived from capital imported to Cyprus.
- 10 years' 'tax holiday' for certain work related to the tourism industry.

Deductions Allowed (Main New Provisions)

Companies and individuals:

- The restriction concerning the allowable amount for donations and contributions to approved charity funds has been removed. However, if a loss is created in the year in which the donation or contribution is made, any part of such loss up to the amount of such donation or contribution allowed will not be carried forward and set off against the income of subsequent years.
- Any interest on business assets acquired and used in the business can be deducted.

Individuals only:

- 20 per cent of income derived by an individual from renting property will continue to be deducted on the gross rents, before the deduction of wear and tear allowances and interest expended. Note that gross rents received, reduced by 25 per cent, will be subject to the Special Contribution at the rate of 3 per cent.

Deductions Not Allowed (Main New Provisions)

The following deductions are not allowed:

- business entertainment expenses; they are now restricted so that they do not exceed, in any year of assessment, 0.5 per cent of the gross income of the business, subject to a maximum limit of CY£5,000.

- expenses for private motor vehicles.

- professional tax paid or payable.

- interest proportionate to the cost of a private motor vehicle irrespective of whether it is used in the business or not, and the cost of any other asset which is not used in the business; this provision will not apply after the expiring of a period of seven years from the date of purchase of the asset.

- tax paid under the Immovable Property (Towns) Tax Law 1962.

Deductions Previously Allowed that Have Been Deleted

Deductions may no longer be made on:

- rent paid by an individual for a house or flat up to CY£300.

- transport fares of individuals who reside in a village or small town.

- investment allowances on new business assets acquired.

- certain allowances in respect of mining operations.

Allowance for Losses

The general provisions for allowance for losses are as follows:

- The five-year limit for carrying forward losses has been abolished and losses from the year 1997 and onwards can be carried forward to subsequent years without restriction until such losses are extinguished.

- Losses incurred from any business carried on outside Cyprus will be allowed as a deduction from a person's profits accrued in Cyprus.

- The accrued losses of a business carried on by an individual or a partnership which has been converted to a company may be transferred to the company and allowed as a deduction from the company's profits.

- The restriction of setting off losses from agricultural, animal husbandry, bird-breeding or fishing business against income from other business or employment income has been removed.

Taxation of Pensions

The taxation of pensions of any individual for services rendered outside Cyprus continues as under the previous Law; that is to say that any sum exceeding CY£2,000 will, in any year of assessment, be liable to tax at the rate of 5 per cent unless the individual elects to be taxed under the normal rules of the Law.

Taxation of Certain Incomes under Special Circumstances

- Taxation of income from ship management will continue at the rate of 4.25 per cent.

- Taxation of gross amount of royalties, premiums, compensations and so on earned from sources within Cyprus by a person not resident of Cyprus will continue as it was under the previous Law – it will be liable to withholding tax at the rate of 10 per cent, but in the event that the royalty right is granted for use outside Cyprus, such income will not be liable to withholding tax.

- Taxation of the gross amount of film rentals earned by a non-resident will remain at 5 per cent.

- Taxation of the gross income derived by an individual not resident in Cyprus from any profession or vocation and the gross income of public entertainers and athletes will continue to be liable to withholding tax, but at the reduced rate of 10 per cent.

Provisions that Have Been Deleted

The following provisions have been deleted:

- the distinction between Cypriot and foreign employees.
- the reduced rate of taxation for exports.
- the taxation of foreign investment income over CY£2,000 at the rate of 5 per cent.

Corporate Tax

The main provisions for corporate tax are that:

- Companies, other than semi-governmental bodies, are liable to corporate tax at 10 per cent of the chargeable income.

- Semi-governmental bodies are liable to corporate tax at 25 per cent of the chargeable income.

- If the chargeable income of a company or a semi-governmental body for the years of assessment 2003 and 2004 exceeds one million pounds, that company or a semi-governmental body will be liable to additional tax at the rate of 5 per cent.

Provisions that Have Been Deleted

These provisions have been deleted:

- the 10 per cent additional tax payable on profits before the deduction of losses brought forward and investment allowances and after the deduction of income subject to corporation tax.

- the reduced corporate tax for companies listing their shares on the Cyprus Stock Exchange for the first time.

Withholding Tax on Dividends

Dividends are exempt from withholding income tax, but there are special provisions under the Special Contribution for the Defence of the Republic Law No. N117(I) of 2002.

International Business Companies: New Provisions as from 1 January 2003

The main provisions as a result of the unified taxation policy are as follows:

• International business companies will no longer be taxable by virtue of their registration in Cyprus but instead will be considered tax residents if they will be managed and controlled in Cyprus.

• International business companies will be taxable as any other local companies at the corporate tax rates prevailing (*see* above) and they will be entitled to the new beneficial tax provisions.

• International business companies will, subject to obtaining the relevant permits, also be allowed to derive income from within Cyprus.

• International business companies will be subject to the provisions of the Social Cohesion Fund Law and will be required to contribute at the rate of 2 per cent on the gross emoluments of its tax resident employees working in Cyprus.

• 50 per cent of income from interest will be exempt from corporate tax but the whole amount of interest received or credited will be subject to the Special Contribution at the rate of 10 per cent. However, interest from ordinary trading activities such as banking and financing activities will be considered as trading income and taxed only at the normal corporate rates.

Other Beneficial Provisions

There are other beneficial provisions:

• Dividend income will be exempt from corporation tax.

• Dividend income will also be exempt from the Special Contribution provided the direct holding is at least 1 per cent of the share capital of the overseas company. This exemption will not apply if the company paying the dividend engages in more than 50 per cent of its activities in producing investment income and the foreign tax burden on the income of the company paying the dividends is substantially lower than that in Cyprus.

• International business companies will be exempt from deemed dividend distribution provisions.

• Profits from activities of a permanent establishment situated outside Cyprus are completely exempt. This exemption will not apply if the permanent establishment directly or indirectly engages in more than 50 per cent of its activities in producing investment income and the foreign tax burden on the income of the permanent establishment is substantially lower than that in Cyprus.

• International business companies holding royalty rights will continue to be exempt from any withholding tax on royalties payable if the right is granted for use outside Cyprus.

• Profits from buying and selling shares will be exempt from tax.

Transitional provisions for International Business Companies trading at 31 December 2001

International Business Companies established in Cyprus before 31 December 2001 and during the year of assessment ending 31 December 2001, which earned income from sources exclusively outside Cyprus, will have the option to elect to be taxed as before for the years of assessment 2003, 2004 and 2005 at the rate of 4.25 per cent provided that an irrevocable election is made and that they will continue to derive income from sources exclusively outside Cyprus.

International Business Companies that have elected to be taxed at the rate of 4.25 per cent for the years 2003, 2004 and 2005 will be exempted from the payment of the Special Contribution.

Allowances and Deductions for Individuals

Tax relief is available on up to one-sixth of taxable income paid for premiums to:

• widows and orphans pension funds or schemes established under any law in Cyprus or comparable law outside Cyprus.

• pensions, provident or other society or fund or scheme established in Cyprus or abroad.

• an insurance company under an annuity contract.

• an insurance company for pension schemes or medical schemes.

• the General Health Scheme Law of Cyprus or under comparable law in force abroad.

• life assurance policies made on his or her life but not on the life of the spouse by the other spouse. The premiums payable on life assurance policies made on the life of the spouse by the other spouse under the provisions of the old income tax law will continue to be allowed.

The deductions for interest of up to CY£500 paid in respect of a loan obtained for the acquisition of a dwelling house remains for the year 2003 only.

Provisions that Have Been Deleted

These provisions have been deleted:

• the provision for reduced rates of income tax (50 per cent) allowed to foreign employees of international business companies.

• old age allowance.

- spouse allowance.
- displaced persons allowance.
- child allowance (replaced by government grants).

Income Taxes for Individuals

Before 2003 the maximum rate of income tax for individuals was 40 per cent. Since 2003, the maximum rate has been reduced to 30 per cent but income bands are increased, as shown below.

For the year of assessment 2003:

Chargeable income	Tax rate
Up to CY£9,000	nil
CY£9,001–12,000	20%
CY£12,001–15,000	25%
CY£15,001 and over	30%

For the year of assessment 2004:

Chargeable income	Tax rate
Up to CY£10,000	nil
CY£10,001–15,000	20%
CY£15,001–20,000	25%
CY£20,001 and over	30%

Defence Tax on Dividends

Every resident who receives a dividend from a company is liable to Special Contribution at the rate of 15 per cent, except on:

- dividends paid from one Cyprus resident company to another.

- dividends received from an overseas company by a resident company of Cyprus or a company which is not a resident of Cyprus but has a permanent establishment in Cyprus, holding directly at least 1 per cent of the share capital of the overseas company. This exemption does not apply if the company paying the dividend engages in more than 50 per cent of its activities that produce investment income and the foreign tax burden on the income of the company paying the dividends is substantially lower than Cypriot tax.

Defence Tax on Deemed Distributions

Seventy per cent of the distributable accounting profits after tax accruing in the year of assessment will be deemed to be distributable as dividends to its shareholders as at the end of a period of two years from the end of the year of assessment to which the profits relate, and the shareholders concerned will be assessed for Special Contribution at the rate of 15 per cent on such dividends. The amount of the deemed dividend will be reduced by any actual dividends distributed during the period of two years from the end of the year of assessment to which the profits relate. In the case of liquidation of a company, the total profits of the last five years prior to liquidation, which have not been distributed or which have not been deemed distributable dividends, will be deemed to be distributable on its liquidation and be subject to Special Contribution at the rate of 15 per cent.

In the event of reduction of the capital of a company and payment to the shareholders of any amounts up to the amount of undistributed chargeable income of any year that arises before the deductions for losses brought forward from previous years, but after deducting those amounts that have been deemed distributable dividends, such amounts will be deemed distributable dividends subject to Special Contribution at the rate of 15 per cent.

Every company that falls within the provisions of deemed distribution of dividends will submit to the director of the Department of Inland Revenue the relevant return of deemed distributions and pay the Special Contribution in accordance with such returns.

The provisions of deemed dividend do not apply to the proportion of profit attributable to shareholders who are non-residents of Cyprus. An individual receiving a dividend does not further suffer income tax on the dividend income.

Defence Tax on Other Incomes

The following provisions apply:

• Every individual or company resident in the Republic who receives or is credited with interest, except interest from saving bonds, development bonds and from deposits with the Housing Finance Organisation received or credited to individuals, is liable to the Special Contribution at the rate of 10 per cent. Interest includes a deemed 9 per cent interest on non-interest-bearing loans provided to directors/shareholders of a company controlled by less than five persons.

• In the case of an individual whose income does not exceed CY£7000 per annum, the Special Contribution withheld exceeding the rate of 3 per cent will be refunded.

• Every individual who receives or is credited with interest from saving bonds, development bonds and from deposits with the Housing Finance Organisation as well as interest received by a provident fund is to continue to pay the Special Contribution at the rate of 3 per cent.

• Every individual or company who receives rents will be liable to the Special Contribution at the rate of 3 per cent on the gross rents reduced by 25 per cent.

• Every semi-governmental body will be liable to pay the Special Contribution at the rate of 3 per cent on its chargeable income except incomes from dividends, interest and rents before the deductions of losses as provided under section 13 of the income tax law.

• Credit relief will be allowed for foreign tax paid on income subject to the Special Contribution.

The following incomes are no longer subject to the Special Contribution:

- emoluments of employees.
- employers' contribution on the emoluments of their employees (replaced by the employer's contribution to the Social Cohesion Fund Law No. N124(1) of 2002).
- income of self-employed persons.
- emoluments of persons holding or exercising an office in Cyprus.
- pensions.
- income of a company carrying on business in Cyprus.
- dividends payable to other Cypriot companies or to residents outside Cyprus.

Exemptions

Gains accruing from disposal of shares listed on any recognised stock exchange are exempt from tax. *The provisions exempting aliens, Cypriots established abroad and international business entities from tax on gains accruing from disposal of property held outside Cyprus, and on gains accruing from disposal of shares listed on the Cyprus Stock Exchange, have been repealed.*

Gains accruing from disposal of immovable property held outside Cyprus and shares in companies, the property whereof consists of immovable property held outside Cyprus, are exempted from capital gains tax.

Transfer of Property in Case of Reorganisation

New provisions have been enacted so that under a reorganisation scheme, no capital gains tax is payable in case of transfer of property or shares in companies, the property whereof consists of immovable property, until such property is disposed by the new company.

The Social Cohesion Fund Law No. N124(1) of 2002

For the purposes of this law, 'emoluments' include any allowance, whether in money or otherwise, payable as a result of the exercise of any office or the rendering of any employment and any amount payable by way of thirteenth salary or otherwise in excess of the usual remuneration compensation for each specified period, but it does not include any other grant or retirement benefit or any sums payable by an approved provident fund.

Under the provision of this law all employers will contribute to the Social Cohesion Fund at the rate of 2 per cent on the emoluments of their employees, except on the emoluments of foreign employees employed in Cyprus by:

- foreign governments.
- international organisations.
- companies that are the owners of a Cyprus ship.
- companies that derive income from ship management.

• international business companies which have opted to be taxed for 2003, 2004 and 2005 at the rate of 4.25 per cent as provided under section 46 of the Income Tax Law 2002.

Immovable Property Taxes

	Applied until end 2002 (%)	Applicable from 2003 (%)
Up to CY£100,000	nil	nil
CY£100,001–250,000	2	2.5
CY£250,001–500,000	3	3.5
CY£500,001 and over	3.5	4

The immovable property tax is payable annually. It may be thought of as the equivalent of British 'rates'. When thought of in this light, it will be seen to be most competitive in comparison with the UK.

Under the Assessment and Collection of Taxes (Amendment) Law No. N122(1) of 2002, interest on arrears of tax payable – tax not paid within the prescribed time – is subject to 9 per cent interest charge. Previously interest on tax not paid within the prescribed time but paid within six months from the due date was subject to a 5 per cent interest charge.

VAT

As we go to print, the 2004/05 general rate of VAT is 15 per cent. With minor exceptions, VAT is charged on the same range of goods and services as in the UK. Since 1 May 2004, VAT is charged on buildings for which town planning permission and building permits have been applied for since 1 May 2004 (i.e. on new property). Your lawyer will endeavour to make the property developer responsible for the VAT.

The Double Taxation Treaty

The sole purpose of the Double Taxation Agreement between the Republic of Cyprus and the United Kingdom is to prevent the same income being taxed in both countries. Specific provisions cover:

• **income by way of dividends and (bank) interest received.**

• **income from property lettings – it is taxed in the country in which the property is located.**

• **pensions received from the UK; and there is different treatment of government-related pensions – government pensions are taxed in the UK, non-government pensions are subject to tax in Cyprus.**

• **capital gains tax.**

Cypriot residents deriving income from the UK and wishing to claim relief from the UK under the Double Taxation Agreement should complete form X/INDIVIDUAL for relief from UK income tax and form X/INDIVIDUAL/CREDIT for claim of the tax credit for dividends paid by UK companies. These forms will be certified by the local Cypriot income tax office and forwarded by them to the Inland Revenue in the UK.

Your lawyer, financial adviser or accountant will be able to give you further detailed advice depending on your specific circumstances.

Tax Rates and Allowances for 2005

At the time this chapter was written (November 2004), no announcement has been made by the Ministry of Finance about any changes in the tax rates and allowances set for 2004. Be aware, though, that it is not unknown in the Republic of Cyprus for laws to be passed retrospectively – theoretically the government could publish tax amendments at any time in 2005 to be applied from 1 January 2005.

When is Tax Payable?

Tax due from earned income is collected by the employer regularly throughout the year, in much the same way as the PAYE system in the UK. All other income is payable according to provisional assessment. Each year individuals submit a provisional assessment of their taxable income for that year. The tax for that year's assessment is paid in three instalments, on 1 August, 30 September and 31 December of the same year. Form 101 details the actual income earned and must be submitted by 30 April of the following year. The Cypriot tax authority then issues an income tax assessment and any balance due must be paid by 31 August in the same year.

Inheritance

Just as in the UK, British residents in the Republic of Cyprus may dispose of their assets as they please. So, too, may Cypriots. The inheritance and intestacy provisions in the Republic of Cyprus are broadly based on English law.

Making a Will

Given that dying intestate causes many problems to surviving relatives, most people will wish to give formal notice of their intentions about the disposal of their assets at the time of death by drawing up a will. Indeed, most British retirees taking up residence on the island will already have done so. So what do you need to do in Cyprus? Contrary to popular belief, there is no need to make a will in Cyprus, providing that a will exists elsewhere and that that will provides for the distribution of one's worldwide assets. The legal requirement for a will is slightly different in Cyprus from the UK in terms of the way it is signed, so if the will is not valid in Cyprus but is in the UK, application for probate must first be made in the UK, and then in Cyprus.

Probate

A will has no effect until it has been admitted to probate and probate has been granted by the appropriate court – either in the UK or in Cyprus or both. If one has assets both in the UK and Cyprus it is necessary for probate to be granted in both countries. The deceased's lawyers will apply for probate in one country and will apply to the courts of the second country to reseal the grant of probate that was made by the first country.

It doesn't matter to which country the first application is made except that the legal requirements for a will to be valid in Cyprus are different from the UK in one important aspect: in Cyprus each sheet (not necessarily a page) of paper that comprise a will must be initialled or signed by the testator and two witnesses and the last sheet must be signed by the testator and two witnesses. Thus if the will document is valid in the UK but does not comply with Cyprus requirements, application for probate must first be made in the UK and then application should be made to the probate register of the local district court in Cyprus to reseal the UK grant of probate.

If a will is made in Cyprus there is provision, but no requirement, that the will may be deposited in court by the testator accompanied by a declaration that the sealed envelope contains his or her last will. If the registrar does not personally know the testator, someone who is personally known by the registrar must swear an affidavit identifying the testator.

The Cyprus Bar Council has set the minimum fees for drafting a will. The minimum fee for listing the disposal of assets up to CY£10,000 is CY£68, and this sum increases in increments. For assets in excess of CY£100,000 the amount payable is CY£352 plus 0.07 per cent of the value of assets in excess of CY£50,000. If an advocate is appointed as administrator of an estate, remuneration is set at CY£375 plus 1.5 per cent of the value of the estate in excess of £10,000 plus 1.5 per cent of the amount payable to the heirs. In practice testators negotiate a fee with their lawyer, as do the heirs with the executor.

Investments

There is no particular reason why moving to Cyprus will require you to make radical changes to your long-term investment strategy, but moving here does open the door to some types of offshore assets that, because you were previously subject to UK taxes, you may not have previously considered. This implies that you intend to do something about your status with regard to domicile and/or residence.

There is a plethora of British financial advisers in Cyprus. Most are *bona fide*; some are not. It is a requirement of law in Cyprus that an independent financial adviser is licensed by the Central Bank of Cyprus. (Under EU regulations not yet enacted by the House of Representatives, the regulatory body will change from the Central Bank to the Capital Markets Committee (Cyprus) – effectively implementing an even stronger control over financial advisers.) Similarly to appointing a lawyer or accountant, when appointing a financial adviser, seek verifiable references and check that fellow expats have received satisfactory service. Just as with your accountant, it is important to brief your financial adviser with the full details of your existing portfolio and your intentions in the short, medium and long term. If you are considering using trusts in combination with a change of domicile and/or residence to minimise your tax liabilities and your estate's future inheritance tax liabilities, decide what you want to do and when to do it before, or as soon as, you take up residence in Cyprus.

Trusts

Trusts, both in the UK and overseas, are a most tax-efficient way of keeping your property and investments out of the clutches of the tax authorities. The legal effect of a trust is that you voluntarily divest yourself of capital; this capital is placed in the hands of one or more trustees, usually a professional company offshore – in a country which imposes particularly low rates of tax. Since you no longer control the assets that make up the trust, they are not considered to be your assets for tax purposes. The trustees hold the capital assets that constitute the trust for the benefit of whomsoever you choose – a charity, a relative, your children's education, even yourself. In setting up the trust you declare under what terms and conditions income is distributed and under what terms and conditions capital is devolved.

During your life you will only be liable to tax on whatever interest is paid to you by the trust, and on your death the assets making up the trust are not subject to inheritance tax, providing that seven years have elapsed since the trust was created. Should you die before seven years then part of the trust capital, on an apportionment based over seven years, will fall into your estate for the purpose of calculating inheritance tax. Note that in the Republic of Cyprus there is no inheritance tax, so the seven-year deemed devolvement of capital is irrelevant.

Setting up a trust correctly is essential if it is to work properly and save you and your estate money, and for this it is advisable to seek professional advice. A competent accountant, financial adviser or lawyer will be able to set up the trust in the most beneficial way for tax purposes, while drawing up the trust deed in such a way as to ensure your intention will be honoured by the trustees.

Recording Your Investments

Keep a record of your investments and update this list whenever you buy or sell any particular asset. The record of your investments should be a complete list of your assets, including assets under management, share certificates and so on under your own management, a note of the trusts that you have established (not that these form part of your worth) or of which you are a beneficiary, savings certificates, building society accounts and all your bank accounts (it is surprising how many bank accounts one may have established in different countries if you are a somewhat nomadic expat). It is also advisable to update the value of your portfolio every few months. If your investments are managed by a firm of professional financial advisers or investment managers they will automatically revalue your portfolio at least quarterly; the more professional financial advisers will do so weekly with a (password protected) online valuation so that you can keep an eye on the performance of your assets whenever you choose and wherever you may be. When choosing a suitable financial adviser, it would not be a bad idea to ask how often he or she proposes to update the valuation of your portfolio. Have a detailed conversation with your financial adviser at least annually to review the performance of each individual asset and to take new investment decisions in the light of individual asset performance, market trends and any changes in your own investment policy.

Keep the most up-to-date valuation together with your will somewhere secure and preferably in a fireproof safe – maybe with your lawyers or your bank. It's important to let your family know where these details are kept.

Conclusion

Approached sensibly, purchasing a property in Cyprus is not a difficult or risky thing to do and you may take courage from the fact that thousands of Brits have done so before you.

A key object of these two chapters on making the purchase and the financial implications of buying a property in Cyprus is to encourage you to seek professional advice each step along the way – and to satisfy yourself that this professional advice is coming from someone who is competent, honest and independent. To help you, in the resources section at the end of this book (**References**, pp.179–96) we have included the addresses of various professional bodies and associations from whom you will be able to obtain membership lists. See *A Directory of Services*, in 'English-Language Press and Magazines', p.181, for a publication by the author of these two chapters, which recommends the names of actual lawyers, accountants and other advisers who have been vetted or recommended by fellow British expats.

Settling In

07

Making the Move

Now that you have bought your place in the sun, there are various practicalities to consider before you're actually sitting by your pool watching a Cypriot sunset as the *souvlaki* grills on the barbecue. The easiest way to tackle the mammoth task of relocating is to make a list of all the things you need to do in preparation for the big move, including:

- obtaining the necessary permits.
- making sure you have a valid passport and a photocopy of it for safe-keeping.
- getting the necessary documentation to take your pets to Cyprus, including a passport, and making sure that their vaccinations are up to date.
- checking local Internet providers on the island, unless you have a webmail account.
- possibly buying a mobile phone to use until your landline is connected.
- opening a bank account in Cyprus and making sure you have access to funds until a new bank account is up and running.
- notifying all the relevant bodies of your change of address.
- arranging for mail to be redirected.
- taking out health insurance in Cyprus, or checking to see whether your existing insurance covers you there.
- if you are taking prescription medicine, making sure you have enough supplies until you are registered with a doctor in Cyprus.

What to Bring and What to Leave

Before you start getting quotes from removal companies think about what you really need to take. Furniture is fairly cheap to buy on the island and you may find it better value to store or sell what you have in the UK and start again when you get to Cyprus.

Bring lots of summer clothes; you'll find yourself changing several times a day in summer. Bring all your swimwear as well – it will wear out quickly. The choice of children's clothes is not very good, so bring everything you can. Likewise winter clothing; do not underestimate how cold it gets on winter evenings.

As far as household appliances go, you may want to bring your washing machine but be warned that the water in Cyprus is very hard and it may not last long. You can rent a machine for around CY£10–12 per month. It is advisable to have a dishwasher as well; you should not leave crockery lying around because of the problem of attracting insects in the heat. You may find yourself vacuuming more than at home in summer as the island gets very dusty. Bring your TV, video and DVD player; you may find lounging around inside in the air-conditioning when it is 40°C outside is a welcome pastime! Cyprus has the same electricity cycle as the UK so you will not need adapters or new plugs. The following items are cheaper to buy on the island than in the UK and are readily available: plastic containers for food, computers, garden furniture, portable air-conditioning units, toiletries, nappies and baby food.

If you have a reasonably new car, you may as well bring that, as Cyprus drives on the left and new vehicles are expensive. Besides, the depreciation on a car in the UK means that you will probably save money by driving or shipping it to Cyprus rather than selling it back home and buying a new car when you arrive. *See* 'Cars', p.135, for information about bringing your car to Cyprus.

Removal Companies

The most efficient way to move your belongings to Cyprus is to freight them by sea. You are allowed to import all your household goods, furniture and personal effects without paying duty. The only charge is a small fee levied on used electrical items, which is payable at the port at the time of entry.

Choosing a Removal Company

When choosing a removal company there are various considerations:

- **Will they give you an estimate free of charge?**
- **Are they members of the Fédération Internationale des Déménageurs Internationaux (FIDI) – bonded, quality overseas agents who carry out the destination portion of your move?**
- **Are they members of the British Association of Removers (BAR) Overseas Group? Ask to see the company's BAR Overseas Group membership certificate when the estimator visits – only BAR Overseas Group members are qualified and uniquely bonded to carry out international moves.**
- **Do they offer a door-to-door service including packing and customs clearance at the other end?**
- **Do they have adequate modern, alarmed storage facilities, as your goods may not be shipped immediately?**
- **Do they use their own packing crews, or sub-contractors? Many companies – even large ones – use sub-contracted labour, which is less of a guarantee of safe, quality packing.**

Get a couple of quotes from different companies to compare prices. Expect a 20ft container to cost roughly £2,885 plus VAT, and for the shipping to take between three and five weeks. For a list of removal companies, *see* p.181.

Retirement

Cyprus is a perfect spot for retirement, as many have discovered – warm, relaxed, friendly and affordable. Health care is good (*see* pp.139–41), although you won't find the sophistication of specialist medical facilities for ongoing conditions that you might expect in the UK. Procedures for obtaining a residence permit and claiming your pension are described below.

Getting a Residence Permit

You can start your retirement on a temporary residence permit (for which you need a bank account in Cyprus and a sales agreement on a property), which is valid from one to four years. In order to settle in Cyprus permanently, and to live on earnings derived from your pension and/or other income from sources outside Cyprus, you have to apply to the chief immigration officer for approval under Category F of Regulation 5 of the Aliens and Immigration Regulations of 1972–1996 on the form M67. *See* 'Residence', p.9.

You also have to submit a short CV and documentary evidence that you have a secured annual income (such as pension, dividends from investments, interest from deposits) of a sufficient amount to support yourself and your family while in Cyprus. The annual income must be at least CY£5,600 per person, plus CY£2,700 per dependant. Only original or officially certified copies of the documents showing your secured annual income are accepted.

If your application for a residence permit is finally approved, you will not be allowed to engage in any form of business profession or occupation, whether paid or unpaid, while residing in Cyprus and you will have to support yourself and all your family from your own income.

For further information contact:

- **Migration Department**, Ministry of the Interior, 1457 Lefkosia, Nicosia, **t** 22 80 45 02, **f** 22 80 45 87, **migration@crmd.moi.gov.cy**.

Claiming Your Pension

You can claim your UK state pension directly in Cyprus, although you must advise the Pension Service in the UK when you relocate to Cyprus, so the relevant forms can be sent to you when you near retirement age. You will usually be paid straight into your bank or building society account in the UK or your bank account in Cyprus, if you have one. Or, if you wish, you can choose to have payment by payable orders sent straight to you by post. Whichever you choose, payment is made every four or 13 weeks in arrears.

The minimum monthly amount of a Cyprus pension in 2004 was CY£149.89 for a beneficiary with no dependants, CY£199.85 for a beneficiary with one dependant, CY£224.84 for a beneficiary with two dependants and CY£249.82 for a beneficiary with three or more dependants. Payment of the old-age pension begins from the day on which the insured person acquires entitlement to it and continues for the rest of the person's life.

The pensionable age in Cyprus is 65, although you can defer payments till you are 68 if you want to. For further information contact:

- **Department of Social Insurance** at 7 Byron Avenue, 1465, Nicosia, **t** 22 40 17 72, International Affairs and EU branch (for co-ordination of social insurance systems between EU states).

Deaths

When someone dies a doctor issues a death certificate (or a coroner issues a report in specific cases) and a form is completed and furnished to the local office of the eparch. For further information, contact the Holy Archbishopric of Cyprus: **t** 22 55 46 00.

See also 'Making a Will' pp.117–8.

Working and Employment

Working in Cyprus

Anyone, provided they are an EU citizen, can seek employment in the Republic of Cyprus without the burden of requiring a work permit. The recent growth of the Cyprus economy has led to job creation, resulting in increased employment, especially among women, who have traditionally made up a smaller percentage of the workforce than men. Some 11.7 per cent of the workforce is made up of foreign workers, many in hotel services and construction rather than management jobs. Cyprus is increasingly a service centre, with big growth in tertiary industries like tourism and banking, at the expense of primary and secondary industries such as agriculture. Tertiary industries now occupy more than three-quarters of the entire workforce, the total of which is some 327,000.

The number of jobs for graduates has also increased as more management positions become available, and some 32.5 per cent of workers are now graduates. There are labour shortages in the areas of hotels, restaurants and construction, as well as manufacturing and the retail trade. All of these sectors have a high staff turnover. Cypriots have a tremendous sense of pride in their service and many deeply resent the labour shortage in the hotel industry and the consequent dilution of the Cypriot 'essence' of hospitality, but this increasingly diverse environment is a fact of life. Seasonal job opportunities are available in restaurants, bars, clubs, shops, watersports concessions, tour companies (as a guide) and hotels.

If you want to work in Cyprus, you could expect to find a job in hotel management, banking, property services or tourism, among other areas. Don't assume that everybody will want to speak English in the workplace; being able to speak Greek is a tremendous advantage. Many Cypriots will speak Greek together and lapse into English, or vice versa. Greek is not an easy language to learn as there's a whole new alphabet involved, so start well before heading to Cyprus in search of work (*see* pp.150–51).

Finding a Job

The best way to find employment is to search the job pages in the local English language newspapers, or approach the local employment bureaux listed in the Cyprus *Yellow Pages*. Word of mouth is also a good source of information, so network as much as possible and keep your ear to the ground.

In order to get a job, bring an ID card or passport, copies of your application for a residence permit, copies of educational qualifications, any disability certificates if you have a medical condition that will affect your work, and your degree certificate or documentation about other qualifications you hold.

Jobs are often advertised in the two English-language newspapers, the *Cyprus Mail* and *Cyprus Weekly* (**www.cyprusweekly.com.cy**), and you can also place your own ad offering your services, a practice that is perfectly acceptable in Cyprus. See 'English-Language Press and Magazines', p.181, for contact details.

Government jobs (mainly for Cypriot citizens) are advertised in Greek in the government *Gazette*, published every Friday and available on subscription from the **Government Printing Office**, Michail Karaoli Str., 1445 Lefkosia (Nicosia), **t** 22 40 58 46, **f** 22 30 31 75.

Some other addresses that may be of use are:

- **Cyprus Chamber of Commerce and Industry**, PO Box 1455, Lefkosia (Nicosia), **chamber@ccci.org.cy**.

- The **Employers and Industrialists Federation** (Cyprus), PO Box 1657, Lefkosia (Nicosia), **oeb@dial.cylink.com.cy**.

- **EURES**, the European Job Mobility Portal, **http://europa.eu.int/eures/home.jsp**. There is a long section on living and working in Cyprus.

The Public Employment Service

The Public Employment Service (PES) is attached to the Department of Labour of the Ministry of Labour and Social Insurance and operates centrally and at district level. There are five district offices and services are free to job seekers. The PES is a kind of job centre and provides various types of assistance, for instance information about terms of employment and labour legislation – particularly useful if the forms are in Greek. Offices are open daily 8–12am and Thursdays 8–12am and 3–6pm.

Local district labour office contact numbers:

- **Famagusta District Labour Office: t 23 81 20 52.**
- **Larnaca District Labour Office: t 24 30 45 67.**
- **Limassol District Labour Office: t 25 80 44 00/15.**
- **Nicosia District Labour Office: t 22 30 35 55.**
- **Paphos District Labour Office: t 26 82 27 99.**

Tax and National Insurance

Tax and National Insurance (NI) are payable at local rates. Income tax is currently 20 cents in the pound for any earnings in excess of CY£10,000. This rises to 25 cents in the pound for earnings over CY£15,000 and then 30 cents in the pound for earnings over CY£20,000. There is a reciprocal arrangement with the UK for NI contributions, so these do count towards your UK contribution record, but will only be registered on your record once you have paid your first NI contribution back in the UK. For more on taxation, *see* pp.100–117.

Setting up a Business

EU citizens can now live, work and establish their own business in Cyprus; they can own 100 per cent of their business and do not need to provide a minimum investment. EU citizens may establish a local company through which they pursue their business or practise their profession. Successful businesses have been set up in hairdressing, video retail, physiotherapy, bars and cafés, internet cafés and property maintenance.

EU citizens can establish their own local company in which they become 100 per cent shareholders and then obtain work and residence permits. The EU citizen becomes a company employee and as such is subject to local income tax and social security regulations. Similarly, the company is subject to compulsory VAT registration if its turnover exceeds the limit of CY£9,000 per annum. Once you have reached the VAT threshold, you must charge VAT on all invoices issued after you have registered.

There are some restrictions in the following areas:

- **An EU citizen can own up to 25 per cent of a real estate company and may apply for up to 49 per cent, but that is subject to more stringent criteria and would depend on the merits of the individual application.**
- **Investment in banking is restricted to 59 per cent of the equity capital.**
- **Financial services and stockbroking are subject to more stringent criteria (although you can invest freely in the Cyprus Stock Exchange).**
- **Certain professions or businesses require a permit from the government or other regulatory professional bodies.**

A company can have one or more shareholders. The whole process of setting up a company takes about seven to 10 weeks. You will need CVs and passport copies of the directors and shareholders, the names of shareholders and division of shares, the names of directors and a brief description of the company's activities. Companies must have insurance to cover their employees. Accounting and book-keeping must comply with the VAT regulation and directors must prepare end-of-year accounts for auditing. For more on company taxation, see 'Taxation', pp.102–20.

Money and Banking

Money

The currency of the Republic is the Cyprus pound – CY£, which is divided into 100 cents. Notes and coins currently in circulation are:

- **banknotes: CY£20, CY£10, CY£5, CY£1.**
- **coins: 1 cent, 2 cents, 5 cents, 10 cents, 20 cents, 50 cents.**

The Cyprus pound is pegged to the euro; Cyprus plans to adopt the euro in 2007 or 2008.

Import and Export of Banknotes

You can import any amount of local or foreign bank notes. You should declare to Customs any Cypriot and foreign banknotes for the purposes of deposit with banks in Cyprus, purchase of goods or immovable property, or re-export. You can export any amount of Cypriot or foreign banknotes declared on arrival. You can also export up to the equivalent of US$1,000 in Cypriot or foreign banknotes which you imported, even if you did not declare them on arrival. In addition, visitors may take out with them up to CY£100 in Cypriot bank notes.

These banks are authorised dealers reporting to the Central Bank of Cyprus and allowed to deal in foreign currency: Alpha Bank Ltd, Arab Bank Plc, Bank of Cyprus Ltd, Commercial Bank of Greece (Cyprus) Ltd, Co-operative Central Bank Ltd, Cyprus Popular Bank Ltd, Hellenic Bank Ltd, National Bank of Greece (Cyprus) Ltd, Société Général Cyprus Ltd and Universal Savings Bank Ltd.

Banking

If you are planning to live in Cyprus, or spend a significant amount of time there, it's worth opening a local bank account. Commercial banks in Cyprus offer a wide range of banking services in Cyprus pounds, as well as in foreign currencies, and have correspondents in most major cities around the world. They are also full members of SWIFT, the Society for Worldwide Interbank Financial

Telecommunication. Commercial banking is based on UK banking law and practice and commercial banks are supervised by the Central Bank of Cyprus.

There are many different types of account, similar to the range on offer in the UK. If you have a standard personal account you will receive a cheque book and a debit card, and be able to withdraw cash with no notice; if you choose the right bank, full online banking facilities will be available. Immediate access savings accounts pay a small interest rate, while notice accounts and fixed deposit accounts pay more. There are also accounts for children. Shop around before you open an account – like the UK banking system, the Cypriot system is highly competitive and there are always special offers to be had. *See* 'Banks in Cyprus', p.179, for a list of banks.

Banking Hours

Banking hours vary according to the time of year:

- **Sept: Mon–Fri 8.15am–1pm, Mon also 3.15–4.45pm.**
- **Oct–April: Mon–Fri 8.30am–1pm, Mon also 3.15–4.45pm.**
- **May–Aug: Mon–Fri 8.15am–1pm.**

Banks are closed at weekends and on public holidays and Easter Tuesday. Christmas Eve is a working day for banks.

There are **ATMs** in all major towns and tourist centres, although you may be charged a commission to use them. Banks at Larnaca and Paphos international airports provide 24-hour exchange bureaux services, and similar facilities are available at Limassol harbour.

Hotels, large shops and restaurants normally accept credit cards and travellers' cheques. Banknotes of major foreign currencies are also acceptable, although you will invariably lose on the exchange rate. Rates of exchange are published daily in the local press and are broadcast through the media. Further information of Cyprus's banking system is available at the Central Bank's website (**www.centralbank.gov.cy**) or the website of commercial banks.

Credit Cards

More than 15,000 shops, restaurants and hotels accept major credit cards, and establishments with EPOS (a 'live' credit card machine) also accept also Visa, Electron and Maestro. Usually the card symbol is displayed in the shop window or at the reception. Eurocheques and travellers' cheques are also accepted by all banks, shops, restaurants. You will find petrol pumps that take credit cards.

You can withdraw cash at the following establishments with these cards:

- **American Express: Cyprus Popular Bank Ltd.**
- **Diners Club and Carte Blanche: Bank of Cyprus Ltd.**
- **Mastercard: Alpha Bank Ltd, Bank of Cyprus Ltd, Co-operative Bank, Cyprus Popular Bank Ltd, Hellenic Bank and National Bank of Greece.**

- Visa: Alpha Bank Ltd, Arab Bank, Bank of Cyprus Ltd, Commercial Bank, Co-operative Bank, Cyprus Popular Bank Ltd, Hellenic Bank and National Bank of Greece.

Lost Cards

The local contact number for lost cards is **t** 22 86 81 00; contact the card issuer as soon as you realise your card is missing.

Cars

You need a car to live or even holiday in Cyprus. The rules covering importing or buying a car have changed since the island joined the EU – excise duty and road tax are now based on the size of the engine, heavily skewed towards higher tax for larger engines. Despite this, a lot of Cypriots favour large, four-wheel drives.

As of May 2004 there is no import duty on cars, but a new excise duty has been introduced when buying a car, payable at the time of purchase of the vehicle. The duty is calculated according to the size of the engine. There are also rates imposed on registering a new car, or re-registering a car bought duty-free before May 2004, again, based on engine size.

Petrol and diesel are much cheaper than in the UK, as is insurance.

Importing Your Car

Goods in free circulation in the EU move from one member state to another without payment of further Customs import duty. To be exempt from paying further import duty in Cyprus, proof of Community status of the goods must be provided. If you are transferring a car for private use to Cyprus from another member state, you may prove its Community status by producing:

- **for a brand new or used vehicle, a T2L or T2LF document (which can be obtained from Customs & Excise in the UK or through your vehicle supplier or the shipper).**
- **for used vehicles, the number plates and the vehicle registration document issued by the previous member state.**

Even if they have been bought in the EU, excise duty must be paid on:

- **saloon-type vehicles.**
- **jeep-type, off-road vehicles (4x4).**
- **double cabin cars.**
- **vans of tariff heading 87.04 having a gross weight not exceeding 2,032kg and a net cargo space not exceeding 2 cubic metres.**
- **motorcycles with an engine of a cubic capacity exceeding 100cc.**

If you accompany your vehicle from another member state of the EU, provided it is in free circulation, you may leave the port or airport immediately without any Customs procedures. If your vehicle is brought in unaccompanied by ship, you are required to furnish proof of Community status before you are allowed to remove the vehicle from the port. In both cases, you are required to declare the vehicle to the nearest Customs station within 24 hours from the date of its arrival using form ED5 (in Greek and English), in order to pay the excise duty and VAT, if the latter is payable. If a public holiday or weekend follows the date of arrival, you must make the declaration on the first working day after the 24-hour deadline expires.

Brand new vehicles, which at the time of their arrival in the Republic have no number plates of another member state, are liable to VAT in addition to the excise duty payable. The value for VAT calculation is the sum of the purchase price plus the transportation costs and insurance up to the point of entry in the Republic, plus the excise duty. On collection of the excise duty and VAT (if the latter is payable), Customs will issue form C72A. The vehicle and relevant documents must then be taken to the Inland Transport Department for inspection and registration purposes. For further information contact:

- **Department of Customs and Excise**, Corner M. Karaoli and Gr. Afxentiou 1096, Nicosia, **f** 22 23 20 31, **headquarters@customs.mof.gov.cy.**
- valuation section at **Customs Headquarters, t** 22 60 17 53 or **t** 22 60 17 48.

You can bring your car to Cyprus without paying excise duty for six months. Thereafter, it must be registered with a Cyprus plate and the duty paid, or else be re-exported. You are allowed to bring your vehicle on this basis if you are the owner or if you have the written authority of the owner and if:

- **your normal residence is in another member state.**
- **you are bringing it for your private use only.**
- **you intend to use it during your stay in Cyprus for a period not exceeding six months, consecutive or not, per year.**

Each person may transfer only one vehicle, and the person making a transfer must hold a valid driving licence. The vehicle may not be sold, placed for sale, hired out or loaned without payment without the prior approval of the director of the Department of Customs and Excise.

Driving Licences

Visitors in Cyprus may drive using a pink British–EU licence, provided it is valid for the class of vehicle they want to drive. If you want to get a Cyprus driving licence you have to convert your national licence to a Cypriot one or take the driving test. The Cyprus licence costs CY£35 pounds for a lifetime, but there is no real requirement to convert.

Rules of the Road

These rules apply:

- Hands-free driving is forbidden, so you may not use a mobile phone while driving unless you have an earpiece.

- The prescribed limit in breath is 39 micrograms of alcohol per 100ml of breath. The prescribed limit in blood is 90mg of alcohol per 100ml of blood.

- You will see plenty of motorcyclists riding without helmets but this is illegal and foolhardly. Driving without a helmet, and driving while using a mobile, can result in a fine of CY£500.

- Parking and waiting is prohibited along a double yellow line.

- Along a single yellow line, loading and unloading is allowed but parking is prohibited at all times.

- International road traffic signs are in use, and placed on the left hand-side along the roads and highways.

- Distances and road speed limits are posted in kilometres and kilometres per hour (kmh), respectively.

- The maximum speed limit on the motorways is 100kmh and the lower speed limit is 65kmh. On all other roads the general speed limit is 80kmh, unless a lower one is indicated. In built-up areas generally the speed limit is 50kmh, unless a different one is indicated.

- The use of seat-belts is compulsory (front and back).

- Children under the age of five must not under any circumstances sit in the front passenger seat. Children from five to 10 years old may occupy the front passenger seat only if an appropriate child's seat belt has been fitted. If you are renting a car to start with, request a child seat and inspect it carefully, or bring your own.

- Parking is free in most areas, although there are parking places in the town centres charging around CY£1 per day. Parking meters do not operate on Saturday afternoons, Sundays and public holidays.

- Rush hours in the towns are approximately 7.30–8am and 1–1.30pm, and in late afternoon 5–6pm or 6–7pm in summer.

Petrol

Motor fuel and unleaded petrol may be bought in unlimited quantities at petrol stations, and common brands are: Agip, EKO, Esso, Exxon Mobil, Lina, Lukoil and Petrolina. Petrol is sold by the litre and prices fluctuate. In 2004, including 15 per cent VAT, they were:

- 47.5 cents per litre for premium petrol (super).

- 46.3 cents per litre for unleaded petrol (super).
- 45.2 cents per litre for unleaded petrol 95 ROM.
- 31 cents per litre for diesel oil.
- 33 cents per litre for diesel low sulphur.

Petrol stations are open:

- April–Sept: Mon–Fri 6am–7pm, Sat 6am–3pm; Oct–Mar Mon–Fri 6am–6pm, Sat 6am–3pm.
- Nicosia district: closed Wed pm.
- Limassol, Larnaca, Paphos and Famagusta districts: closed Tues pm.

Petrol stations in Nicosia and all seaside areas are equipped with petrol vending machines, which accept bank notes and credit cards. Vending machines operate during non-working hours, on weekends and on holidays. Petrol stations in rural areas may be found open on weekends and on holidays. A list of petrol stations can be found in the *Yellow Pages* of the phone directory.

Home Utilities and Services

Electricity

Electricity is controlled by the Electricity Authority of Cyprus (EAC) and can be supplied anywhere in the non-occupied part of the island. If you are building a property, you have to apply for your supply using form EAC585. Your property will be inspected for compliance with safety rules and you will need to pay a deposit of CY£75 and sign form EAC13. You should include your name, the postal address and telephone number, as well as Land Registry Office (LRO) plan details of the premises, where electricity supply is required (sheet or plan number and plot number). You will also need:

- the building permit.
- the LRO plan of the building certified by the issuing authority (official seal).
- details of the electrical load to be installed in addition to the normal load (lighting, water heater, cooker, refrigerator, small appliances) such as air-conditioning units and storage heaters.

When the house to be supplied is in a rural area, in order to benefit from the EAC's Rural Area Policy (lower capital contribution towards the cost of supply), you have to submit a written confirmation from the district officer, certifying that you are entitled to be included in the Rural Area Policy Scheme.

Bills are dispatched every two months by post to all urban, suburban and major rural areas. For small rural areas, EAC dispatches bills through the local co-operative societies, and in areas where there are no co-operative societies EAC personnel dispatch bills. You can pay at a customer service centre, by post, at a bank or co-op, by direct debit, or even straight out of your salary if you work for a large organisation. When you buy or rent property, you need to either transfer the existing electricity contract to your name or, in the case of a new property, establish a new one. In order to have an electricity supply in your name you should produce your passport and a contract of sale, or your rental agreement, to the clerk at the new connections counter.

The EAC requires a deposit of CY£10 plus CY£3.25 for a change of name. A typical annual electricity bill is around CY£200.

- **EAC customer service centres:** 55 Ag. Andreou Str., PO Box 50121, 3601 Lemesos, **t** 25 84 90 14/6; 57 Constantinou Palaiologou Str., PO Box 40186, 6301 Larnaka, **t** 24 20 40 00; 13 Tepeleniou Str., PO Box 60057, 8100 Pafos, **t** 26 84 11 50.

Gas

Only bottled gas is available in Cyprus for domestic use. Gas is widely available and costs CY£2–3 for a 10kg bottle, or slightly more if you have it delivered. A 10kg bottle should last about three months, depending on what you use it for.

Water

Water is charged for quarterly. There is an initial connection fee of CY£32; the standing charge varies according to the municipality that you live in. It is usually between CY£4 and CY£9 per quarter for a supply of 40 cubic tonnes. Customers who exceed the 40 cubic tonnes are charged more. If you intend to be absent from Cyprus for long periods, it is advisable to pay your water bill in advance or alternatively get someone reliable to do it for you; you do not want to be cut off.

In areas where the water is supplied from wells, the private owner of the well(s) (this includes the church) will charge according to their own scales. Ask the individual supplier what the rates are.

Contact details for some of the water authorities are:

- **Limassol: t** 25 83 00 00.
- **Paphos: t** 26 94 03 51.
- **Larnaca: t** 24 82 24 00.

Communications

Cyprus has one of the most advanced and cheapest telecommunication systems in the world. ISDN, ADSL and standard dial-up PC networking are also easily accessible. The Cyprus Telecommunications Authority (CYTA) is responsible for the provision, maintenance and development of telecommunications facilities, both local and overseas. Since the beginning of 2003 the telecommunications market has been liberalised so is now open for other telecommunications providers. Services provided by CYTA include fixed and mobile telephony, ISDN, DSL and Internet.

Telephones

Getting a landline connected costs CY£100, and is refundable if/when you leave or sell the property. CYTA does not require a deposit from home-owners as long as you remember to take a copy of the sale agreement with you when you set up your account.

You can call or fax anywhere in the world from Cyprus. The following reduced rates apply:

- **national calls: weekdays from 8pm to 7am and all day Saturday, Sunday and on public holidays.**

- **international calls: weekdays from 9pm to 8am and all day Saturday, Sunday and on public holidays.**

For directory enquiries ring:

- **192 (national).**

- **194 (international).**

Although practically everybody has a mobile phone, Cyprus still has payphones and public card-phones taking coins or cards. Telecards of £3, £5 and £10 can be purchased at any CYTA shop, at banks, post offices, kiosks and other shops. Coin-operated payphones accept 2, 5, 10 and 20 cent coins. While it may seem old-fashioned to use a payphone, it's cheaper than using your UK mobile to call the UK in the weeks before your phone line is installed.

CYTA COMMcard

CYTA COMMcard is a prepaid calling card that allows you to make calls from a mobile phone, a hotel phone or any other fixed telephone and charge the calls to the card instead of the phone you are calling from. Again, this can be useful before your own landline is installed.

Mobiles

Cytamobile-Vodafone (**www.cytamobile-vodafone.com.cy**) is the CYTA mobile telephony brand, following a CYTA partnership agreement with Vodafone in the beginning of 2004. You can use your mobile phone in Cyprus, provided that a roaming agreement between Cytamobile-Vodafone and your mobile service provider is in place. For an up-to-date list of coverage, see the website. There is good coverage all over the southern part of the island and you will soon find that Cypriots are obsessed with their mobile phones, which ring constantly. Once you've moved to Cyprus you will need a Cypriot mobile provider or your bills from the UK will be enormous; each time someone calls you from Britain, you pay the international portion of the call. If you're in Cyprus with a Cypriot phone, your callers from the UK pay the international element of the call.

Mobile Phone Payment Schemes

• **Pay monthly**: there are two Cytamobile-Vodafone pay monthly plans currently in existence: light, for customers who do not wish to make many calls, and classic, for customers with average to high use. To connect to either one of the pay monthly plans, the customer needs to sign a contract with CYTA.

• **Soeasy pay as you go**: soeasy is the Cytamobile-Vodafone pay-as-you-go plan, for which you don't need a contract. You pay for the calls in advance. All you have to do is to buy a soeasy connection pack and top-up your account using top-up cards. The soeasy connection pack and top-up cards are available throughout the country at kiosks and other points of sale. There are three different values of top-up cards, worth CY£5, CY£10 (with a CY£1 free bonus) and CY£20 (with a CY£3 free bonus)

• **Cybee services**: Cybee services are offered to all Cytamobile-Vodafone customers regardless of whether they are connected to a pay monthly or pay-as-you-go plan. Services include SMS, WAP, or web.

Internet and E-mail

Cytanet

Cytanet is the largest internet service provider in Cyprus and offers Internet services to individuals, corporate customers and other Internet service providers based in Cyprus or neighbouring countries. Cytanet provides connections via the telephone network (at 56kbps), the ISDN (at 64kbps and 128kbps) and Asynchronous Digital Subscriber Line (ADSL) (at 640kbps). For more information, **t** 8000 8080 free of charge or e-mail **cytanet@call-centre.cyta.com.cy**.

Broadband Networks and Services

Many people have broadband at home now (in urban areas), and it is useful if you want to send and receive digital pictures from friends and relatives at home, or send relatively large files. Various providers can supply the service, via CYTA's network. A typical broadband package includes a permanent connection to the broadband network; a fixed monthly charge, with no per minute charge; the ability to talk on the phone and at the same time surf the Internet or connect to a company's intranet; and fast connection with speeds up to 20 times faster than are available without broadband.

Education

Education in Cyprus is free and you can send your children to a local Cypriot school if you are living on the island. Standards are reasonably high. Lessons are in Greek; if your children are not fluent Greek speakers they will be given extra Greek tuition locally, sponsored by the government, so that they can catch up – which they invariably do with great speed. If you want to send your child to an English-speaking school, *see* 'Private Education'.

The State System

Pre-school Education

There are state baby nurseries for children of up to three years of age. Then pre-school education is provided by Greek-language state schools for children aged from three years to five years and eight months. Attendance is voluntary and costs less than what the private sector charges.

Primary and Secondary Education

Primary education lasts for six years leading to a leaving certificate. It is provided free of charge at state schools for children aged from five years and eight months to 11 years and eight months. Age is the only criterion for the entry of children into primary education.

Public general secondary education also extends over six years and is free for children until they are 18. It is divided into two three-year cycles: three years at the *gymnasion* for children from 11 years and eight months to 15 years, followed by three years at the *lykeion* for children aged from 15 to 18.

Higher Education

Education is compulsory until the age of 15, but most Cypriot students stay on till 18 and then go on to higher education. Cyprus has one university and 24 colleges and institutions of higher education. Some 70 per cent of school leavers go on to college or university, although many go overseas to Greece, the UK and the USA.

The University of Cyprus, which opened in September 1992, comprises four schools (Humanities and Social Sciences, Pure and Applied Sciences, Economics and Management and Letters). Studies are organised in terms, and subjects taught are counted in credits. Degrees last at least eight terms.

Private Education

Pre-school Education

There are private nurseries for children from the age of three, which cost CY£70–150 per child per month. Pre-school education is available in Greek-speaking schools and in schools teaching in other languages until children go to primary school.

Primary and Secondary Education

Cyprus has a number of private English-speaking schools, in Larnaca, Limassol, Paphos, Nicosia and on the army bases. They tend to provide small classes, high academic standards and a good range of extra-curricular activities. Expect to pay fees from around CY£2,800 per year for junior school and CY£4,000 per year for seniors. All of these schools ask students to sit an entrance exam in Greek and mathematics and many have a waiting list, so start your research long before you move.

You'll find a lot of Greek Cypriot families send their children to private English-speaking schools to get a grounding in English and to enter the British educational system. Sometimes up to 30 per cent of students at private schools are from local Cypriot families.

There are two primary schools on the British army bases and one secondary school on the Episkopi Garrison, all with an excellent reputation. They take non-army children for a fee. Cyprus also has more than 30 private secondary schools teaching in Greek, English, French or Russian, with fees of CY£2,000–3,000 per year. Contact details for some of the main English-speaking schools are:

- **American Academy**, Larnaca, **www.academy.ac.cy**.
- **American International School Cyprus**, Nicosia, **www.aisc.ac.cy**.
- **English School**, Nicosia, **www.englishschool.ac.cy**, **t** 22 79 93 00.
- **Foley's Grammar and Junior School**, Limassol, **t** 25 58 21 91, **www.foleysschool.com**.
- **Grammar School**, Nicosia and Limassol, **t** 25 72 79 33, **www.grammarschool.ac.cy**.
- **International School**, Paphos, **t** 26 23 22 36, **www3.spidernet.net/ web/isop/**.
- **Akrotiri Primary**, Akrotiri Garrison, **t** 25 96 61 67, **http://sceschools.com/ schools/CYPRUS/AKROTIRI.HTM**.
- **Episkopi Primary**, Episkopi Garrison, **t** 25 96 34 25, **http://sceschools. com/schools/CYPRUS/EPISKOP.HTM**.
- **St John's School**, Episkopi Garrison, **t** 25 26 38 88, **http://sceschools.com/ schools/CYPRUS/STJOHN.HTM**.

Health and Emergencies

State Health Care

Health care in Cyprus is generally very good. If you are travelling as a visitor (for less than 90 days), you can use the E111 form for subsidised emergency medical treatment at government hospitals now that Cyprus is a member of the EU – but this should never be a substitute for proper travel insurance. Out-patient and in-patient treatment is charged for. Citizens of the European Union on state retirement pensions who transfer their residence to Cyprus are provided with treatment free of charge when they present form E121.

Free medical care in government hospitals is only available for low-income families, government employees and refugees, so most expats resident in Cyprus take out private medical insurance (see 'Private Health Care', below). Government general hospitals and private clinics and hospitals are mostly concentrated in urban areas, while health centres, sub-centres and dispensaries function in the rural areas. A lot of doctors were trained in the UK or USA and most speak some English. Cyprus also has a growing number of people visiting for 'medical tourism' – face lifts and tummy tucks – as it is considerably cheaper in Cyprus than in the UK. So if you're planning any plastic surgery, save it till you arrive!

Dentists, and dental specialists, are available everywhere and their fees are low compared with European standards. Dentists are of a high standard and dental surgeries are well equipped with the latest facilities.

Hospitals

Some of the main hospitals in Cyprus are:

- **Larnaka General Hospital: t** 24 80 05 00 or **t** 24 80 03 69.
- **Lefkosia General Hospital: t** 22 80 14 00/75 (Accidents and Emergency).
- **Lemesos General Hospital: t** 25 80 11 00 or **t** 25 30 57 70.
- **Kyperounta Hospital: t** 25 53 20 21.
- **Pafos General Hospital: t** 26 80 32 60 or **t** 26 30 61 00.
- **Paralimni Hospital: t** 23 82 12 11.
- **Polis Hospital: t** 26 32 14 31.

Private Health Care

All government-run hospitals and some private clinics have accident and emergency departments for emergency cases.

Private medical insurance is very reasonable, from around CY£130 a year, but even if you pay as you go, a private consultation will only cost about CY£15. Of course, paying ad hoc like this is much less attractive if you need an operation or ongoing treatment. **Inter Global Insurance Services Limited, t** (01252) 745910, **www.interglobalpmi.com**, provides medical insurance for people who live in Cyprus.

Pharmacies

Almost all brands of manufactured medicines are available in Cyprus and pharmacists are a very useful source of advice if you haven't got the time or the inclination to go to the doctor. Local newspapers list the pharmacies that are open during the night and on weekends and holidays, as well as the names of doctors who are on call at weekends and holidays.

Emergencies

Information about private doctors on call on at weekends and public holidays is given by the following telephone numbers:

- **Famagusta area: t** 1433.
- **Larnaca: t** 1434.
- **Limassol: t** 1435.
- **Nicosia: t** 1432.
- **Paphos: t** 1436.

For information on night pharmacies, call **t** 192 or listen to the automatic recording on:

- **Famagusta area: t** 1403.
- **Larnaca: t** 1404.
- **Limassol: t** 1405.
- **Nicosia: t** 1402.
- **Paphos: t** 1406.

Everyday Health Matters

Water is safe to drink in Cyprus, as water pollution is negligible and every home has fresh running drinking water. Tap water in hotels, restaurants and in public places is safe to drink, although it is always advisable to wash fruit before eating it.

Cyprus is also free from dangerous infectious diseases and no vaccinations are required to enter the country. The biggest health hazard is the sun, which should be treated with respect. Cover up at all times and make sure children are fully protected, even more so if they have light skin.

Cyprus has its fair share of mosquitoes, which, although not malarial, are a real nuisance. Use screens on windows if you like the windows open, and have coils in bedrooms at night, as well as using insect repellent. Don't have standing water close to your house – in a garden pond, for example.

Cyprus also has three species of venomous snake: the cat snake, Montpellier snake and blunt-nosed viper. Other, non-venomous snakes that live only in rural areas will bite if cornered. If you are bitten, restrict movement as much as possible and get to a doctor fast.

It could be argued that passive smoking is a health hazard in Cyprus, as so many Cypriots smoke. Unfortunately, this is a fact of life and short of campaigning against smoking in public places (and upsetting your Cypriot friends) there is not much you can do about it, other than eating outside when at restaurants wherever possible, and asking people not to smoke in your home or car. Public pressure does eventually change situations: Cyprus Airways became a mainly non-smoking airline some time ago, although it was one of the last to implement the policy, and smoking on the Cyprus–Moscow route is still allowed.

Cyprus has a very strict policy towards drugs and importing drugs; possession and use are all strictly prohibited.

Welfare Benefits

The UK and Cyprus have a reciprocal agreement to protect the benefit rights of those moving between the two countries. For full details, visit the website of the Department of Work and Pensions (**www.dwp.gov.uk/international**) as the rules are complicated. The website is presented in plain English.

Job Seeker's Allowance

According to the Department of Work and Pensions, if you have paid enough Class 1 National Insurance (NI) contributions, you will get a personal rate of contribution-based Job Seeker's Allowance (JSA) as long as you are available for and actively seeking work. Contribution-based JSA may be paid to jobseekers in European Economic Area (EEA) countries (of which Cyprus is one).

If you are getting UK contribution-based JSA, and you have been registered as available for work, usually for four weeks, at a UK Jobcentre Plus office or Jobcentre, you may be able to carry on getting UK contribution-based JSA for up to three months while you look for work in Cyprus. But you must have been getting contribution-based JSA before you go abroad. UK contribution-based JSA is paid by the employment services in Cyprus, in Cyprus pounds, at the rate of contribution-based JSA you were paid in the UK, and is authorised on form E303. This form is issued by the Pension Service.

If you can get UK contribution-based JSA in Cyprus, you can get a letter from your Jobcentre Plus office or Jobcentre to help you in registering for work there. Give it to the authorities that run the employment services in Cyprus. If you can get UK contribution-based JSA in Cyprus and you are going to look for work, you will also be given form E303, which will be sent to a liaison office in that country.

In Cyprus, you must register for work and be available for work. You can only get benefit while you are registered at the employment office in Cyprus. Normally, as long as you register before the end of seven days after you left the UK, you may carry on getting your UK contribution-based JSA without a break in your entitlement. But you should note there may be a delay before you are paid in Cyprus.

Statutory Maternity Pay

Statutory Maternity Pay (SMP) is paid by employers to help women take time off work when they expect a baby. If you work for a UK employer, have done so for at least 26 weeks of the 66 weeks before your baby is due, and your earnings are on average at least equal to the lower earnings limit in the appropriate reference period, you can get SMP while you are in another EEA country such as Cyprus. Also, a woman who is absent from Great Britain in an EEA country during her SMP pay period, but who is normally in employment in the UK, may continue to receive SMP. You do not need to be a national of any EEA country to get SMP in another EEA country. SMP is paid for up to 26 weeks. The rate of benefit depends on your average weekly earnings.

UK Maternity Allowance in Another EEA Country

If, for any reason, you cannot get SMP in another EEA country, but you were last insured under the UK scheme, you may be able get UK Maternity Allowance instead if:

- **you are living or working there.**
- **you are looking for work there and you are getting UK contribution-based Jobseeker's Allowance.**
- **you are already getting Maternity Allowance in the UK and you go back to the country where you usually live or you go to live in another EEA country; but you must get your Jobcentre Plus or social security office to agree that you can carry on getting your benefit.**
- **the Department of Health tells you that you can go to another EEA country to get medical treatment.**

Leaflet T6, 'Health Advice for Travellers', tells you more about this. You can get a copy from any UK post office or from **www.dh.gov.uk/travellers**. If these regulations do not apply to you, and you are going to another EEA country for a short visit, you may still be able to get Maternity Allowance. But you must be going abroad to get medical treatment for a medical condition that started before you left the UK, or you must have been unable to work for at least six months, with no gaps, before you go.

If you have your baby in any other EEA country, the rules for deciding if you may get UK Maternity Allowance are just the same as if you were living in the UK, unless you can get the same sort of Maternity Allowance from the EEA country you are living in. If you are getting Maternity Allowance and you are going to another EEA country, check with your Jobcentre Plus or social security office well before you leave.

Maternity Benefit from Another EEA Country

If you have been working in another EEA country you may have become insured for sickness since the last time you arrived there. If you have, and you claim maternity benefit under that country's scheme, your UK insurance may help you get it. The authorities there will ask the Inland Revenue NI Contributions Office for details of your UK insurance record.

The Inland Revenue NI Contributions Office will send on to them form E104. They will usually need to get in touch with the employer you used to work for in the UK before they can send form E104. The authorities who run the foreign maternity scheme will decide your claim using their own rules.

Crime and the Police

Cyprus has a crime rate 10 per cent that of most west European countries and around 6 per cent that of the UK. The low incidence of crime among Cypriot nationals is accounted for by the closeness of family ties, the emphasis on upholding the family's honour and reputation, and the social pressures for education and achievement. You'll find that people often leave their cars unlocked, or doors and windows open. This takes a bit of getting used to when you first arrive. You should, however, play safe and keep valuables locked away.

The main objectives of the Cyprus police are to maintain law and order throughout the Republic, to preserve peace, to prevent and detect crime, to apprehend offenders, to protect the population and public installations, to improve the movement of road traffic and to reduce road accidents. Cyprus shares with the rest of Europe a threat from international terrorists and the Foreign Office warns that, like everywhere else, attacks could be indiscriminate and against civilians. The presence of the United Nations peacekeeping force and British army may also provoke terrorist attacks, although it hasn't so far.

Theft is the most common crime in Cyprus, with fraud second in line. Murders, sex offences and violent crime are very uncommon. The occasional torching of cars is reported in the press, but this is mainly thought to be in-fighting between criminals. Cyprus has a strictly enforced zero tolerance policy towards drugs. Being caught in possession of any type of narcotic will usually lead to a prison sentence or a hefty fine.

When in Cyprus, do not attempt to make fraudulent claims on your insurance policy. The police investigate such claims and prosecute visitors for this offence. Prison sentences and heavy fines have been imposed. Avoid taking photographs near potentially sensitive areas such as military establishments and along the Green Line in order to avoid any misunderstandings.

The emergency number for police is **t** 199 or **t** 112.

Taking Your Pet to Cyprus

Taking your pet to Cyprus is much easier now that the country is a member of the EU and pet passports are in operation. You can bring a dog or cat and take it back to the UK, subject to meeting the criteria, without the misery of quarantine. If the animal has a passport, you do not need to apply for an import licence. Think about whether your dog or car will be able to withstand the heat in Cyprus, though; a fluffy, long-haired cat, for example, may find the climate very uncomfortable. Note that the following breeds cannot be brought into Cyprus: American pit bull or pit bull terrier, Dogo Argentino, Fila Brasileiro or Japanese tosa.

To bring a dog or cat to Cyprus, you must have:

• an EU Pet Passport issued by your vet. To obtain this, you must first have your pet microchipped by your vet, who must vaccinate your pet against rabies. If you intend to return to the UK then the vet must obtain a blood sample 30 days after the rabies vaccination and submit it for testing. Assuming that this result is OK, the details of the blood test will be entered into the Pet Passport.

• an antiparasitical treatment against fleas, ticks and worms containing the active substances Fibronil and Praziquantel 24 to 48 hours before departing for Cyprus. If this is not carried out, on arrival in Cyprus your pet will be subject to one month's quarantine and payment of CY£26 at the airport.

• a fitness to fly certificate. Airlines require assurance that your pet is healthy enough to fly. Therefore your pet must be inspected by a vet shortly (preferably within a week) before the flight and then if all is well issue a fitness to fly (or private health) certificate. This is a document provided by any vet describing your pet(s) and confirming that on the date they were examined they were deemed to be free of clinical signs of disease and were of a satisfactory condition to be transported by air. It should state the name of the owner and address, the destination airport and the final destination address. The certificate is valid for up to 10 days (though some airlines deem them to be valid only for two days).

• a travel box that complies with IATA regulations for the movement of live animals.

Your pet will be checked over by a vet on arrival at the airport before being released. The total cost of taking a pet to Cyprus can be as much as £600 for the animal's flight plus another £20 for the vet's inspection at the airport.

For a list of useful addresses and websites, *see* 'Pets', p.182.

Food and Drink

Cyprus Cuisine

Cyprus cuisine is closely related to that of Greece, but the island's unique position at the crossroads of Europe, Africa and the Middle East has added spicier dimensions that make it particularly delicious. It's more varied than Greek food and uses plenty of fresh local ingredients, herbs, spices, and, of course, olive oil.

The typical taverna meal is *meze*, short for *mezedes*, or 'little delicacies'. You never really know what's coming but it's almost always a vast amount. A typical *meze* will start with pitta bread and *dips* *hummous*, *tzatziki* (or *talatouri* as it's sometimes called here), taramasalata, aubergine dip and tahini. Next comes *loukanika* (coriander-seasoned sausages, soaked in red wine and smoked), *koupepia* or *dolmades* (vine leaves stuffed with minced meat and rice), *lountza* (smoked pork), grilled halloumi – a saviour for vegetarians in Cyprus. Fish is also

---

Halloumi

Halloumi is the traditional white cheese of Cyprus and has been produced by the island for centuries. It's a semi-hard cheese, prepared from sheep and goat's milk with the addition of mint. Fresh curd is submerged in hot whey to soften and stretch it, similar to the way mozzarella is made. The young cheese is then aged in baskets and folded into wedges about the size of a large wallet. The milk is produced in the villages surrounding the Avdhimou area between Limassol and Paphos districts. The soft, springy, oval-shaped curd has a mild yet tangy flavour.

Halloumi cheese is delicious when grilled or fried; it retains its texture and shape and bubbles nicely under the grill. Many Brits add it to their traditional fry-up in the morning, with bacon and eggs, or you can serve slices of it with salad instead of the usual crumbled feta. Cypriots swear that the best way to eat it at breakfast is to serve it with wedges of ripe watermelon. Halloumi can also be grated on pizza, served in sandwiches, or used in pasta dishes. You can marinade it, or serve it grilled on big portabello mushrooms.

served – *kalamari* (squid) , octopus, sea bass and red mullet. All this is accompanied by a large Greek salad, or farmer's salad – tomato, cucumber, green peppers, olives and crumbled feta, drizzled with olive oil and lemon.

Only now does the main course come: *sheftalia* (minced pork with herbs), *souvlakia* (kebabs with lemon juice and herbs), moussaka or *stifado* (rich beef and onion stew). *Kleftiko* is lamb or goat, wrapped in foil and baked with bay leaves in a sealed oven, making it wonderfully tender. *Yemista* is also popular – baked vegetables stuffed with rice and mince. Other common vegetable preparations are potatoes in olive oil and parsley, pickled cauliflower and beets, courgettes, *kolokasi* (a sweet potato-like root vegetable) and asparagus.

Cypriot desserts often consist of fresh fruit, served alone or with a selection of sweet pastries or fruit preserved in syrup. These include *loukoumades* (Cyprus doughnuts with honey syrup), *daktyla* (ladyfingers with almonds, walnuts and cinnamon) and *shiamali* (orange semolina cakes cut into squares). *Baklava* (filo pastry with nuts, drenched in syrup or honey) is delicious and more than enough to finish you off after a spread like this.

In cafés, popular snacks include *kolokoti* (a pastry triangle stuffed with red pumpkin, cracked wheat and raisins), *pastellaki* (a sesame, peanut and honey syrup bar) and *galatopoureko* (a cream-stuffed filo pastry). A traditional sweet treat is *loukoumia* (cubes of gelatin flavoured with rose water and dusted with powdered sugar).

As well as countless tavernas, you'll find international food of every persuasion – English (in pubs), Chinese, French, Indian, Japanese, Thai and fast food. There are upmarket restaurants in Nicosia, in the old part of Limassol, and dotted along the coast in five-star hotels, some of them overlooking the sea. Larnaca seafront is great for fish tavernas. Some of the agrotourism establishments in the mountains and small villages serve fabulous organic food.

Drinks

Coffee

Cypriots drink coffee really strong, in tiny cups. The coffee is boiled in the cup with the water and served black with sugar. For a *metrio* add one spoon of sugar; for a *glyko* add two spoons of sugar. If you want instant coffee, ask for Nescafé. Quite a few places can make cappuccino and latte as well. Off the beaten track, don't expect to find decaf.

Brandy Sour

Brandy sour is practically a national drink, consisting of Cyprus brandy and lemon squash (made from Cyprus lemons) with angostura bitters and soda water, on the rocks. It's very refreshing. Cypriot brandy is good alone, too, and has a mild taste. It's usually served at weddings.

Beer

There are two breweries, Carlsberg and Keo, although plenty of places serve draught and bottled beer, as well.

Wine

Cyprus was the only place in Europe not to be affected by the Phylloxera beetle, which, after arriving on vine samples shipped from the USA, decimated European vineyards in the 1860s and 1870s. Consequently, many of the vines in the mountains behind Limassol and Paphos are over 150 years old. Red wines are made from the mavro grape, as well as maratheftiko and ofthalmo, while whites come mainly from the Xynisteri, producing a fresh, crisp taste. Cabernet sauvignon, grenache, carignan noir, mataro, chardonnay and semillon have also been introduced and blended with the native grapes.

Cyprus is not famed for the brilliance of its wines, but like some other countries keeps the best for itself, rather than exporting everything. There are four big producers – Keo, Etko, Sodap and Loel – with wineries dotted all over the hills and even on the coast. Some 20 smaller growers also produce 10,000 to 100,000 bottles a year. There are several labels worth trying. Keo Aphrodite is dry and fruity, while Othello is a powerful and full-bodied red. Sodap's Afames is mellow and medium-bodied, from the Troodos, one of the best wine-growing regions. Arsinoe is another dry, fruity white, made from the traditional Xynisteri grape by Sodap. If you want to try some produce from smaller growers, take a trip to Omodhos or Kilani village, where you can taste and buy direct.

Other Drinks

As well as wine, Cyprus produces sherries, vermouth, and ports. The traditional ouzo is a strong distillation of grape juice taken watered, when it looks like milk. It tastes like aniseed and is familiar to many Grecophiles. Zivania is another strong distillation. The pink cinnamon flavoured variety is a speciality of the Kykko Monastery in the heart of the Paphos Forest. You'll no doubt come across a sickly orange liqueur, Filfar, popular as an aperitif or in cocktails. It's made from Cypriot oranges and is best mixed with orange or lemon juice and ginger ale or soda, and served in a long glass, on the rocks.

Commandaria

Today no Cypriot wine enjoys greater renown than Commandaria, a sweet, robust fortified dessert wine that is said to be the oldest named wine in the world. It's the only appellation-controlled wine on the island. Once called 'Nama', it so reminded Marc Antony of Cleopatra's kisses that he gave the whole island to his legendary lover because of it. Nama was renamed after Richard the Lionheart sold Cyprus to the Knights Templars (the Grand Commandarie was the estate of the Knights Hospitallers at Kolossi). The oversized Commandaria grapes are grown on the high southern slopes of the Troodos Mountains (particularly in the villages of Zoopiyi, Kalokhorio and Agios Konstantinos), picked late in the season and sun-dried to enhance the sugar content. The wine is produced by fermentation in open jars.

Shopping

Arts and handicrafts aside, Cyprus is not the world's most exciting shopping destination. You'll find familiar brands of things like clothing, but a narrower choice than in the UK. A recent survey by the Armies Family Federation revealed that 46 per cent of families posted to Cyprus were unhappy with the shopping facilities. In Cyprus, once purchased, goods are non-returnable and refunds are not available.

Food tends to be of high quality, fresh and locally produced. Imported biscuits and chocolates are very expensive. Local pork is usually good, and fresh vegetables and fruit are a speciality of Cyprus. Reasonably priced melons, oranges, grapefruit, cherries, mandarins, grapes and strawberries are readily available, but usually only during the appropriate season. Cypriots tend to shop for food in supermarkets – there's no fashionable backlash against supermarkets similar to the situation in the UK; in Cyprus, a hypermarket is considered a good thing and a prestigious place to shop. In Limassol, there's a covered market just north of St Andrew's Street, selling meat, fruit and vegetables. Look out for roadside fruit and vegetable sellers in the countryside, too.

Leather goods, shoes and luggage are good value, and there is a wide choice of furniture that suits most tastes. Designer clothes, however, are thin on the ground and women's fashions tend to be sold through smaller, independent stores or in the hypermarkets like Ermes. Spectacles cost half as much as they do in the UK, so there's no need to stock up before leaving!

You'll find familiar names like Miss Selfridge, Esprit and Next in Nicosia, as well as Debenhams, Adams, and Villeroy & Boch. The latter three are part of the big Ermes Group, which also has department stores in Larnaca, Limassol, Nicosia and Paphos. Other familiar brands include the Body Shop, the Early Learning Centre, Marks & Spencer, Morgan and Mothercare. Jumbo, situated just outside Limassol, is very similar to Toys R Us in UK, with reasonable prices. Swedish furniture giant IKEA is rumoured to be opening on the island in 2006, and will no doubt do very well.

Chris Cash and Carry is a large hypermarket chain, with stores in Paphos, Larnaca and Limassol (three), selling a huge range of food, reasonably priced alcoholic drinks, fresh meat and fish, clothing, appliances, home improvements goods – practically everything, in other words. Orphanides, another big hypermarket, has seven stores and two shopping centres, spread across all the main towns. It stocks Iceland products.

Opening Hours

Shop opening hours are different in winter and summer, as follows:

- winter (Nov–Mar): Mon, Tues and Thurs 9am–7pm, Wed 9am–2pm, Fri 9am–8pm, Sat 9am–3pm; Sunday is not a working day, although shops in tourist areas may well be open.

- summer (April–Oct): Mon, Tues and Thurs 9am–8.30am, Wed 9am–2pm, Fri 9am–9.30pm, Sat 9am–5pm. From 15 June to 31 August, the shops are closed 2–5pm. Sunday is not a working day.

Official public holidays for shops are: 1 Jan, 25 Mar, 1 Apr, Easter Monday, 1 May, 1 Oct, 28 Oct, 25 Dec and 26 Dec. During the Christmas period, which begins on 12 December and ends on 30 December, and the Easter period, which begins 10 days before Easter Sunday, the shops are open for longer.

All urban areas have **kiosks** that are open for longer than the shops or even for 24 hours a day; they sell cigarettes, soft drinks, mineral water, and magazines and newspapers. A large number of **bakeries** stay open until 11pm, selling bread, other bakery products, and milk and other dairy products.

Media

Newspapers

The *Cyprus Weekly* is an independent English language newspaper published every Friday, with a diverse selection of news, politics, business, environment, arts and sports. The *Cyprus Weekly* is rivalled by the daily *Cyprus Mail*, which has a good Sunday 'What's On' section including chemist and Sunday petrol station details. Both newspapers cover the political division between north and south Cyprus in great depth and have a somewhat gossipy, tabloid feel in most of their coverage. The *Financial Mirror* is the island's leading business newspaper, published weekly in English. **Foreign newspapers** are expensive – perhaps CY£1.20 for *The Times*. They usually arrive one day after publication. Most English magazines can also be bought, although they're not cheap. English-language books are sold in the main tourist centres.

Television

The public broadcasting service is the Cyprus Broadcasting Corporation (CYBC), which transmits island-wide on three radio and two television channels. CYBC is a non-profit organisation that uses its entire income for the promotion of its main mission: the objective provision of information, culture and entertainment for the people of Cyprus.

There are six Cypriot Greek TV stations available at the moment free of charge. Approximately 30 per cent of the programmes are broadcast in English and all foreign films are broadcast in their original language, with Greek subtitles. Residents can also subscribe to the Cypriot cable service LTV to watch US and UK sports and programmes. There are also a number of satellite services available including Sky and a range from European, Russian, Middle Eastern and Indian TV satellites.

Radio

There are also numerous radio stations, which are broadcast in Greek and English. CYBC has three channels – One, Two and Three. One and Three broadcast in Greek, while Two has English language news. the BBC World Service is at 89.9FM, 1323AM, broadcasting around the clock. The forces (BFBS) broadcast in English on a number of frequencies, and you can even find *The Archers*!

Commercial radio stations include Astra, for music, news, sport and chat; Kiss FM for dance and pop music; Napa Radio, for more dance music; ditto Mix FM; Sky Radio; Melody, which includes some Greek music; Logos Radio; Radio Elios; Coast FM in Limassol; and Super FM.

Learning and Speaking Greek

If you plan to work in Cyprus, learning Greek is highly recommended. It's a good idea to start well before you leave, as Greek is not an easy language and involves learning an entire new alphabet. You will need good Greek if you are to be taken seriously in the job market, although it's possible to get by with basic knowledge if you are working in a service industry like tourism or real estate. You will find that if you work for Cypriots they will converse in a mixture of Greek and English in the office, and it helps to understand what's going on. If you send your children to Cypriot school, they should be given extra, free tuition in Greek to help them catch up.

Formally, and in written form, standard modern Greek, the Dimotiki dialect, is used in Cyprus. However, orally and informally there is a distinctive Cypriot Greek dialect (*Kypriaki dialectos*). The Cypriot Greek dialect, although it observes the grammar and syntax of the Greek language, reflects in its vocabulary the historical influence of the island's various occupiers, among them the Arabs, English, French, Turks and Venetians. These words are not found in Greek and reflect Cyprus's relative separation from the Greek mainland. There is a stronger pronunciation of most letters in Cypriot Greek (except the vowels) that is different from 'Greek' Greek, for example, 'and' in Greek is pronounced like 'ke', while in Cypriot Greek, it is 'je'. These variations and the 'borrowing' can often render the Cypriot Greek dialect incomprehensible to non-Cypriot Greeks!

How to Learn the Language

There are many different ways to learn a language: online, in evening classes, with a private tutor, from a CD, or through total immersion, when you go and live in the country and stay with a local family, attending school during the day. Learning online is a challenge, as you have to be really self-motivated to do it. There is a large online facility at **www.kypros.org**, with courses in ancient and modern Greek (you want modern for Cyprus). The course is run in conjunction with the Cyprus Broadcasting Corporation and is free. Visit **www.cybc.com.cy/ Learn.htm**.

There are numerous private Greek-language tutors in the UK, particularly in London. Evening classes are run by almost all local education authorities, too. In Cyprus, the University of Cyprus runs Greek language classes in its School of Modern Greek. You can choose between a four-week summer class, Monday to Friday, five hours per day, and a one-term course, held twice a year, lasting 13 weeks and amounting to 260 teaching hours. For more information, contact **t** 22 43 47 90, **f** 22 34 55 63, **smgreek@ucy.ac.cy**, **www.ucy.ac.cy/publications/ school/english/intensive_courses.htm**.

Politics

Cyprus is a presidential republic. The president serves a five-year term, and exercises executive power through a Council of Ministers appointed by him. The Legislature comprises an 80-member House of Representatives, elected for a five-year term, although 24 seats reserved for Turkish Cypriot MPs were vacant in late 2004. The head of state is President Tassos Papadopoulos (since 28 February 2003), serving a five-year term. The president is both the head of state and leader of the government. He appoints the Council of Ministers, the cabinet of the Republic of Cyprus. The main political parties are the Restorative Party of the Working People (AKEL), Democratic Rally (DESY), Democratic Party (DEKO), United Democratic Union of Cyprus (KISOS) and the United Democrats Movement (EDI).

The last parliamentary election took place on 27 May 2001. The Restorative Party the Working People (AKEL) and Democratic Rally (DESY) won the most seats with 20 and 19 seats respectively. Democratic Party (DEKO) won nine, United Democratic Union of Cyprus (KISOS) four, and the remaining four parties, one seat each.

The current president of the House of Representatives, who is elected by a majority of MPs, is Demetris Christofias, the leader of AKEL.

Politics is one thing that everybody talks about in Cyprus. All Cypriots feel passionate about the 'situation' and everybody wants it resolved, although on their own terms. Everybody was affected by the Turkish invasion of 1974 and many people lost land, homes and relatives. Over 1,500 people seized by the

Turkish troops are still missing. Turkish families suffered losses, too, and both sides blame one another for failing to co-operate with the humanitarian issue of finding or identifying the missing. The Committee on Missing Persons in Cyprus (CMP) has recently been revived after five years of inactivity.

How the Problem Began

Following independence in 1960, tension between the Greek and Turkish Cypriots increased and culminated in serious intercommunal fighting in December 1963. From then until 1974 there were occasional outbreaks of further violence and the Turkish Cypriot minority retreated into small enclaves. A UN force was established in 1964. In July 1974 Turkish troops landed in northern Cyprus following a coup on the island by extremists against the elected president, which was backed by the military junta then in power in Greece. The invading forces landed off the northern coast of the island around Kyrenia. By the time a ceasefire was agreed three days later, Turkish troops held 3 per cent of the territory of Cyprus. Five thousand Greek Cypriots had fled their homes.

On 14 August 1974, just as agreement seemed about to be reached, the Turkish army mounted a second full-scale offensive, which increased its hold to include the booming tourist resort of Famagusta and the rich citrus-growing area of Morphou. All in all almost 36 per cent of the territory of the Republic of Cyprus came under Turkish military occupation, an area Turkey still holds today, despite international condemnation. As a result, 28 per cent of the Greek Cypriots were turned into refugees and 70 per cent of the economic potential of Cyprus came under military occupation. Moreover, thousands of people, including civilians, were killed.

The island has been effectively partitioned ever since. The 'Green Line' – the buffer zone dividing the two parts from the coast northwest of Morphou through Nicosia to Famagusta – is patrolled by United Nations troops. In 1983 the Turkish Cypriots announced the establishment of the 'Turkish Republic of Northern Cyprus' ('TRNC'). In common with the rest of the international community, apart from Turkey, Britain does not recognise any state in Cyprus other than the Republic of Cyprus.

The Future

Numerous attempts have been made to reunify the island, none of them successful. UN Secretary General Kofi Annan made what seemed like serious progress towards a result in 2004, as Cyprus prepared for EU accession in May. Negotiations reached a point where a referendum was held in April. The referendum in the Turkish Cypriot community was carried by a large majority (65 per cent voted yes); but in the Greek Cypriot community the settlement proposals were opposed by a large majority (76 per cent voted no). Cyprus entered the EU on 1 May 2004 as a divided island.

Since then, Turkey has agreed with the EU that membership talks will begin in October 2005. Part of the deal for these talks to begin is for Turkey to recognise the Greek Cypriot government. It is hoped that Turkey's accession to the EU, if it happens, will come hand-in-hand with the Cyprus problem being resolved.

If you want to discover more about the modern history of Cyprus be aware that a lot of websites are heavily biased either towards the Greek or Turkish argument, some to the point of ranting. For a broad overview of the country and a reasonably neutral assessment of the political state of affairs of Turkey, start with the Foreign Office at **www.fco.gov.uk**.

The Family and Everyday Life

The Cypriots may seem very 'British' in essence but there are important cultural differences to understand if you want to integrate yourself into Cypriot society. In Cyprus, family is more important than anything else. Many Cypriot women do not work once they have children, and the role of homemaker is valued. Grandparents and other relatives help with childcare. Children stay at home for many years, usually until they marry, and are not likely to move very far away from the family residence. Cypriots, both men and women, love to talk about their children and question other parents about their offspring. Children are a great conversation topic or ice-breaker! If you have Cypriot friends, you are also likely to be invited to family gatherings. It is polite to return the invitation.

In business, Cypriots are entrepreneurial and service-orientated. They like to do things well but there is also a strong desire to make a fast buck, particularly with the current property boom. People work hard but the work ethic is much healthier than that of the UK. Cypriots are visibly less stressed than the pale-faced Brits pouring off the aircraft in Larnaca and Paphos for their annual fortnight in the sun!

Cypriots do not share the same love of the beach and the outdoors as the holi-daymakers to whom they play host. Many will be happy to live in an apartment in town rather than a suburban house with a garden. Anything more than a 10-minute commute is jokingly referred to as a long distance, so urban living is popular. Gardening is definitely not on; rather than cultivate flowers, a city-dwelling Cypriot will probably buy a plot in the countryside for growing olives, pomegranates, oranges and lemons to squeeze over the *souvlaki*.

Typical interests include the village café or pub, backgammon and chess for men, particularly of the older generation, and family life, shopping and home-making among women. Football is a passion, with many staunch supporters of

British teams on the island. Families will go on outings at the weekend, either to the beach, or to Akamas Peninsula if they live in the west, or inland to the Troodos mountains.

The Role of Women in Cyprus

Women in Cyprus in the workplace enjoy nothing like the freedom or equal rights of women in Britain, despite what the EU laws say. Sexism is rife, particularly among older Cypriot men, even if it is not maliciously intended. Women in a Cypriot company will almost always have to answer to a man and, however educated or senior their position, will be expected to perform secretarial duties and make the coffee.

There are jobs for women, naturally, including British women (many of whom are employed in the hospitality business and in real estate), but advancement to senior level is difficult. Having said this, there are more and more female role models for young Cypriot women, including politician Kate Clerides, daughter of former Cyprus president Glafcos Clerides. There are many active women's groups who campaign for peace between the north and the south, among them Women Walk Home, Women's Civil Initiative for Peace, Actions in the Mediterranean and Hands Across the Divide.

Whether they intend to work or not, women in Cyprus marry young. There is usually intense family pressure to find a husband and produce grandchildren. An engagement is cause for great celebration and a broken engagement is regarded by the family as a shameful tragedy. A very small percentage of the population still practises arranged marriages. Most couples marry in the Greek Orthodox church, usually on a Sunday, followed by a lavish ceremony involving the entire local community, the bride in a frothy white dress, singing, dancing and *bouzouki* music. In urban communities the invitation to the wedding is often in the form of an advertisement in the paper, ensuring a large turnout. Many Cypriot girls still come with a dowry, usually in the form of property, although in practice both sides of the family will contribute towards the couple's first home.

Diversity and Tolerance

Homosexuality has only been legal in Cyprus since 1998. The Cypriot mentality is typically Mediterranean and machismo is rife. Close-knit family ties and the strong influence of the church mean many gay men don't come out, or are forced to move away from their families to live in places like Limassol, Larnaca or Paphos, where they can live a more open life. However, there are plenty of gay-friendly bars and restaurants, and certain beaches, that are popular with gay holidaymakers and Cypriots alike, and the atmosphere is one of tolerance.

Racism is an extremely sensitive subject in Cyprus. On an island famed for its hospitality, xenophobia has no place. But Cypriots have enormous national pride and the very essence of the country – the famous Cypriot hospitality – is being undermined in the eyes of many by the need to import foreign workers. Ten years ago all the workers in a hotel would be Cypriot. Today, they're from Russia, Bulgaria, Romania and any number of other, mainly East European countries, as are labourers on building sites and petrol pump attendants. Now that Cyprus is a member of the EU, the foreign workforce is likely to expand further. Some Cypriots openly express dismay about this – but the jobs need to be filled.

There's also an ongoing problem of the ingrained suspicion and, in places, hatred of Turkey. Having said this, though, there are Turkish Cypriots who live in

Aphrodite's Legacy

It was around 1200 BC when Aphrodite, Goddess of Love and Beauty, emerged from the gentle jade-coloured sea foam at Petra tou Romiou, a craggy boulder which rises up out of the water next to the white cliffs between Pissouri and Paphos. The name Aphrodite, in fact, means 'born in the foam'. She was the most ancient goddess in the Olympian pantheon.

Aphrodite led a colourful life. An awestruck Paris, son of King Priam of Troy, once gave her a golden apple in recognition of her astonishing beauty. Zeus put Aphrodite in charge of wedlock and arranged her marriage to the good but ugly craft-god Hephaistos. She took solace in the strong arms of Ares, god of war, but then fell in love with Adonis.

Eros, Aphrodite's son, accidentally wounded her bosom with one of his arrows. Reeling from the wound, she took solace in her mineral pool, the famed Baths of Aphrodite on the Akamas Peninsula. The hunter Adonis was within sight that day, and the love he inspired in Aphrodite was the greatest and most painful she would ever know. Adonis, however, was killed by a boar, a jealous Ares in disguise. Aphrodite heard his cries from her swan-drawn chariot, high above the island's highest forested peaks. She summoned Menthe, the spirit of mint, who sprinkled nectar on his blood, and red anemones burst from the earth, their petals scattered by the wind. ('Anemos' in Greek means wind.)

The goddess left many legacies. The Italian poet Arioste named 'Fontana Amorosa' the natural spring on the Akamas Peninsula from which Aphrodite used to drink. Take a sip from it and you may fall in love. Take a dip in the sea at Petra tou Romiou under a full moon and you may discover the secret of eternal youth. Or swim in the shaded Baths of Aphrodite on Akamas to improve your fertility.

In the 12th century BC, an elaborate sanctuary was built in her honour her at Palea Pafos (present-day Kouklia) – the most significant of a dozen such consecrated sites in Cyprus. You can see artefacts from the site in the Cyprus Museum in Nicosia, adorned with erotic scenes. The Baths of Aphrodite, the grotto where Aphrodite purified herself after her many trysts, is a popular tourist site now, and the Fontana Amorosa is a few miles further on.

the southern part of the island in villages alongside Greek Cypriots. There is a genuine desire to solve the Turkish 'problem'. Expats should find Cyprus a conservative and patriotic but essentially easygoing, friendly place to live.

Religion

The Orthodox Church of Cyprus is extremely powerful and until the Turkish invasion of 1974 was the biggest landowner. It still owns large tracts of land today, much of it prime seafront plots devoted to agriculture. Its foundation is attributed directly to Sts Barnabas, Paul and Mark (in AD 45). The church makes a significant contribution to the historical, cultural and social life of Cyprus.

The overwhelming majority of Cypriots – around 78 per cent – belong to the Orthodox Church, and many Cypriots attend on church on Sunday mornings and religious holidays, although church-going is on the decline among young people. Other religions in Cyprus include Muslim (18 per cent), Maronite, Armenian Apostolic and 'other' (4 per cent in total). There are churches of many denominations on the island – Anglican, Roman Catholic, Coptic, Russian Orthodox, for example – but there are no synagogues, Buddhist or Hindu temples. You can attend a Greek Orthodox service if you wish; the services are all in Greek. *See* 'Church Services in Cyprus', pp.182–3, for details of service times.

Cyprus has some wonderful monasteries to explore, not least the one in the centre of lively Ayia Napa. Pick up the Cyprus Tourism Organisation's publication '10,000 years of History and Civilisation', which has a guide to the monasteries and how to see them. Many are in remote mountain areas and some are closed to the public. Most, in any case, are kept locked as they house beautiful icons and frescoes, so you need to ask at the village café or taverna if the priest can be summoned to show you round. One, Stavrovouni, is only open to men. Chrysorogiatissa Monastery, 25 miles from Paphos in the mountains, is spectacular, with its own winery, producing some of the best vintage wine on the island. Kykkos is the most famous, housing a rare and valuable icon to St Luke. There's a small museum, as well. When you visit monasteries or churches, observe local custom and dress respectfully; also, do not use flash photography.

Getting Married in Church

You can get married in Cyprus, if you possess the right documentation, at a civil ceremony or in church. Anglican or Catholic weddings can be held in a number of pretty chapels, mostly associated with hotels like the Anassa in Latchi and the Elysium in Paphos. There are further possible wedding venues in Ayia Napa, Derynia, Larnaca, Limassol, Nicosia, Peyia, Pissouri, Protaras or the Troodos Mountains.

Letting Your Property

08

Cyprus is a good investment opportunity for a number of reasons. First, it is one of the few true year-round destinations in Europe and even the traditionally quieter areas like Ayia Napa and Protaras are becoming livelier in the winter months. Rental income can be maximised over a much longer period than with other holiday destinations where there are short, intense summers lasting only three months. Other bonuses include the ease of communication, as practically everybody in Cyprus speaks English, the low crime rate, the high quality of life, the relatively low cost of living, low taxation and a sophisticated infrastructure.

The government's investment in tourism facilities like golf courses and marinas, and its commitment to diversifying the market coming to Cyprus are also good pointers for the buy-to-let market. Another positive factor is the opening up of air routes to the island, with Cyprus Airways now seeing competition from low-cost carriers like Helios Airways, which, in addition to bringing down flight costs, opens up links with regional airports in the UK.

The lettings market in Cyprus is healthy at the moment. Some would say booming, but they are probably estate agents. The sharp upward trend in the market of the last few years has levelled off slightly, and the cost of buying and living on the island has certainly risen in the year since Cyprus joined the EU. But, either way, the signs for the future are positive. Independent holidaymakers, as opposed to those who book packages, are on the increase. New businesses are are being set up now that Cyprus is a member of the EU and the whole process has become easier; these new businesses lead to demand for corporate lets. The number of people buying is on the increase, and these buyers need somewhere to rent in the short term while they get a feel for the island, and while their own property is being built.

Property prices (and therefore rental prices) are, however, likely to rise, and too steep an increase could make the island less competitive in comparison with other sunshine destinations. Cyprus is in a transitional period until 2008, when VAT will be imposed on land, so the market is predicted to keep increasing as people buy to beat the deadline. Also, Cyprus has limited remaining plots on the beach, with vast tracts of seafront already developed, so seaside locations will only increase in price and should command the highest of all rental prices. One has to assume that at some point the market will right itself and property prices will stabilise.

If you are buying now, you should be able to help finance your home in Cyprus by letting it out, at least with demand for rentals outstripping supply for the next few years. This might be a commercial venture, where the home is a business and is (ideally) filled with tenants for most of the year. Or it may be a more casual arrangement, whereby the home is let to friends and family informally. Neither, particularly the latter, can be absolutely guaranteed to cover the cost of your mortgage, whatever you hear from estate agents and developers. The market may be buoyant at the moment but there are no certainties with property other than that the mortgage will have to be paid. Competition is also a lot stiffer than it was. Many new developers have sprung up, former contractors who have decided to have a go at making some money themselves. You will be competing against any of these who decide to let, as well as buy-to-let schemes.

Prices change all the time so it is difficult to pinpoint the exact return you can expect. But generally speaking the monthly income from rental should certainly exceed the mortgage payments and capital growth is currently between 5 and 7 per cent. With a big enough deposit, and a constant stream of tenants, your buy-to-let investment could be self-funding.

If you're planning to finance your property primarily by letting, this should be a major factor throughout your whole selection process. Your main goal is to maximise profit, and this should influence the location of the property, its size, style and amenities. Put yourself in the position of your would-be tenants and what they will want: neutral décor, a pool, at least one en-suite bathroom, perhaps. If you're only planning to let to family and friends casually, this is less important, but you should consider matters like storing your own belongings, and creating enough space to accommodate your tenants' holiday wardrobes, and the supply of extra bed linen for them.

If you're aiming to participate in a buy-to-let scheme, the considerations will be different again, as you should be aiming for long-term lets and need to think about what type of person might rent your property and why. You may, in these schemes, be more influenced by the developer with whom you have chosen to work; in many buy-to-let projects in Cyprus, the developer takes the risk and guarantees the rent for the first couple of years, while you simply put in the money.

This chapter refers mainly to the 'serious' letting business, although casual letters and those in buy-to-let schemes may want to bear in mind some of the points, as well. Casual letters, for example, should certainly draw up a contract, even if they are only letting to friends.

Location, Choice of Property and Letting Potential

Location

Location, location, location is the most important factor to bear in mind when planning to let a property. If you seriously want it to be a business venture, a decent house or apartment in a thriving tourist or business area should do well, while a traditional house in a mountain village will attract a specialist market only. If your heart is set on the latter, you should consider any lettings a bonus, rather than a necessity to finance the whole venture. Always, keep in mind that the best investment is property on or near the beach. Demand for these properties is very high, yielding both high resale values and high rental return. The property will cost you a lot more in the first place, though.

The success of a letting venture will depend on the tourist traffic to an area, its attractions and services, the size of the property, the seasonality of the area and what the lettings market will bear. A lavish five-bedroom villa in Coral Bay will probably be harder to let than a two-bedroom town house in Kato Paphos, for example. A large house in Ayia Napa may be a tough one on which to make a profit, as the resort is more seasonal than Larnaca, Limassol and Paphos. An apartment in Nicosia will probably attract a business market.

Paphos is one of the most popular regions, although it is also the most expensive. The best areas are reckoned to be Kato Paphos, Tomb of the Kings, Universal, Chloraka and Peyia. Protaras and Ayia Napa are not yet fully fledged year-round resorts, although this is changing. Summer rentals are practically guaranteed and command high prices, and the season is getting longer. Nobody can predict the future but when the two halves of the island are reunited, this area will take off because of its proximity to the beautiful town of Famagusta, located on a sweeping bay and formerly one of the leading resorts on the island. In the Protaras area, Kapparis and Pernera are good for maximising holiday lets. Areas around Paralimni and Dereynia are reckoned to be better for 12-month rentals.

If you intend to go to the residential lettings market, Nicosia, Limassol and Larnaca, close to business and commercial centres, are your best bet. Property in the villages outside Larnaca is still very good value, yet with houses and plots right on the beach and easy access from the airport and the town. Detached villas in the suburbs, ideally with a pool, appeal to the family market.

As for the type of property, agents in Cyprus reckon that a one-bedroom apartment will provide the best annual return – in 2004 an average of 7 per cent per annum, island-wide. According to surveys, Nicosia yields the best return in terms of area, with a 6.8 per cent average for 2004. This is because of the demand for corporate lets, where people are prepared to pay more, and also because property in the capital is reasonably priced. One-bedroom apartments in Nicosia are in particular demand.

If you intend to employ a letting agency to let out your property, don't buy without consulting them and finding out which areas do best for holiday lets and what size of property it is easiest to keep filled all year round. Some letting agencies won't even touch a property without a pool, so think very carefully about this. Make sure you speak to agents who deal with the whole of the island (meaning the southern, Greek-speaking part) as well as those that specialise in specific areas. Some agents let property in the Turkish-occupied north as well as the south but you need to be clear that they understand that the markets attracted to the two are completely different. *See* 'Letting and Managing Agents', pp.163–4. If you plan to let your property yourself, make sure you understand your target market – families, couples, retired, young, active? If you're planning to advertise on the internet on an English-language website, you'll probably attract British customers, so be sure to bear their tastes in mind when choosing and equipping your property.

Climate

Climate is not a particular consideration in Cyprus as there is little variation along the coast. Larnaca and the eastern resorts of Ayia Napa, Protaras and Paralimni are slightly drier and less humid than the west, while Nicosia is hottest in summer. What you should bear in mind, though, is when you will occupy the property yourself. January to March is the low season when you are least likely to attract holiday lets – but do you want to spend your hard-earned holiday in your hard-earned place in the sun in the middle of winter, in a very sleepy resort, when the weather can be rainy and dull? If you're planning to use the property yourself in winter, you might want to consider somewhere nearer a year-round town like Larnaca or Limassol.

Attractions

Cyprus is relatively small and very easy to drive around, but you should also bear in mind the attractions of each area when choosing a property with letting potential. The water parks and sandy beaches of Ayia Napa and its neighbours will appeal to the family market, while Paphos has history and culture in the centre of the town, at the Tombs of the Kings and on the waterfront, as well as three excellent golf courses, in demand year-round, so it is good for winter lettings. Limassol also has a historic centre, with easy access to the Troodos Mountains an added bonus. 'New' areas around these main tourist centres are doing well at the moment, as well as brand new 'discoveries' like Ormidia (between Larnaca and Protaras), Pyrgos (just outside Limassol) and Souni (between Limassol and Paphos). Bear in mind that most holidaymakers want a sense of atmosphere; they have chosen Cyprus for its local character, after all. So even if you're buying on a new development, choose one in a village with a 'real' centre with a bit of tradition – pretty church, a taverna, views and local walks.

Local Facilities

If you are aiming for short-term holiday lets, look at the facilities in the imme-diate area. Tavernas and bars within walking distance are a huge bonus, as is a supermarket or at least a grocery shop. Proximity to the beach is ideal, but beachfront property is very expensive and in Limassol and Paphos you are unlikely to have this. Larnaca has the advantage of being a busy, lively town with an excellent beach right along the seafront, so an apartment in the centre should do well. Many people in holiday lets in Cyprus will not balk at driving to the beach; they'll probably have a rental car in any case if they intend to explore.

A pool is almost essential for a successful holiday let, particularly as the beaches in many parts of the island are not spectacular, and the heat is so intense in summer. Even a shared pool is better than no pool. Big balconies, a roof terrace, a bit of outside space – all these will appeal to a British market keen to spend as much time outside as possible.

The Right Property

Once you've decided on a location, be sure to choose the right type of property. It's hard to describe many older, town-centre homes in Cyprus as architecturally beautiful, but make sure you style the property well for its photograph, which is likely to be the basis on which most tenants make their decision. Potted geraniums, a smart front door, pretty shutters, a tidy lawn – all make a difference!

In some parts of the world tenants are attracted to older properties with character, but in Cyprus anything in an urban location is likely to be boxy-looking; it's the village and mountain properties that ooze style and authenticity. So, unless you're buying a photogenic stone house in the mountains surrounded by vineyards, by all means go for a new-build on an attractive development as your letting investment; one near a golf development will have added attractions and a specific market. It will be easier to maintain and if it's brand new it will be under guarantee. Almost all new-builds in Cyprus have great entertaining space and an open-plan interior design. But check this, particularly if you are buying off-plan; a family holiday home should have space for the whole family to eat together, and a well-organised kitchen.

The number of bedrooms is critical. For the family market, two or three is ideal – many rental agencies say there is a shortage of two-bedroom properties, which are the best size for a family of four. For long-term lets, smaller properties do better – one or two bedrooms should suffice. Four-bedroom villas are certainly spacious, but you'll need to find large families, groups of friends or people prepared to pay extra and perhaps not use one of the bedrooms.

The Right Price

It goes without saying that for a commercial venture you want to pay as little as possible for a property and maximise the letting return on it. Its likely increase in value is also important. Keep an eye out for up-and-coming areas where new property is cheap. In addition to the traditional areas (Paphos, Peyia, Limassol), the surroundings of Limassol are getting more popular because of their 'village' atmosphere and the proximity to the town. There are several satellite villages around Paphos representing good value, while established suburbs like Peyia, with its lovely views and pretty houses, are very expensive now. Some of the villages west of Larnaca are tipped to be the next big thing and you can pick up a spectacular house for a bargain price – but you will have to word your marketing material carefully to point out their advantages for rentals. Even visitors very familiar with Cyprus may not have heard of some of these places; on all their previous trips they will have driven straight past them on the motorway.

If you plan to use the property yourself, do the maths on the return you need to make to leave a few weeks free for your own holiday. If, for example, you're aiming for year-round tenants, remember to factor in, say, a month for your own use, and never base your calculations on 100 per cent occupancy for the rest of the year, unless you already have a waiting list!

Letting and Managing Agents

In an ideal world, you would find your tenants yourself and not have to pay anybody a management fee or a commission. But realistically this requires a level of commitment that most people do not have time for, particularly when they are living in another country. It is therefore far simpler and less stressful to use a managing agent. Although you will have to pay them a fee or a commission, by using their services you are more likely to fill your property with tenants year-round. There is no shortage of managing agents in Cyprus and standards vary. As with any country, the business has its sharks who may try things like renting your property on the quiet and pretending to you that it is empty, or creaming off some of your rent, or charging you a registration fee and then doing very little to let your property. Fortunately, people like this are few and far between and as you get to know more people on the island you can always ask friends to check up on the property when you are not there.

Managing agents in Cyprus charge between 20 per cent and 40 per cent of gross letting income. To get into their catalogue, contact them the summer before you want to let, although the Internet allows much shorter lead-times, so if you need to let quickly, choose an agent with a good website.

There are many things to look out for when choosing a letting agent, not just what they charge. How do they market the property? On the Internet, in their own newspaper, in the Cypriot press, via direct marketing like e-mail and SMS alerts? Do you pay for listing the property, or do you only pay a marketing fee once it is let? What commission do they charge, if any? How many would-be tenants are registered with the company? What are its opening hours? How are prospective tenants dealt with? What kind of feedback is provided to you and how often? What information is sent to tenants, or shown to them online – floor plans, photographs, 360-degree images? Always check an agent out. Ask for references from current owners, and to see income statements from other properties. Ask about how and where they advertise, and check that you have access when you want – some are not keen to let the owner use the property during peak weeks. Be sure to have done your research into the going rate for property similar to yours before you hire an agent.

What to Expect from a Management Contract

Management contracts normally last a year and cover everything from cleaning between lets, to pool maintenance, house and garden maintenance, meeting and greeting guests, and being on hand to help with problems. They will also make periodic checks when the property is empty, and assist you if a difficult tenant refuses to leave. The managing agent should handle all your paperwork and collect the funds from rentals.

On a long-term rental contract, apart from finding the tenants, you should expect them to clean the property between tenants, prepare the rental contract, take copies of tenant identification and hold the tenant's deposit, prepare and check the property's inventory, greet new tenants and hand over the keys, keep on top of tenants' payments, check them out when they leave, return deposits and send you a report after each rental finishes.

If you are participating in a buy-to-let scheme, the agent may well furnish the property for you, manage it and act as your signatory. Other services a mainte-nance contract might include are: utilities connection and bill payment, appliance checks and maintenance, rubbish disposal, laundry, window cleaning, decorating, pest control, keyholding, post-collection and forwarding, emergency maintenance and providing a 24-hour helpline number for landlord, tenants and guests.

Marketing

If you are not using a letting agent, marketing a property is a necessary evil and you won't get any rentals without it unless you're incredibly lucky! Decide on your target market and tailor your marketing material accordingly. For example, if you are aiming at families, point out any safety features of the prop-erty, the availability of outside space, any facilities for small children, and things for families to do in the area.

Decide what medium is most appropriate to your property. For example, a website is fine but only if you're equipped to run it, update it and respond to e-mail enquiries. If you're not computer literate, you will need to rely on someone else to maintain your website for you, which can be frustrating.

Try to find out what level of response to expect from different media and set yourself a budget. Ask other owners in a similar position what works for them. Maximise any medium you use by responding to enquiries quickly and building up a database. Keep in touch with your past customers

Pricing Your Property

The letting market in Cyprus is very competitive with hundreds of properties listed for rent every month. Be sure to price your property correctly; there are masses of websites offering property to rent, so you can easily get a feel for prices in your chosen area. Pick up local agents' free newspapers while you're on the island, and speak to as many as possible. Find out about services like car hire as well – you may be able to make extra money by arranging a rental car for your tenants and taking a commission.

When you're setting the price, ask yourself a few questions. Will you accept children? Pets? Groups of young singles? Corporate lets? What will your payment terms be? Have you factored in all the running costs and expenses as well as the mortgage payments? Consider what length of rentals you are looking for. You could opt for one- or two-week blocks, or you could be more fluid, accommodating the growing 'long weekend' market. Or perhaps a mixture of the two, aiming for higher occupancy in summer, when you should be able to sell one- and two-week blocks, and flexible periods in the low season. Bear in mind Christmas and Easter and whether you'll need to go for, say, a 10-day rental at Christmas to get in two weekends, if Christmas Day falls on a Saturday.

Remember to adjust your rates for seasonality. High season is July and August, mid-season June, late September and October – and even perhaps Christmas and Easter. Mid-season rates are usually about 25 per cent less than high season. Keep an eye out for special events in Cyprus which might suddenly push rates up and offer an opportunity for you to create an extra 'high season' week.

Broadly speaking, you should budget for an occupancy level of worst-case 60 per cent during the high season, and 30 to 50 per cent during the low season. Holiday lettings should command around CY£60 per day in the high season for a two-bedroom property with a swimming pool, while a two- or three-bedroom villa with a private pool should bring in revenue of around CY£150 per day. Long-term lettings command a monthly rather than a daily rate. Expect to earn up to CY£400 per month for a two-bedroom apartment, depending on the area, and CY£1,000 per month for a three-bedroom villa with a pool.

Word-of-Mouth Recommendations and Repeat Bookings

Starting from scratch can be daunting, but once you've got a client base established, remember that one loyal customer is worth at least two new ones. If you do it right, repeat business and word-of-mouth recommendations will be your most valuable marketing tools. The way to ensure loyalty is to make sure the property lives up to the client's expectations, and that the administration runs smoothly. Enquiries need to be followed up quickly and efficiently, and any problems on site need to be sorted out with speed. Without going mad on lavish fittings, don't cut corners on quality.

Give your customers an incentive to recommend you to their friends – a case of wine if their friends book, for example. Be sure to contact your database anew every year and plant the idea of a holiday in Cyprus in their minds. Personalise all your communication with them. Develop a newsletter to keep people informed about fun and interesting things happening on the island. Follow up every booking with a questionnaire and a personal call or letter.

You can also maximise word-of-mouth recommendations by making contacts on the island. Befriend the local taverna owner. Make yourself known in the village; you never know who will drop in at the taverna asking casually about property in the area. If you're buying a new property, it always helps to befriend the developer, too, as they handle enquiries all the time. Find out what special interest societies operate in the area. For example, if visitors are coming to the Limassol Wine Festival or the Cyprus Rally, they will need somewhere to stay. You can always offer commission to any locals who place guests in your property. Last, get to know other property owners and pass on contacts. If you send an enquiry to a neighbour when your own property is full, they should do the same for you.

Advertising

Press advertising is expensive and somewhat random. Choose your medium carefully; one small ad in a UK national newspaper will be expensive but if it is placed alongside a Cyprus feature it could generate a big response. Consider ads in property magazines and high-circulation local papers. Advertising in specialist magazines – birdwatching, archaeology, walking – pays off for some but is more of a risk.

If your property is likely to appeal to people already in Cyprus, place ads in Cypriot newspapers as well; the *Cyprus Weekly* and the *Cyprus Mail* have huge property sections. When you advertise in the Cypriot press, bear in mind that there's a certain way of wording the ad. You should state the plot size, the percentage of the plot built on, and the amount of outside space. If you are letting through an agent, ask if they have their own newspaper, or will market the property in the local press for you, and also to markets other than Brits – Greeks, Russians, Germans, for example.

If you are paying to advertise on a website, be careful. Don't fall for the number of 'hits' a website claims to have; many of these are hugely exaggerated, unless the site owner can show you proper statistics, of course. If the site looks good, works efficiently and comes up in Google or Yahoo! when you search on 'Cyprus' and 'Property', it is more likely to get a lot of visitors. As with any advertising, try it for a while and if it doesn't work for you, try something else.

Your Own Website

There are hundreds of properties in Cyprus advertised on the Internet. While your own small website is unlikely to be indexed by search engines – and so will not come up on a search for 'Cyprus property' – it is still the cheapest and most effective form of brochure to which you can refer people once they have made their enquiry. All they have to do is visit the site and print off the information, saving you all the cost.

A site of a few pages costs practically nothing to start. Domain names are cheap to register (literally just a few pounds for a .com address) with companies like 1&1 Internet and a simple, clean design can be prepared easily, either by you or a web designer. Put pictures of your property up at the correct resolution (so the page doesn't take too long to download) and add as much written description as you can. As you become more experienced, you can add things like a visitors' book, client testimonials, FAQs and local information.

Your site should include up-to-date rates and a means to contact you by e-mail or phone. Trying to add things like real-time availability is probably beyond the sphere of most property owners. You can, however, set up online payments using a system like Paypal (**www.paypal.com**) whereby people can pay to rent your property using their credit card through Paypal's secure site. You do not need to set up a secure site yourself to do this.

Friends and Family

Spread the word through friends and family, as well as work colleagues. If you aim for a realistic 60 per cent occupancy, and aim to spend, say, two months of the year in the property yourself, you only need to find 10 to 15 clients a year, assuming bookings are for two weeks. It should not be hard to get this ball rolling with a decent network of acquaintances!

Make it clear to friends and family that they are expected to pay, and to pay on time. They should have the same terms as everybody else, and the same inventory check. It is important to be firm with everybody, nearest and dearest included, that your insurance does not cover their personal property, to avoid any nasty falling-out in the event of disaster.

Managing Viewings

If you're in the long-term letting market, you should expect people to come for viewings. A few simple tricks of the trade can turn these into business! Clear all clutter, and make sure the kitchen surfaces are clean and empty. Minimise what's on show in your bathroom and make sure it's spotless. Fresh flowers, healthy houseplants and bowls of fruit make a good impression. The old trick of brewing coffee just before people come works well, as do vanilla-scented candles or pods of vanilla in a warm oven. Windows should be clean and any paint jobs that need doing patched up. Show the property with lights on.

Outside, make sure the rubbish is cleared away and the lawn and garden plants are in good condition. Put toys and outdoor clutter away and make sure the pool is clean, and terraces and balconies swept. Show the guests round in a logical progression of rooms, making sure you reveal the property's best feature – a view, a lovely pool or garden, for example, with enthusiasm. They will probably ask to look round alone, but be on hand to answer any questions and be sure to get any of the property's big selling points into the conversation.

Equipping the Property

Once you have selected your property, equip it with the facilities your tenants will expect. The only way to get repeat business is for the property to exceed the guests' expectations. Many of the developers will help you furnish your new-build. Kleanthis Savva in Paphos (**www.ksavva-developers.com**), for example, is particularly good, with a large showroom of furniture and kitchen and bathroom fittings. The office has several English staff who will accompany new owners on shopping trips to the many furniture suppliers around Paphos and offer them help.

Furnish inexpensively (although not at rock-bottom prices – you want it to last) as things will get broken. Theft is rare in Cyprus but tenants inevitably treat a rental property less carefully than their own home. If you are aiming at the higher income bracket, things like dishwasher, microwave and satellite TV, as well as comfortable garden furniture, are mandatory. A telephone is not standard and most people have mobile phones in any case.

It goes without saying that a rental property needs to be well maintained at all times, and that its external appearance is impressive, as this is the first view your guests will have. Other than that, the property should have facilities to suit the needs of your target audience, for example, a travel cot and high chair in good working order if you are trying to attract young families.

Documentation

Send your guests as much information as possible before they arrive. You can get a supply of maps and brochures free of charge from the Cyprus Tourism Organisation. You should also supply directions on how to get to the house, emergency contact numbers and the contact number for whoever will be letting them in. Holiday renters appreciate some kind of guestbook inside the house, with details of restaurant recommendations, things to do and comments from other guests. The more personal recommendations you can give, the better. The property should also come with an inventory and whoever is handling the meeting and greeting needs to check this at the beginning and at the end of the let, and take money for any repairs off the deposit.

Meet and Greet

It is always a good idea to have somebody meet and greet your guests, to hand over the keys and answer any questions they may have. This person can also keep an eye on the property for you.

Cleaning

Any rental property should be spotlessly clean. If you are not using a managing agent, you should be able to find a local cleaner, although this may not be so easy if you are in a rural area of Cyprus, as the cleaner may not have a car. Provide them with a list of exactly what you want doing and make sure that they have all the equipment they need.

Kitchen

Make sure the kitchen has everything a holidaymaker will need. As big a fridge as you can manage will be welcome particularly in the heat of summer, and for families. A microwave is useful for young families. Make sure the gas bottle is full and that the clients have a telephone number to call should it run out. Check that there is enough cutlery and crockery for the number of people in the let, as well as sufficient cooking equipment.

Bathroom

Most people appreciate it if you supply towels as part of the service, even if you charge a deposit for them. Soap and toilet roll are also an appropriate gesture, particularly for people arriving on flights at unsociable hours when the shops are shut. If you don't want your bathroom towels to be used around the pool or on the beach, say so, and think about supplying separate beach towels.

Laundry Facilities

A washing machine and tumble dryer are standard in a holiday rental property and are especially important in Cyprus, where the hot weather generates a lot of washing. You could be generous and provide enough washing powder for a couple of washes, to save your clients having to buy a big box.

Bedrooms

Bed linen must be spotless and in good condition. It is worth investing in good quality beds when you equip your property, as they will last a lot longer. Supply waterproof removable mattress covers if you are expecting small children.

Living Areas

Keep furniture and upholstery in good condition and try to introduce some touches of Cyprus into the property, unless, of course, you are going for something ultramodern and minimalist. Make sure the fireplace is clean and working for winter lets. You are not, however, expected to provide fuel, although you should make it clear what kind of fuel can be burnt in this fireplace and where the tenants can buy logs if they want them.

Air-conditioning

Air-conditioning is a huge bonus for holidaymakers not used to the heat. If you don't have it, make sure you do have ceiling fans that work.

Swimming Pool

The pool should be clean and well maintained, with a properly functioning filter that your clients will hopefully not have to touch. In Cyprus, you do not have to heat a swimming pool in summer, although you will need to if you think your guests will want to swim in December and January. Make sure the pool has features like a net for scooping out debris, and a cover if appropriate. If the pool is fenced for the safety of young children, you should point this out in your marketing literature as many families would consider this a bonus.

Welcome Pack

All arriving guests appreciate a basic welcome pack including things like bread, milk, teabags, coffee, sugar, breakfast cereal and juice. You can make more money by offering a shopping service for them and stocking the fridge before they arrive. Another nice touch is something inexpensive like a bottle of chilled Cypriot wine, or locally produced olive oil.

Formalising the Letting

Any letting agency will have its own contracts for you and your tenants to sign. You may want to have these checked over by a lawyer. If you handle the lettings yourself, you still need a contract in line with Cypriot law, which should be drawn up by a lawyer. You should be protected in the event of a dispute with the tenants, and the tenants need to be clear what the rules are for breakages, damage to the property, what is and what is not covered in the insurance (tenants' personal property is not usually covered) and those relating to the development or village – loud music late at night, for example, or pets.

Security deposits, monthly rent, payment terms, occupancy dates and other conditions must be discussed and agreed before signing the lease. Note that in Cyprus with long-term rentals the payment of utilities such as gas, electricity, refuse collection and telephone bills is generally the responsibility of the tenant; in short-term rentals the responsibility lies with the landlord.

Whether you go for a long-term or short-term rental, you or your appointed agent will have to check your property regularly to make sure that it is maintained correctly and well looked after. If you have tenants in situ, you'll need to give them enough notice before doing so. One day in advance is sufficient in Cyprus. You are generally responsible for repairs to the property with the exception of breakages by tenants, minor repairs and normal wear and tear.

References

Glossary of Useful and Technical Terms

Annual percentage rate (APR)
This is a value created according to a government formula intended to reflect the true annual cost of borrowing, expressed as a percentage.

Appreciation
The increase in the value of property owing to changes in market conditions, inflation or other causes.

Asset
Items of value owned by an individual, for example, money in the bank, stocks and shares; property and debts owed to an individual by others.

Building density
The percentage of a given plot of land on which you are allowed to build; anything from 10 per cent or less on agricultural land to more than 100 per cent in an urban area.

Building zone
A zone in a given area which has been allocated for development. A building zone may be surrounded by agricultural land, on which you cannot build, or on which building is severely restricted.

Buy-to-let
A scheme whereby you invest in a property with the sole intention of letting it out for profit.

Capital gains tax
A tax levied on capital gains.

Commission
The estate agent's cut on your purchase. Typically, this is 4 or 5 per cent of the purchase price and is paid by the vendor.

Contract price
The price you will pay for a property; a matter of negotiation between you and the seller.

CREAA
The Cyprus Real Estate Agents' Association, a body that is supposed to regulate the activities of estate agents on the island. Any agent that is a member should display its licence number in its office and on its letterhead.

Credit
An agreement in which a borrower receives something of value in exchange for a promise to repay the lender at a later date.

Debt	An amount owed to somebody else.
Default	Failure to make a mortgage payment within a specified period of time.
Deposit	A sum of money given in advance to secure your interest in a property. Typically, this is CY£2000.
Depreciation	A decline in the value of property; the opposite of appreciation. Depreciation is also an accounting term which shows the declining monetary value of an asset and is used as an expense to reduce taxable income.
Developer	An individual or a company who acquires land and builds property on it with a view to selling that property. Not to be confused with an estate agent.
Donum	A unit of land at measurement: 1,335 sq m (14,000 sq ft).
Equity	A homeowner's financial interest in a property. Equity is the difference between the fair market value of the property and the amount still owed on its mortgage.
Estate agent	A middleman who sells the property of developers or private individuals for a commission.
Immovable property	Property including land and buildings.
Inspection trip	A visit to Cyprus, often funded or part funded by a developer or estate agent with a specific few to showing properties to serious potential buyers.
Joint ownership	The most common way in which expats purchase property in Cyprus. Your portion is your portion and your partner's is theirs. When one of you dies then that person's portion will be dealt with in accordance with Cyprus law.
Liabilities	A person's financial obligations, including long-term and short-term debt as well as any other amounts that are owed to others.
Liquid asset	Any asset that is easily converted into cash.
Maturity	The date on which the principal balance of a loan, bond or other financial instrument becomes due and payable.
Notice of completion	The sale agreement will include a clause that the developer must provide you, or your attorney, who is usually your lawyer, with notification that the works for a particular stage are complete and that payment for that stage is now due. That official notification, a 'notice of completion', will be signed either by the architect or by the supervising civil engineer. After service of the notice of completion, the sale agreement will allow you a short period of grace to make the payment.

Off-plan　　　　　Buying a property which is not yet built, simply from looking at the plans.

Pink slip　　　　　Colloquial term for a Cypriot residence permit.

Power of attorney　A legal document that authorises another person to act on one's behalf. A power of attorney can grant complete authority or can be limited to certain acts and/or periods of time. If you are living in the UK, you would typically grant power of attorney to your lawyer in Cyprus so that they can act on your behalf.

Principal　　　　　The amount borrowed or remaining unpaid. The part of the monthly payment that reduces the remaining balance of a mortgage.

Specific performance　The primary purpose of specific performance is to protect the purchaser. While specific performance requires both parties to perform, specifically, their obligations under the terms of the sale agreement, the vendor will always be protected by the wrongful act of the purchaser. The most common reason for invoking the specific performance law is when a property developer unreasonably delays transferring title.

Stage payments　　There is no given formula for stage payments; larger developers will tend to be strict in the contractual terms that they lay down whereas smaller developers will be more fluid.

Stamp duty　　　　Stamp duty is payable by the purchaser on signature of contract at the rate of CY£1.50 per CY£1,000 up to CY£100,000 and CY£2 per CY£1,000 thereafter.

Title deeds　　　　The document that states that you are the owner of a property.

Transfer fees　　　A fee charged by the district land registry based on the market value of property. This is paid by the purchaser.

Internet Vocabulary

If you are planning to research property in Cyprus, it helps to be Internet-savvy! Don't ever try to buy property or pay over any money to a website.

Bandwidth　　　　How much you can send through a connection. Usually measured in bits per second. A fast modem can move about 57,000 bits in one second.

Blog or web log　　A blog (short for 'web log') is a type of web page that serves as a publicly accessible personal journal (or log) for an individual. You might want to start one to record your day-to-day life in Cyprus for friends back home to read – it could be the next Peter Mayle-style bestseller!

Broadband

This refers to high-speed data transmission in which a single cable can carry a large amount of data at once. The most common types of Internet broadband connections are cable modems (which use the same connection as cable TV) and DSL modems (which use your existing phone line). With broadband, you can be on the phone at the same time as surfing the Internet. You will need it if you want to send and receive large files, for example, family photographs.

Bulletin board

Online chat where members can exchange views. **CyprusLife@groups.msn.com** is a great discussion site about expat life in Cyprus.

Cyberspace

This simply refers to the virtual world of computers. For example, an object in cyberspace is a block of data floating around on some computer system or network.

Domain

This is the name that identifies a website. Websites ending .gov are government-related; .edu or .ac are educational establishments; and, geographically, .co.uk relates to the UK and .cy to Cyprus. You can set your website up to be a .com or a .biz or a number of other suffixes, regardless of your geographical location.

Download

To copy something from a primary source to a more peripheral one, as in saving something found on the web to diskette or to a file on your local hard drive.

E-commerce (electronic-commerce)

Business transactions done over the internet. Websites such as Amazon.com, Buy.com and eBay are all e-commerce sites. The jargon terms 'e-business' and 'e-tailing' are often used synonymously with e-commerce.

FAQ

Stands for 'frequently asked questions'. A FAQ page would be useful on your website to answer the most common questions, for example, 'How far is the property from the airport?', and 'Do you accept children?'.

Gigabyte

A gigabyte consists of roughly 1 billion bytes. To be exact, there are 1,024 megabytes or 1,073,741,824 bytes in a gigabyte, but 1 billion is a much easier number to remember. Because of the large size of today's hard disks, storage capacity is usually measured in gigabytes.

HTML

Hypertext Markup Language. A standardised language of computer code, used in all web documents, containing the textual content, images, links to other documents and formatting instructions for display on the screen.

ISP or internet service provider   A company that sells Internet connections.

PDF   Abbreviation for portable document format, a file format developed by Adobe Systems, that is used to capture almost any kind of document with the formatting in the original. Viewing a PDF file requires Acrobat Reader, which can be downloaded free from **www.adobe.com**.

Router   This is a hardware device that routes data (hence the name) from a local area network to another network connection. It's part of the kit you will need to set up broadband access.

Search engine   A means of searching for other websites and topics; **www.google.com** or **www.google.co.uk** are regarded as the best but you can also search with engines like **www.yahoo.com** if you prefer.

Spam   Junk e-mail or postings on a bulletin board.

Greek for Survival

Greek Vocabulary

Né	Yes
Óhi	No
Efharistó	Thank you
Efharistó poli	Thank you very much
Parakaló	Please or You are welcome
Signómi	Excuse me
Yá sou	Hello
Andío sas	Goodbye
Kaliméra	Good day/morning
Kalispéra	Good afternoon/evening
Kaliníhta	Good night
Ti kánis?	How are you?
Kalá	Good
Áshima	Bad
étsi ke étsi	So-so
Héro polí	Nice to meet you
Den katalavéno	I do not understand
Pos to léte sta [Aggliká]?	How do you say this in [English]?
Miláte Aggliká	Do you speak English

The Greek Alphabet

Capital	Lower-case	Greek Name	English
Α	α	Alpha	a
Β	β	Beta	b
Γ	γ	Gamma	g
Δ	δ	Delta	d
Ε	ε	Epsilon	e
Ζ	ζ	Zeta	z
Η	η	Eta	h
Θ	θ	Theta	th
Ι	ι	Iota	i
Κ	κ	Kappa	k
Λ	λ	Lambda	l
Μ	μ	Mu	m
Ν	ν	Nu	n
Ξ	ξ	Xi	x
Ο	ο	Omicron	o
Π	π	Pi	p
Ρ	ρ	Rho	r
Σ	σ or ς	Sigma	s
Τ	τ	Tau	t
Υ	υ	Upsilon	u
Φ	φ	Phi	ph
Χ	χ	Chi	ch
Ψ	ψ	Psi	ps
Ω	ω	Omega	o

Directory of Contacts

Major Resources in Britain and Ireland

Cyprus High Commission
93 Park St, London W1K 7ET
t 0870 005 6711
f (020) 7491 0691
w www.cyprus.embassy
homepage.com

Cyprus Tourist Office, 17 Hanover St,
London W1S 1YP, **t** (020) 7569 8800

(020) 7569 8808, **f** (020) 7499 4935,
w www.visitcyprus.org.cy
e informationcto@btconnect.com

Embassy of the Republic of Cyprus
71 Lower Leeson St, Dublin 2, Ireland
t (01) 676 3060, **f** (01) 676 3099
e embassyofcyprusdub@eircom.net
Tourist Section:
t (01) 662 9269
Ambassador: HE Mr Andreas
S. Kakouris.

Major Resources in the USA

Cyprus Tourism Organisation
13 East, 40th St, New York, NY 10016
t (212) 683 5280
f (212) 683 5282
e gocyprus@aol.com
cyprustourism.org

Embassy of the Republic of Cyprus
2211 R. St NW, Washington, DC 20008
t (202) 462 5772
t (202) 462 0873
f (202) 483 6710
w www.cyprusembassy.net

British Resources in Cyprus

British High Commission
Alexandrou Palli, PO Box 21978,
CY1587, Lefkosia
t (00357) 22 86 11 00
hotline t 90 91 66 66 (daily service)
f (00357) 22 86 11 25 or f 22 86 12 00
office hours: weekdays 7.30am–2pm
(except Tues 7.30am–1pm and
2–5.30pm); consulate section:
weekdays 7.45am–12.30pm; for visas:
Mon, Tues, Thur, Fri 7.45–11.30am
e infobhc@cylink.com.cy

Irish Embassy, 7 Aiantas Str., 1082
Nicosia, or postal address,
PO Box 23848, 1686 Nicosia
t (00357) 22 81 81 83
f (00357) 22 66 00 50

US Embassy, 2407 Engomi, Nicosia
t (00357) 22 39 39 39
f (00357) 22 78 09 44

Professional Bodies in Cyprus

Association of Insurance Companies
PO Box 22030, 1516 Nicosia
t (00357) 22 76 39 13
e cina@cytanet.com.cy
w www.iac.org.cy

Association of Valuers and Surveyors
PO Box 20724, 1663 Nicosia
t (00357) 22 75 12 21 or t 25 36 87 57
f (00357) 22 67 08 76
contact Varnados Pashoulis
e var@cytanet.com.cy.

Cyprus Bar Association (Lawyers)
PO Box 21446, 1508 Nicosia
t (00357) 22 78 00 60

**Cyprus Civil Engineers and
Architects Association**
PO Box 21825, 1513 Nicosia
t (00357) 22 75 12 21
w www.cceaa.org.cy

**The Cyprus Real Estate
Agents Association**
17 Hadjiloizi Michaelides Street,
PO Box 50563,
Limassol CY 3041
t (00357) 25 36 74 67
f (00357) 25 36 51 88
e solo@cytanet.com.cy

**Institute of Certified Public
Accountants of Cyprus**
41 Themistokli Dervi Street,
Hawaii Tower, 5th Floor, Office 503,
1066 Nicosia,
or PO Box 24935, 1355 Nicosia
t (00357) 22 76 98 66

**Preservation Section of the
Department of Town Planning**
1454 Nicosia
t (00357) 22 40 82 10/7/3
f (00357) 22 408262

Financial Advisers

The Regulatory Body for Financial
Advisors is the **Central Bank of Cyprus**
(**w www.centralbank.gov.cy/**). All
licensed financial advisers are listed
on what is known as the CIFSA list.

Banks in Cyprus

Most of the banks listed here have
branches in all the major towns.

Alpha Bank
213A Arch. Makarios III Ave and
2 Grivas Dhigenis Ave,
Corner Maximos Plaza,
PO Box 51746,
3508 Limassol,
t (00357) 25 83 2600
f (00357) 25 58 96 69
42–44 Arch. Makarios III Avenue
PO Box 60016, 8100 Paphos
t (00357) 26 84 30 00
f (00357) 26 95 01 45

Bank of Cyprus Ltd
1 Saripolou Str, 3036 Limassol
t (00357) 25 84 50 00
f (00357) 25 37 36 99
Evagora Pallikaride and Antrea
Tsielepou Corner
PO box 60034, 8123 Paphos
t (00357) 26 84 62 00
f (00357) 26 94 36 03
w www.bankofcyprus.com

**Barclays Bank Plc, International
Banking Unit**
PO Box 27320, Nicosia 1644
t (00357) 22 65 54 40/21
f (00357) 22 75 42 33
e bbcorp@spidernet.com.cy

Central Bank of Cyprus
w www.centralbank.gov.cy/

**Commercial Bank of Greece (Cyprus)
Ltd**, L 203 Christodoulou
Chatzipavlou, 3036 Limassol
t (00357) 25 74 75 00

Co-operative Central Bank Ltd
84 Gladstonos, 3040 Limassol
t (00357) 25 82 05 70

Cyprus Popular Bank Ltd
Main Branch (020)
121 Makariou III Ave, 3021 Limassol
t (00357) 25 81 50 00
w www.cypruspopularbank.com

Hellenic Bank (Finance) Ltd
56 Makariou III Ave, 3065 Limassol
t (00357) 25 56 46 86

Hellenic Bank (Investments) Ltd
2 Riga Feraiou, Shop 25,
3095 Limassol
t (00357) 25 34 30 30

Hellenic Bank Ltd, Main Branch
52 Gladstonos, 3041 Limassol
t (00357) 25 50 20 00
w www.hellenicbank.com

Housing Finance Corporation
77 Makariou III Ave, 3067 Limassol
t (00357) 25 57 60 30

Laiki Bank, Corner, Athinon Road and N. Xiouta Street, 3041 Limassol
t (00357) 80 00 20 00
f (00357) 25 81 51 91
10 Apostolou Pavlou Avenue
8046 Paphos
t (00357) 80 00 20 00
f (00357) 26 81 61 82

Estate Agents

ECR Properties
t (020) 8347 0055
f (020) 8347 5577
w www.ecrpro.com
in Cyprus
t 25 81 76 60
f 25 81 76 61

Halcyon Properties
t (01323) 891639
f (01323) 892954
w www.halcyon-properties.co.uk

Headlands
w www.headlands.co.uk.

Living Cyprus
t 07050 262596 or 659909
w www.living-cyprus.com
and sister website
w www.cypruspropertydreams

Antonis Loizou and Associates
t (00357) 22 42 48 53
e enquiries@aloizou.com.cy
w www.aloizou.com.cy

Nicholas & Tsokkas
t (00357) 26 93 09 35
f (00357) 26 22 04 38
w www.cypruspropertyfinder.com

Property Finders International
t 0845 330 1449
w www.newskys.co.uk

Serious About Cyprus
t (01234) 401557
w www.seriousaboutcyprus.com

w www.forsalecyprus.com
British-run website for direct sales and rental of property (no agents) as well as sale of boast and motor vehicles.

Real Estate Support Services

Absolute Property Services Ltd
w www.absolutelycyprus.com
Property maintenance service set up by a British expat.

Select Cyprus Pools
PO Box 66351 8830 Polis Chrysochous
t (00357) 26 81 7219
f (00357) 26 81 7220
e info@cypruspools.biz
w www.cypruspools.biz
British-run pool maintenance in the Paphos/Latchi area.

Holiday Companies Specialising in Cyprus

Amathus Holidays
t (020) 7611 0901
w www.amathusholidays.co.uk

Olympic Holidays
t 0870 429 4141
w www.olympicholidays.co.uk

Planet Holidays
t 0870 066 0909
w www.planet-holidays.net

Rent Cyprus Villas
t 0870 199 9966
w www.rentcyprusvillas.com

Sunvil Holidays
t (020) 8758 4747
w www.sunvil.co.uk/cyprus

Removal Companies

Bishops Move
t (020) 7501 4930
f (020) 7622 1794
w www.bishopsmove.com

Excess Baggage
freephone t 0800 783 1085 or
t (020) 8324 2066, f (020) 8324 2095
e sales@excess-baggage.com
w www.excess-baggage.com

PSS International Removals
Head Office, 1–3 Pegasus Road
Croydon, Surrey CR9 4PS
t (020) 8686 7733
f (020) 8686 7799, sales@p-s-s.co.uk
w www.pss.uk.com

English-Language Press and Magazines

Cyprus Mail
24 Vassilious Voulgaroctonou Str.,
PO Box 21144, 1502 Nicosia
t (00357) 22 81 85 85
f (00357) 22 67 63 85
e mail@cyprus-mail.com or
advertising@cyprus-mail.com

Cyprus Weekly
PO Box 24977, 1306 Nicosia
t (00357) 22 66 60 47
f (00357) 22 66 86 65
e weekly@spidernet.com.cy
w www.cyprusweekly.com.cy

The Cyprus Croc
PO Box 54359, 3723 Limassol
t (00357) 99 52 44 45
f (00357) 25 58 53 21
e editor@crocguides.com
w www.crocguides.com.
An annual listings magazine with
details of leisure and cultural events,
sporting amenities, and articles for
tourists and resident expatriates. It is
distributed free by the Cyprus
Tourism Organisation and may be
found in all tourist information
offices.

A Directory of Services
PO Box 54359, 3723 Limassol,
t (00357) 99 52 44 45
f (00357) 25 58 53 21
e editor@crocguides.com
w www.crocguides.com (click link:
A Directory of Services).
Annual listings magazine with
details of individuals and companies
wishing to do business with the
expatriate community.

Moving to and Living in Cyprus
PO Box 54359, 3723 Limassol
t (00357) 99 52 44 45
f (00357) 25 58 53 21
e editor@crocguides.com
w www.crocguides.com (click link:
Moving to Cyprus).
A definitive guide to the Republic
of Cyprus.

Internet Sites

w www.crocguides.com
Online and print guide aimed at English-speaking visitors and residents, full of insider tips on restaurants and cultural events.

w www.cyprus-freemasons.org.cy/
Freemasons in Cyprus.

w www.palc.com.cy/
The Paphos Adonis Lions Club.

w www.royalbritishlegion-cyprus.com
Royal British Legion based in Limassol.

w www.ukca.com.cy
UK Citizens Abroad.

http://groups.msn.com/CyprusLife
Larnaca-based chat forum run by British expats.

Pets

Animals By Air Ltd
Second Floor, Unit 1, Building 307, Freight Terminal, Manchester Airport, Manchester M90 5PL
t 0870 833 8020
f 0870 833 8021
e enquiries@AnimalsByAir.co.uk

BARC – British Forces Animal Rehoming Centre
t (00357) 25 96 37 33
e admin@barc-cyprus.org
w www.barc-cyprus.org
Site aimed at the forces but contains lots of useful information about taking a pet to Cyprus.

Department of Veterinary Services
Nicosia, PO Box 2006
t (00357) 22 30 52 11

Ministry of Agriculture
CY1417 Lefkosia
t (00357) 22 80 52 01/8
f (00357) 22 33 28 03
e vet.services@cytanet.com.cy

w www.defra.gov.uk.
Check for up-to-date info on taking animals abroad or back to the UK.

Church Services in Cyprus

Nicosia
Anglican Church (St Paul)
Leoforos Vyronos
t (00357) 22 67 78 97
Sun at 9.30am, 6pm

Roman Catholic Church (Holy Cross)
Pyli Pafou
t (00357) 22 66 21 32
f (00357) 22 66 07 67
Mass daily at 6.30pm, except Tues at 7.30am (Greek); Sun at 8am, 9.30am, 6.30pm (English)

Limassol
Anglican Church (St Barnabas)
Archiepiskopou Leontiou A' 153A
(opposite the Lemesos old Hospital)
t (00357) 25 36 27 13. *Sun at 10am*

St Catherine's Catholic Church
28 Oktovriou 259
t (00357) 25 36 29 46
f (00357) 25 34 62 90
Daily Mass at 6.30pm; Sun at 8am, 9.30am (Greek) and 11am (Latin), 6.30pm (English)

Paphos

Anglican Masses at Agia Kyriaki,
Chrysopolitissa Church, Kato Pafos
Res. Chaplain
t (00357) 26 95 24 86
Sun at 8.30am and 6pm; Wed at 9am

Roman Catholic Mass at Agia Kyriaki,
Chrysopolitissa Church, Kato Pafos
t (00357) 26 93 13 08, 26 95 34 59
f (00357) 26 93 13 08
Sun at 10am (Latin), 12 noon (English),
1pm (German)

Roman Catholic Mass at Pissouri
Beach area,
c/o **t** (00357) 26 93 13 08
Sun at 6pm

Polis, Pafos District

Roman Catholic Mass at St Nicholas
Church
t (00357) 26 93 13 08. *Sun at 10am*

Larnaca

Anglican Church (St Helena)
St Helena Bldg, Leoforos Gr. Afxentiou
and Ag. Elenis

t (00357) 24 65 13 27 or 24 62 72 18
Sun, Holy Communion at 9.30am,
evening worship at 6.30pm

Santa Maria Catholic Church
Terra Santa 8
t (00357) 24 64 28 58
f (00357) 24 63 69 53
Masses Mon–Sat at 8am (Latin);
Sat at 6.30pm (English);
Sun at 8am (Greek)
and 9.30am (English)

International Evangelical Church
(Presbyterian and Reformed)
Stylianou Lena 57
t (00357) 24 65 70 57 or 24 65 23 31
Worship every Sun at 10.30am and
7pm

Ayia Napa

Ecumenical Centre – Agia Napa
Monastery
c/o **t** (00357) 24 64 28 58
Mass every Sun for Roman Catholics at
5pm (Apr–Dec in English)

Cypriot Holidays and Celebrations

Public Holidays

1 January	New Year's Day
6 January	Epiphany
25 March	Greek National Day
1 April	Greek Cypriot National Day
1 May	Labour Day
15 August	Feast of the Assumption
1 October	Cyprus Independence Day
28 October	Greek National Day (Ochi Day)
24 December	Christmas Eve
25 December	Christmas Day
26 December	Boxing Day

There are also variable holidays for Carnival, on Green Monday, on Good Friday, on Easter Monday and on Kataklysmos (Pentecost or Festival of the Flood). *See below* for more information about these celebrations and p.186 for a list giving the exact dates of the variable holidays from 2005 to 2008.

1 January: New Year's Day

New Year, rather than Christmas, is when families exchange gifts. On New Year's Eve, a traditional cake, *Vasilopitta*, is baked, with a coin hidden in it. Children go out carol singing and some families play a fortune-telling game with olive leaves. The cake is cut the following day, with one slice for Jesus, one for the house and one for any family members who are absent. The person who gets the coin is considered lucky for a whole year.

6 January: Epiphany

Epiphany is one of the most important Greek Orthodox religious celebrations of the year. It is also known as the Feast of the Light, since it commemorates Christ's baptism in the River Jordan, symbolic of the spiritual rebirth of man. It is celebrated in a number of seaside towns in Cyprus (Larnaca hosts a dramatic service by the sea).

On the eve of Epiphany, known as *kalanda*, people gather in church for the blessing of the waters, which are supposed to have held evil spirits for the past 12 days. After Mass, the priest visits all houses to cleanse them from the demons, or evil spirits, known as *kalikandjiari*. According to Cypriot tradition, these demons appear on Christmas Day, and for the next 12 days play evil tricks on people. On the eve of their departure, housewives throw pancakes and sausages on their roofs, where the demons are believed to dwell, in order to please them, so that they will leave contented without causing any trouble.

On the day of Epiphany, a special celebration takes place at all seaside towns. After the Epiphany Mass the archbishop or one of the bishops leads a procession down to the sea, where a ceremonial baptism is performed. During the ceremony the leading priest throws the holy cross into the sea. Young men dive into the water to retrieve the cross and return it to the priest. Doves are released and at the same time boats sound their horns.

Carnival

Carnival is a two-week period of festivity, before the 50 days of Easter. The first week is called the Meat Week (*Kreatini*), as it is the last week for eating meat before Easter. The second week is known as the cheese week (*Tyrini*), when cheese and other dairy products may be consumed.

Carnival festivities begin on the Thursday of the Meat Week. The last Sunday of the Cheese Week is the highlight of the Carnival, when parties are held all over the island. Limassol is the centre of the festivities, with fancy dress parades and balls. Carnival parades and fancy-dress balls are very popular and take place in most towns. However, Limassol is the most famous town for the Carnival festivities, and this is where most parties and balls take place.

Green Monday (variable)

A celebration 50 days before Greek Orthodox Easter. Although this is the first day of Lent, Green Monday is a day of celebration and vegetarian picnics in the countryside. This is followed by 50 days of fast, during which strict Christians prepare themselves to receive the Redeemer. Some people follow a vegetarian diet, but not many nowadays.

25 March: Greek National Day

Celebrated all over the island with parades, dancing and sporting events.

1 April: Greek Cypriot National Day

The anniversary of the start of the liberation struggle of the Greek Cypriots against British colonial rule in 1955.

Good Friday and Easter Monday (variable)

Easter is the biggest feast of the Greek Orthodox calendar and is a wonderful time to be in Cyprus. On Thursday before Easter, after morning Mass, people bake Easter breads, pastries and cheese pies known as *flaounes*. Eggs are dyed red. On Thursday evening, a representation of Christ's Crucifixion takes place in Church, where icons are draped in black. Good Friday is again a day of mourning, in which the village sepulchre is decorated with flowers and paraded around the parish during evening Mass. On Saturday, during morning Mass, as the priest announces Jesus' resurrection, the black drapes drop from the icons and the members of the congregation rap their seats to express their joy. At midnight, there is another Mass, followed by a bonfire on which an imaginary Judas is burned, known as *lampradjia*. Traditional Easter fare is lemon and rice soup (*avgolemono*) with the red-dyed eggs.

1 May: Labour Day

A May day holiday, as in the UK.

Kataklysmos (Festival of the Flood) (variable)

A uniquely Cypriot celebration. *Kataklysmos* (Pentecost) refers to the destruction by flood of all living creatures on earth, apart from Noah and his family, and later, Deukalion and his wife, who were saved in order to give birth to a new and moral generation. The ceremonies for *Kataklysmos* last for a few days and take place in all seaside towns and resorts. Singing, dancing, folk festivals, boat races and water fights (to symbolise purification of body and soul) take place everywhere.

15 August: Feast of the Assumption

1 October: Cyprus Independence Day

Cyprus Independence Day is celebrated with a military parade in Nicosia and a reception at the Presidential Palace in the evening.

28 October: Greek National Day (Ochi Day)
Celebrated with student parades all over the island.

24 December: Christmas Eve
On Christmas Eve, special bread (*koulouria*) and pastries (*kourapiedes*) are baked while children go carol-singing. Traditionally, children bring good health and fortune, so the householders always reward them with a small sum of money.

25 December: Christmas Day
Most people attend Mass on Christmas Day, followed by egg-and-lemon rice soup for breakfast. This is traditionally a day of visiting friends and relatives.

26 December: Boxing Day

Variable Public Holidays 2005–2008

	2005	2006	2007	2008
Green Monday	14 Mar	6 Mar	19 Feb	10 Mar
Good Friday (Greek Orthodox Church)	29 Apr	21 Apr	6 Apr	25 Apr
Easter Sunday (Greek Orthodox Church)	1 May	23 Apr	8 Apr	27 Apr
Easter Monday (Greek Orthodox Church)	2 May	24 Apr	9 Apr	28 Apr
Pentecost Monday (Greek Orthodox Church)	20 Jun	12 Jun	28 May	15 Jun
Easter Sunday (Catholic Church)	27 Mar	16 Apr	8 Apr	23 Mar

(courtesy of Cyprus Tourism Organisation)

Further Reading

Bitter Lemons of Cyprus, Lawrence Durrell (Faber & Faber). Charming narrative first published in 1957.

Landscapes of Cyprus, Geoff Daniel et al. (Sunflower Books). Walks all over the southern part of the island.

Journey into Cyprus, Colin Thubron (Penguin Books). Travelogue of a 600-mile walk around the island in its last year of peace.

Cyprus: The Rough Guide, Marc Dubin (Rough Guides).

Cyprus Insight Guide (Insight Guides).

The Tasty Greek Recipes of Cyprus, Nicholas Adam Nicolaou (Tasty Greek Publications). 85 recipes, six poems and a song!

Climate Charts

Larnaca	Jan	Feb	Mar	Apr	May	Jun	Jul	Aug	Sep	Oct	Nov	Dec
Min (°C)	7	6	8	11	16	20	22	22	20	16	12	8
Max (°C)	16	17	18	22	26	30	32	32	30	27	22	18
Min (°F)	45	44	47	53	61	68	72	72	68	62	54	48
Max (°F)	62	63	66	72	80	87	90	90	87	82	73	65

Nicosia	Jan	Feb	Mar	Apr	May	Jun	Jul	Aug	Sep	Oct	Nov	Dec
Min (°C)	5	5	6	10	15	19	21	21	18	15	10	6
Max (°C)	14	15	18	23	29	33	36	36	32	27	20	16
Min (°F)	42	41	44	50	60	67	71	71	66	59	50	44
Max (°F)	58	60	65	74	85	92	97	97	90	82	69	62

Appendix 1: Checklist – Do-it-yourself Inspection of Property

A lot of these points refer to resale property but they also form a useful checklist for new developments. You can use the list for a preliminary check, and also to brief your surveyor.

Title

Check that the property corresponds with its description:

- Number of rooms.
- Plot size.

Plot

Check the building density permission for the plot:

- Ask the vendor or developer whether the plot is within the building zone and what building permission the surrounding land has. If it is owned by the same developer, what are their plans for it?
- Identify the physical boundaries of the plot.
- Is there any dispute with anyone over these boundaries?
- Is there anything suspicious-looking on your plot such as pipes, cables, drainage ditches?
- Is the plot connected to the mains and does it have sewage disposal or a septic tank?
- Is the plot connected to the electricity network? Are there any unsightly cables or posts that you will need to have moved?
- What access is there to the plot? Does anybody else have access across your land?
- Is there somewhere to park a car?
- Is the plot noisy? If you are buying near an airport, are you under the flight path?
- If you are buying in town, are there any bars or nightclubs nearby which may disturb you?

Garden

- Is there anything in the garden that is not being sold with the property: potted plants, fountains, etc?
- Is the garden overlooked?

Swimming Pool

- What to size is the pool? Is it clean?
- Does the filtration system work?
- When was it installed?
- Who maintains it and how much do they charge?

Walls

This is particularly important when buying an older property.

- Are the walls vertical?
- Are there any obvious cracks?
- Is the stone in good condition?
- Are there any recent-looking repairs to the walls?
- If you are buying an older property, has it been built to withstand earth tremors?

Roof

- Is the roof in reasonable repair?
- If it is tiled, are there any tiles missing?
- Is the water tank on the roof in good condition? How old is it?
- Are the solar panels on the roof in good condition? How old are they?
- If there is a satellite dish, is it included in the sale of the property?

Guttering and Downpipes

- Is everything present? Are the gutters securely attached? Are there any obvious repairs?

Enter the Property

- Does it smell musty?
- Does it smell of dry rot?
- Are there any other strange smells?

Doors

- Do the doors close properly?
- Do the locks work?

Windows

- Do the windows have fly screens?
- Do the windows close properly?
- Do the locks work?

Floor

- Does the floor appear in good condition – without chips or cracks in stone or marble, and no cracked wooden boards?

Underfloor

- Can you get access under the floor?
- If so, is it ventilated?
- Are the joists in good condition?

Attic Space

- Is it accessible?
- Can you see daylight through the roof?
- Will you be able to turn it into an extra room if required?
- How hot is it?
- Is there anywhere to put a window or a skylight and would you get permission to do this?

Woodwork

- Any sign of wood-boring insects?

Interior Walls

- Any sign of recent repair or redecoration?
- Any significant-looking cracks?

Utility Bills

- Are you responsible for your own or are they shared with other tenants in the building?
- Are there any other communal costs you should know about?
- Electricity
- How old is the electricity meter?
- Does the wiring look safe? (In Cyprus, most wiring in new houses runs through the walls so it may be difficult to inspect.)
- Are there enough power points?
- If you have a plug tester, does it show good earth?

Lighting

- Do all the lights work?
- Which light fittings, if any, are included in the sale?
- If you are buying an old house, turn the lights off to see how dark the interior is likely to be during the day.

Water

- Is the property connected to the mains, or does water come from a well? If so, who owns the well and how much will you be charged for water?
- Do all the hot and cold taps work?
- Is there enough water pressure?
- Do the taps drip?

Gas

- Where are the gas bottles stored?
- If you are buying a rural property, can you get gas delivered?
- Does the property have sufficient ventilation?

Central Heating

- Is the property fitted with central heating?
- If you are buying off-plan, is central heating included in the price?
- If so, does it work?
- Is there heat in all the radiators?
- Do the thermostat appear to work?
- Are there any signs of leaks?

Fireplaces

- Are the chimneys unblocked and in good order?
- Air conditioning
- Does the property have central air-conditioning or individual units in some of the rooms?
- If you are buying off-plan, is air-conditioning included in the price?
- Are individual units included in the sale?
- Does the air-conditioning work and is it quiet?
- Do any of the rooms have ceiling fans?
- If there is no air-conditioning, is there a provision for it?
- If you do not intend to have air-conditioning, is there a suitable flow of air through the house when the doors and windows are open?

Telephone

- Is there a phone?
- Does the phone work?
- Is it included in the sale?
- Is the area suitable for a broadband internet connection?
- Is there a mobile phone signal?

Satellite TV

- Does the property come with a satellite dish?
- Does it work?
- Is it included in the sale?

Drainage

- If there is a septic tank, how old is it?
- Who maintains it?
- When was it last serviced?
- Is there a smell of drainage problems in the bathrooms or toilets?
- Does the water drain away rapidly from sinks and showers?
- Do the drains appear to be in good condition?

Kitchen

- Do the cupboards open and close properly?
- Is the tiling secure and in good order?
- Are there enough power points?
- What appliances are included in the sale?
- Do they work and how old are they?
- If you are buying off-plan, is there a good choice of kitchens offered by the developer? If not, why not?

Bathroom

- Is the tiling in good condition?
- Does the shower work properly?
- Is the bathroom adequately ventilated?
- If you are buying off-plan, is the developer offering you a decent choice of bathroom fittings?

Furniture

- Is any of the furniture included in the sale? Remember to ask about garden furniture as well.

Repairs and Improvements

- What repairs have been carried out in the last two years?
- Have any improvements being made to the house?
- If changes have been made, was permission granted and are there builders' receipts and guarantees?
- Is there building consent or planning permission for any further additions or alterations?

Defects

- Is the vendor aware of any defects in the property?

Appendix 2: Checklist – What Are You Worth?

Use this table to assess how much you can afford to spend on a second home.

Asset	Value (local currency)	Value (£)
Current assets		
Home		
Holiday home		
Contents of main home		
Contents of holiday home		
Cars		
Boat		
Bank accounts		
Other cash investments		
Bonds		
Stocks and shares		
PEPs		
TESSAs		
ISAs		
SIPs		
Other		
Value of your business		
Value of share options		
Future assets		
Value of share options		
Personal/company pension – likely lump sum		
Value of endowment mortgages on maturity		
Other		

Index

Titles available in the *Buying a Property* series

Buying a Property: France
Buying a Property: Spain
Buying a Property: Italy
Buying a Property: Portugal
Buying a Property: Ireland
Buying a Property: Greece
Buying a Property: Turkey
Buying a Property: Abroad
Buying a Property: Retiring Abroad
Buying a Property: Cyprus
Buying a Property: Eastern Europe

Related titles

Working and Living: France
Working and Living: Spain
Working and Living: Italy
Working and Living: Portugal
Working and Living: Australia
Working and Living: New Zealand

Forthcoming
Working and Living: USA
Working and Living: Canada
Starting a Business: France
Starting Business: Spain